Mexican Movies
in the United States

Mexican Movies in the United States

A History of the Films, Theaters and Audiences, 1920–1960

ROGELIO AGRASÁNCHEZ, JR.

Foreword by Carl J. Mora

McFarland & Company, Inc., Publishers
Jefferson, North Carolina, and London

Library of Congress Cataloguing-in-Publication Data

Agrasánchez, Rogelio, Jr.
    Mexican movies in the United States : a history of the films, theaters
and audiences, 1920–1960 / Rogelio Agrasánchez, Jr.; foreword by
Carl J. Mora.
      p.   cm.
    Includes bibliographical references and index.

    ISBN 0-7864-2545-8 (illustrated case binding : 50# alkaline paper) ∞

    1. Motion pictures, Mexican — United States — History. 2. Motion
picture theaters — United States — History.   I. Title.
  PN1993.5.M4A37   2006
  791.430973 — dc22   2006012350

British Library cataloguing data are available

On the cover: Teatro Alameda, San Antonio *(photograph by Jim Keller)*, joined
with a crowd at San Antonio's Teatro Nacional *(Ignacio Torres Collection)—*
both courtesy San Antonio Conservation Society

Manufactured in the United States of America

McFarland & Company, Inc., Publishers
  Box 611, Jefferson, North Carolina 28640
   www.mcfarlandpub.com

To the memory of
Nettie Lee Benson,
who sparked my interest in Mexican history,
and Ignacio E. Lozano,
founder of two great newspapers:
La Prensa and *La Opinión*

Acknowledgments

I wish to thank the following institutions and their staff for being so cooperative in my search for documents: City of Corona Library (California), Benson Latin American Collection; Center for American History; Harry Ransom Humanities Research Center; Perry Castañeda Library (The University of Texas at Austin), Arnulfo L. Oliveira Memorial Library — Hunter Room (Brownsville), University of Texas-Pan Am Library; Museum of South Texas History (Edinburg), City of Harlingen Library (Harlingen), City of San Antonio Library, San Antonio Conservation Society, and The University of Texas Institute of Texan Cultures at San Antonio.

Many people who supported this project by paying attention to my inquiries, or by reading parts of the original manuscript are here acknowledged: Cecilia Aros Hunter, Rubén Benavides V., René Benítez, Denise Chávez, Federico Dávalos, Robert G. Dickson, Craig Edge, Gustavo García, Lino García, George Gause, Javier González, Cheryl LaBerge, Eileen Mattei, David McCue, Luis Muñoz, Chale Nafus, Jaime Nicolopulos, Rogelio Nuñez, Enrique Ornelas, Ricardo Ruenes, Carlos Rugerio, Zac Salem, Elizabeth B. Standifird, Esperanza Vázquez, Homero Vera, and Al Zarzana.

I express my appreciation to Carl J. Mora for his genuine interest in this research and for his valuable suggestions. Also thanks to David R. Maciel's cooperation and enthusiasm, and to Manuel G. Gonzales for his cheerful words of encouragement. Professor Gonzales kindly shared with me his findings and interview materials. Javier R. García put at my disposal his maps and photos. Steve Wilson was very helpful and guided me to find documents at the Harry Ransom Center. Individuals who kindly accepted to be interviewed for this book, and who shared their memories and anecdotes of movie going include Carlos Hinojosa, Estela S. De la Fuente, David Mercado Gonzáles, Alberto Huerta, Richard H. Dunlap, Fernando J. Obledo†, and Arnulfo Arias. A special thanks go to my father, Rogelio Agrasánchez, Sr.

Finally, I am indebted to my wife, Xóchitl Fernández, who spent long hours gathering information for this project and helped me in an array of time-consuming tasks: copying documents, scanning photographs, fixing computer puzzles, and so on. Without her support, the completion of this book would have been more difficult and certainly much less enjoyable.

Rogelio Agrasánchez, Jr.
April 2006

Table of Contents

Foreword

by Carl J. Mora

Those of us of a certain age find ourselves feeling somewhat out of place in this early 21st century with its blockbuster films costing tens of millions of dollars and which, thanks to ever more sophisticated computer graphics, increasingly seem to be getting along with fewer and fewer actual human actors. As the years slide by, I tend to look back nostalgically to the middle decades of the 20th century when movies were still relatively low-tech and an acceptable form of entertainment for the entire family.

I grew up in New York City in the 1940s, during World War II. My moviegoing consisted of weekly visits to my neighborhood movie houses in Washington Heights. But, thanks to my father, I was fortunate to have an extra dimension to my cinematic upbringing: in addition to the usual Hollywood fare I concurrently watched a lot of Mexican films in the 1940s and 1950s, classic movies of the "Golden Age."

My father left Mexico in 1918 and went to Cuba where he met and married my mother. In 1921 they relocated to New York City where they settled down for the next thirty-two years. During that time my father maintained a link with his country of birth by taking the entire family on weekly outings to see Mexican movies and the occasional Argentine or Spanish feature. These outings provided me with the raw research material which many years later inspired my studies of Mexican cinema history.

I remember, albeit vaguely, going in the early 1940s to the Belmont Theater on West 48th Street, a few blocks north of Times Square. This was one of the first theaters in New York to show Spanish-language films exclusively. I recall seeing *El monje loco* (the Mad Monk), a series of scary movies made by the later eminent director Alejandro Galindo. I retain an image of a bug-eyed, scraggly haired monk pounding away at a cobweb-covered organ who punctuated his ominous chords with maniacal laughter. In 1950 we saw *Los olvidados*, Luis Buñuel's masterpiece, which at first was screened at the San Juan Theater on 168th Street and Broadway, passing unnoticed by the New York mainstream critics until it was honored at the Cannes Film Festival.

Reading Rogelio Agrasánchez, Jr.'s book has aroused these and other long-dormant memories of seeing Mexican pictures and stars in various New York movie houses. It also reminded me of stopping in San Antonio in 1953 en route to Mexico City. There I encountered a veritable movie palace specializing in Mexican films—a large, clean, modern theater in a good part of the city—a dignified showcase for Mexican cinema. It was probably the famous Alameda Theatre described in detail in this book. But at the time it made me somewhat resentful that none of the New York City movie houses that screened Mexican pictures could compare in magnificence to this beautiful San Antonio movie palace.

In my own work on the history of Mexican cinema, which is based on a Mexican and international perspective, I briefly allude to the importance of the United States as a market for Mexican films of the 1940s through the 1960s. But reading Agrasánchez's exhaustive and loving account of the exhibition of Mexican movies in this country, I have come to realize how critical the Mexican, Mexican-American, and other Latin American audiences in the United States were to the financial success of the Mexican film industry.

This book is not simply an economic analysis, which would be a valuable contribution in itself. Through oral histories, anecdotal accounts, and his own extensive knowledge of Mexican cinema, Agrasánchez has also recaptured the cultural and social history of an entire era that certainly would have passed into oblivion if not for his painstaking research. His serendipitous discovery of the Clasa-Mohme business files, one of the three U.S. distributors of Mexican films, enabled him to render that raw data into the present compelling narrative.

Agrasánchez brings to vivid life an era of Southwest social and cultural history when a plethora of Spanish-language movie houses operated in Los Angeles, San Antonio, El Paso, the Rio Grande Valley, and points in between. For decades they provided both live and screen entertainment to a diverse clientele. Some of these theaters were upscale for middle-class families and others were less desirable catering to a rougher element such as *pachucos* and *braceros*. But they all provided an emotional, cultural, and linguistic link with their homeland for many Mexican immigrants and their descendants from the 1920s through the 1980s. Elsewhere, in New York City for instance, Mexican films provided Spanish-speakers of different national origins with entertainment in their own language as well as exposure to Mexican popular culture.

Agrasánchez's book is indispensable to an understanding of the evolution of Mexican and Latin American popular culture in the North American milieu. It is a contextual link between the past and the complex and still-developing identity of today's diverse Hispanic populations within the multicultural landscape of the United States. This book is a nostalgic reminder as well of an era when movies depended on a good script and character development in stark contrast to the explosions, car chases, and special effects of today's action spectaculars.

Carl J. Mora is the author of *Mexican Cinema: Reflections of a Society, 1896–2004*, 3d edition. He is an adjunct lecturer in the Media Arts Department of the University of New Mexcio and has written numerous articles on varied aspects of Mexican, Spanish, American and British movies.

Preface

My interest in Mexican cinema was borne of collecting vintage film posters, an odd pursuit that requires one to delve into the past. This search for movie memorabilia led me to fading theater buildings and abandoned warehouses. One day in 1988, while digging for posters, I stumbled upon several batches of discarded documents; my instinct told me to pick them up and try to decipher them. A close inspection revealed that these were the files of Clasa-Mohme, Inc., a major distributor of Mexican films in the United States. The surviving correspondence belonged to the company's branch manager in San Antonio, Texas, and consisted of several thousand typewritten pages covering the years 1942–1960. Also included, were theater receipts records and booking files of more than a hundred movie houses, located mostly in Texas.

This fortunate finding made me think that a significant aspect of Latin American life and culture in the United States laid buried in these documents. I soon learned that the majority of the literature about México's cinema had consistently overlooked the importance of theatrical exhibition of motion pictures in the local and international markets. Although the study of Latin American immigrants in the United States has produced quite a number of scholarly books and printed articles, very little has been said about the leisure-time activities of these ethnic groups; with the exception of the work on Hispanic theater done by Nicolás Kanellos. Most publications have centered on the history of labor, health and education conditions, as well as on social and political organization of minorities, to the exclusion of non-productive, recreational habits. Further, no specific accounts address the consumption of Spanish-language movies in this country, other than a thesis concerning Puerto Rican audiences and a couple of articles on theaters in Fresno, California, and El Paso, Texas. Certainly, as a profitable business enterprise and a manifestation of the customs of a people, the matter deserves critical thought.

The arrival of the "talkies" in the 1930s generated an interest in Spanish-language cinema that spread to almost every city in the United States. An age of unparalleled activity in the exhibition of motion pictures from México developed as the United States entered World War II. In New York City and throughout the Southwest, many theaters were converted or built specifically for the Hispanic population. In San Antonio, for example, people gathered at the Guadalupe, Nacional, Progreso and Zaragoza theaters. The jewel that crowned this Texan city in 1949 was the Teatro Alameda, an imposing and beautiful construction with a capacity for 2,500 spectators. But the Alameda was only the tip of the iceberg, the most visible sign of a trend in popular culture. Movie establishments across the

1

land operated on a daily basis, offering to their loyal clientele the latest Mexican films complemented by a Hollywood picture. At its peak in 1951, an estimated 683 screens in the United States exhibited south-of-the-border productions.

Clasa-Mohme and Azteca Films, the major U.S. distributors of Spanish-language movies, released more than two thousand titles during the forties and fifties, a period generally regarded as the "Golden Age" of Mexican film entertainment. These companies, with offices in Los Angeles, San Antonio, Chicago, New York, and Denver, were charged with promoting the movies on behalf of the Mexican producers; they were also a determinant force that shaped the business of hundreds of theaters. In 1957, Columbia Pictures Corporation became the third major distributor of Spanish-language features, a move that signaled the economic importance of the domestic Hispanic market. Steady profits from the theatrical exhibition of Mexican films allowed for a six-decade growth of this industry, a phenomenon that finally ended in the latter part of the 1980s.

Focusing on the years of greatest activity in the film exhibition business–1920 to 1960, the present investigation offers a broad panorama of Spanish-language cinema in the United States. The period examined coincides with a time of intense demographic change in the United States that was abetted by the surge of immigrants from Latin America. It encompasses World War II and its aftermath, a pre-television era, when theater going was the most popular form of entertainment. These circumstances brought unparalleled demand of the Mexican motion pictures, a fact that is made evident in this book. The first chapter introduces the reader to the impact of Spanish-language movies on local audiences. It also illustrates the performance of the film industry as viewed from its distribution and exhibition channels. The following six chapters chronicle the development of this popular medium in a number of cities and communities where Hispanics have settled. Such a sampling ranges from the large urban centers of Los Angeles, New York City, El Paso, and San Antonio, to the flourishing agricultural towns in the Pomona Valley of California and the Rio Grande Valley of Texas. To complement this study, an appendix is added with information on hundreds of U.S. theaters showing Spanish-language films from 1920 to 1960.

The Clasa-Mohme Papers that I salvaged and preserved constitute the basis of this book. In selecting the appropriate material, attention has been given to extract weighty information as well as candid commentary. These documents hold an abundance of facts and a first-hand knowledge of the distribution and exhibition business. The correspondence of the Texas representative of Clasa-Mohme, Gordon B. Dunlap, invites the reader to witness the ups and downs of an entertainment concern that was thriving more than fifty years ago. In addition to this archival source, the indispensable review of contemporary Spanish-language newspapers, magazines and trade publications has yielded a more accurate and enticing narrative. Although this research is by no means exhaustive, the themes it explores might offer a fresh and concise look at the topic, while calling for expanded and ancillary studies. For now, this book takes aim at illuminating an obscure and nearly forgotten aspect of the daily life of Hispanics in the United States: their passion for the movies.

1

The Appeal of Mexican Cinema for Hispanics in the United States

The news—carried by the *San Antonio Express* in 1959—that Texas had "in excess of 150,000 citizens of Mexican descent who were unable to speak English" came as good tidings for one U.S. distributor of Spanish-language movies. This film promoter took a gamble saying that "such people should constitute a most important segment of our customers in this large state: probably the less English they learn, the more they appreciate Mexican pictures."[1] That language and demographics combined held the key to the popularity of this national cinema was not merely a guess but a proven fact. To understand the basis of this view we must put it in its historic context.

Throughout the twentieth century, a constant flow of immigrants from Latin America joined the original Hispanic population residing in the United States. Spanish speakers settled more often in four distinct regions: the Southwest (Texas, New Mexico, Arizona, California and southern Colorado), the Northeast (New York, New Jersey, Washington and Philadelphia), the Midwest (Chicago), and the state of Florida. Mexicans represented the largest group of Hispanics, making their homes in the Southwest and Chicago with more frequency. Puerto Ricans were the dominant Latin American group living in New York City. They also populated the Chicago region, where a growing number of Mexicans began to arrive after the First World War. Finally, Miami, Florida, was the preferred place for a majority of Cubans. Other nationals from Spain, Central and South America, and the Caribbean came to the United States in smaller numbers and settled mainly in the same four regions.[2]

The presence of Hispanics in the U.S. was noticeable since the early decades of the century. By 1930 there were about 683,000 Mexicans living in Texas, while the size of this group in California reached 368,000. Los Angeles alone, with a population of almost one hundred thousand people of Mexican descent ranked as the second largest Mexican city in the world, after the capital of México.[3] The city of New York, on the other hand, registered 100,000 Hispanics in the same year, of which the large majority came from Puerto Rico. These calculations, based on official statistics, however, do not take into account the influx of illegal immigrants to the United States, a most significant trend that continues to this day.

Although differences in national origin and social background exist, Hispanics in the United States more importantly share a common language as well as a cultural tradition

3

that cut across national boundaries, levels of education and economic status. Language, for one thing, has been regarded as a fundamental correlation among people because it "transmits a series of values that give unity to these groups."[4] In this light, language can endow virtual universality to certain expressions of popular culture, such as the motion pictures. Sound movies originating in Latin America in the 1930s and 1940s were, therefore, capable of integrating Hispanic audiences from different backgrounds. This does not mean, however, that vernacular movies necessarily appealed to all segments of the Spanish speaking public. It suggests, rather, that certain Hispanic groups, in particular those who were illiterate in their own language and/or did not speak sufficient English, patronized heavily this form of entertainment.

Since the arrival of the "talkies," México, Argentina and Spain fostered local film production. In the 1930s, an attempt by Hollywood to monopolize the making of sound pictures in Spanish dissolved quickly, leaving these three countries unhindered to develop their own cinemas. Civil war in Spain after 1936, however, limited that nation's efforts. Argentina, on the contrary, seemed to gather momentum in film production throughout the thirties, only to be superseded by México's celluloid output during the following decade. The strides made by the Mexican movie industry corresponded to this cinema's ability to attract an emergent international market. What follows is the stunning story of the appeal of Mexican cinema to the Spanish-speaking population in the United States.

Rising Popularity of Mexican Cinema

The popularity of Mexican films in the United States for a growing number of Hispanics is a phenomenon that dates back to the 1920s. More than a few silent pictures produced in México at that time were brought to the screens of California, Texas, and other states. The Million Dollar Theater in Los Angeles presented in 1920 the historical drama *Cuauhtémoc*, a feature-length movie about the life and death of the last emperor of the Aztecs. Meanwhile, the highly popular serial *El automóvil gris* played at the Nacional Theater in San Antonio. The same year, it screened three melodramas co-produced by stage actress and pioneer film director Mimí Derba: *La soñadora*, *En defensa propia*, and *La Tigresa*. In El Paso, the Teatro Colón released several features like *Alas abiertas*, *El escándalo*, and *Tepeyac*. Films such as the action-packed *El tren fantasma* and the historical tale *El Cristo de oro* had commercial runs in 1928 at the Teatro Chapultepec, in Corona, California. Other silent productions like *El caporal* and *El hombre sin patria* (aka *Los braceros mexicanos*) also played at theaters in different cities of the United States. Although the output of movies had been sporadic, the demand for Mexican-made features was already in place. Hollywood continued to dominate the Hispanic market, but this situation changed radically in the next decade.

The innovation of sound-pictures started a new era of experimentation. In Hollywood, producers did not take long to get underway Spanish-language versions of popular movies. Universal Pictures, for example, shrewdly exploited this practice by shooting *Dracula* (1930) simultaneously in English and Spanish. While Bela Lugosi played Count Dracula in the English version, his look-alike, Spanish actor Carlos Villarías, assumed the same scary character for the Spanish "talkie" being shot at night. The female interpreters in this version were two young Mexican actresses: Lupita Tovar and Carmen Guerrero. A baby-faced Argentine performer, Barry Norton, was cast as Tovar's heroic boyfriend.

Although the mix of Spanish accents did not bother the producers, Latin American

A simple peasant girl is drawn to tragedy after being seduced by a handsome soldier in the movie *Santa* (1931), México's first sound-on-film production. Above: Donald Reed and Lupita Tovar (Agrasánchez Film Archive).

audiences found these movies peculiar. Even though their casts were all Spanish-speaking actors, the distracting mannerisms and forced dialogue resulted in awkward situations. Worse, the stories portrayed in many of these "talkies" did not reflect the true character of Latin American people. Still, the experiment of Hollywood's Spanish versions generated about 180 films before it was given up altogether in the late thirties. Frank Fouce, an important exhibitor in Los Angeles, said that even Hollywood movies with big stars like Carlos Gardel or José Mojica could not compete at the box office with the Mexican pictures. Based on his experience, Fouce stated that an import from across the border usually made twice the money that a local Spanish "talkie" did.[5]

In 1931 México began producing sound films formally, kicking off with the adaptation of Federico Gamboa's popular novel *Santa*. Lupita Tovar, now a recognized star, played the film's title role: a cute and naïve peasant girl who is seduced by a soldier and then abandoned. When Santa goes to the Capital, she is transformed into a notorious prostitute who gradually looses luster and is drawn to tragedy and death. The movie met with success among audiences, instilling the producer's optimism with respect to the future of local film production. A few other attempts followed with equal box-office pull: *Cruz Diablo, Madre querida, Juárez y Maximiliano, María Elena*, etc. One of the first hits was the sentimental drama *Madre querida*, which played to packed houses in the barrios of México City. When released in California, it attracted a huge audience of "more than twenty thousand Mexicans that cried in Los Angeles during its exhibition." The public

The public recognized in *Allá en el Rancho Grande* (1936) the essence of rural México. Stars of the film: Tito Guízar and Esther Fernández (Agrasánchez Film Archive).

welcomed these initial efforts and, upon the release of *Allá en el Rancho Grande* in 1936, the industry's prestige was cemented. This modest picture had a savory combination of action, romance and musical comedy. Its well-picked cast consisted of personalities like young tenor Tito Guízar, beautiful Esther Fernández, folk musician Lorenzo Barcelata, and Carlos López *Chaflán*, a charismatic vaudeville comedian. The public applauded the movie's folklore and musical themes, recognizing in it the essence of rural México. It quickly became a blockbuster and, more importantly, it signaled the establishment of a characteristic Mexican genre, the "comedia ranchera." As a consequence, many films made after this year employed the same basic formula laid down by *Allá en el Rancho Grande*.

With the advent of World War II, the Mexican film industry experienced a boom. The rapid development of this national cinema in the forties was made possible by the new configuration of international relations, particularly since México became an essential ally of the United States during the war. Strategic natural resources, such as metals, were delivered to the neighboring country to be transformed into ships, tanks and heavy artillery. In exchange, México's movie studios received external aid in the form of technical assistance and a steady supply of raw film stock from Hollywood. This convenient partnership, coupled with the experience and artistic capacities of Mexicans, gave rise to a prosperous era of movie making that lasted a full decade and is now generally referred to as the "Golden Age." A government-sponsored Film Bank was also established to foster movie production, which soared to unprecedented levels. An average of 50 pictures a

Cantinflas made everyone laugh "with his flood of double meanings and his gruesome sense of humor." Original one-sheet poster, 1940 (Agrasánchez Film Archive).

year came out of the Mexican studios in the mid 1940's, many of which became classics of international cinematography. As the industry progressed, a wave of Spanish and Latin American artists arrived in México to join the boom of the cinema. Producers hired the most talented individuals and invested more money into their projects. As a result, many of these movies were crafted with excellence, serving as the primary vehicle for promoting the image of a country rich in tradition and culture.

Mexican pictures became so popular in Latin American countries that they often competed with films made in Hollywood. Audiences extending from the Caribbean to Argentina applauded features such as ¡Ay Jalisco, no te rajes!, Me he de comer esa tuna, Flor Silvestre, México de mis recuerdos, Ahí está el detalle, and many others made in the early forties. When these films were brought to the Spanish-speaking public in the United States, the reaction was even stronger, as the people "love to hear their own language, observe, criticize and laud their own customs and habits, and recall their beloved towns and hamlets." Filmed entertainment carried a message that struck a sensitive cord among Mexicans. An editorial observed that "these people who are far away from their own country, are even more patriotic, and eager to see anything connected with the land of their ancestors."[6]

Spanish-language movies found an enthusiastic and steadfast public in the United States, as many Mexican families' favorite place of recreation was the cinema. A Californian poll conducted in 1930 showed that people of Mexican origin in San Diego spent a good deal of money on leisure-time activities, such as the movies. They invested more on amusement "than on any other category of expenditure, except food, clothing, and housing." The average family in the San Diego Mexican community went to the movies fifty times in the year. In Los Angeles things were no different, as the largest proportion of the recreation expenditures by Mexican families was for the movies.[7] Similarly, a distributor of Spanish-language films in Texas pointed out in 1957: "There is no more loyal movie fan in the world than the Mexican or the Latin American; they seem to be willing to spend almost their last dollar for entertainment."[8]

At the start of 1941, approximately 145 theaters in the United States included in their program Spanish-language movies. Four years later, about 300 movie houses were regularly showing Mexican films. This number reached a high point in 1951, when together with schools, clubs and churches, the imported cinema played on 683 screens in 443 U.S. cities.[9] Many of these theaters were small venues operated by local entrepreneurs. In some cases, as in the area near Corpus Christi, Texas, popular carpas or tent shows included movies as part of their program. Stout Jackson, a former champion at weight lifting, owned several carpas where vaudeville shows combined with moneymaking Mexican movies. For over two decades, the Jackson tent theaters provided entertainment to thousands of Hispanics in Robstown, Kingsville and Falfurrias.[10]

The growth of the Mexican movie industry and the coming of boom times to Texas in the mid-forties started an unprecedented era of film exhibition and theater business. The number of theaters in Texas that catered to Spanish-speaking audiences grew steadily during this decade. Movie houses showing imported pictures were springing up everywhere, from El Paso to Brownsville, from Amarillo to Dallas, and beyond. In San Antonio—a city with nearly 100,000 Hispanics—several establishments exhibited Mexican films: the Nacional, Zaragoza, Guadalupe, Obrero and Progreso. Finally, a magnificent movie palace opened in 1949, the Teatro Alameda, built by the influential businessman and head of the Zaragoza Amusement Company, Gaetano A. Lucchese.

The architecturally beautiful Alameda and its annex, called "Casa de México," were a significant meeting point for Hispanics. The theater, a radio station, a photography studio, a restaurant, and other commercial establishments, provided the Mexicans with a link to their culture, language, and favorite pastime, all in one spot. A movie house provided a place of gathering for the family and friends; it supplied entertainment and timely information on the events happening in México (as conveyed by the newsreels). But more deeply the movies satisfied a longing. They were like a mirror that reflected the dreams and atti-

In Texas alone, there were about 147 theaters in the mid-forties catering to Mexicans. Crowd at San Antonio's Teatro Nacional (Ignacio Torres Collection, San Antonio Conservation Society).

tudes of people of Latin American origin. The appeal of the Spanish-language movies made south of the border was suggested by a contemporary editorial of *The Texas Spectator.*

> The Texas-Mexicans wanted pictures with a lot of lusty singing, on the order of Jorge Negrete or the late Lucha Reyes. They wanted some blood and thunder such as they got in the *Charro* pictures (comparable to, although generally better than, American westerns). And they wanted their comedy rough in every sense of that word, which they got from *Cantinflas* with his flood of double meanings and his gruesome sense of humor. The Texas-Mexicans got this in the pictures that Mexico finally began making... These movies are considerably better than American pictures on the whole, because they are more honest. If a man and a woman engage in adultery in a Mexican picture, that fact is made quite plain–at times to the horror of the Catholic Church — and adultery is presented as quite an entertaining pastime. Mexico has apparently never heard of the Hays office or its present equivalent.[11]

Movies with abundant singing and steady action were much in demand in the Southwest. *Charro* films in the style of *Juan Charrasqueado*, which featured virile Pedro Armendáriz and the beautiful Miroslava, attracted large audiences. Movie fans idolized singers/stars like Pedro Infante, Luis Aguilar, and Jorge Negrete. Also, the comedies of *Cantinflas*, or the pachuco *Tin Tan* became box-office hits in the United States. When the film *Sube y baja* was released in San Antonio in 1959, people went back to see it two or three times. This *Cantinflas* vehicle broke all the records for a foreign picture, grossing $32,000 in its first two weeks at San Antonio's Alameda Theater. A distributor in that city

Luis Cruz, owner of the Teatro Chapultepec of Corona, California. Photograph taken in the 1930s (courtesy W.D. Addison Heritage Room, Corona Public Library, Corona, CA).

observed: "I did not imagine that the time would ever come when there would be such worship of *Cantinflas* on the part of the Spanish speaking population."[12]

The Mexican laborers or "braceros," who entered the United States to serve as agricultural workers first during World War II and later in the 1950s, became loyal customers of these movie houses. It is estimated that from 1942 to 1947 about "a quarter of a million Mexicans, all of them male, were employed as braceros throughout the West." At the height of this migrant worker program, in the year 1957, more than 450,000 laborers came to the United States.[13] These figures, obviously, do not count the legions of undocumented workers pouring into the country every year. As a consequence, there was a wave of prosperity for Spanish-speaking theaters during this time. Exhibitors wanting to improve their lot booked Mexican pictures for their shows, as more and more braceros (and "wetbacks") crossing the border to find work demanded entertainment in their own language. In a town like Rio Hondo, in Texas' Lower Rio Grande Valley, a theater owner seized on the opportunity: "I have been playing American pictures all along; but I ran out of bookings, and wanted to try out the Mexican pictures to see what results they would give, and since it is now cotton-picking time, I thought this would be the best time to start. I have heard rumors that we are getting about 2,000 braceros in Rio Hondo this year."[14]

In Arkansas, the cotton season attracted large numbers of contract workers from México. Aware of this migratory movement, more people in the exhibition business prepared to book Spanish-language pictures for their patrons. For instance, starting in September, the owner of the Lake Theater in Lake City requested Spanish product from the distributors in Texas, as "there are going to be several hundred braceros in the area." Even though the Lake had a limited capacity of 180 seats, it was the only theater in town; therefore, the chances for big box-office receipts were good. Other towns in Arkansas, like Osceola, Blytheville, Jonesboro, Marked Tree and Weona had the potential for movies in Spanish. The Clasa-Mohme film exchange in Texas instructed one of its agents to send someone to those cities with a load of movies. The instructions emphasized: "You should, as far as possible, provide him with action pictures, preferably westerns, because almost all of the pickers up there are contract laborers from Mexico without families and they must have the kind of pictures that they can understand." In Knott, Texas, an exhibitor who wanted to maximize profits for his theater requested pictures featuring big names, as "his Mexican clientele liked westerns and musicals with Pedro Infante, Pedro Armendáriz, and Luis Aguilar." The same exhibitor pointed out that he had ambitious plans for the building of a "quonset type theater in Ackerly, Texas, to take care of heavy Sunday afternoon trade."[15]

When the sugar beet season started in Ohio, local exhibitors prepared for the "great many Spanish speaking people in the area made up of both Latin Americans and Porto Ricans." For instance, the owner of the Hollywood Theater in Ottawa, Ohio, a Greek named Theodore C. Chifos, thought he could benefit from this wave of workers. He was confident that the people would rather go to his theater than travel to the nearest town 16 miles away, or to the distant city of Toledo for movie entertainment. Distributors of Mexican films received inquiries from all locations, as scores of theaters were eager to show this type of pictures. Most of the time, the requests represented "temporary business that arises from the heavy immigration of Mexican and other Spanish speaking farm workers who spend three to five months in areas like Michigan," where many contract workers engaged in the sugar beet crop.[16]

Texas and California were the states with the most outlets for Spanish-language movies. In the mid-forties, Texas had about 147 theaters showing Mexican films, whereas California accounted for 100. Colorado registered 65 movie houses for Spanish speakers; New Mexico followed with 64; and Arizona with 41. Florida and New York were also important states with a sizable number of Spanish speakers, who were naturally attracted to films in their own language. Other states like Nebraska, Wyoming and South Dakota, for example, had at least a few movie houses catering to Hispanics.[17]

The names of theaters across the country exhibiting Mexican films were as varied as can be imagined. The spectrum ran from the ostentatious marquees of the Palace, Royal, Million Dollar, Alameda, or El Rey, to the more humble wooden signs of El Jacalito, El Calabozo, El Patio, El Rancho, or El Desplumadero. Many movie houses boasted patriotic or regional names that reminded people of their homeland, such as: México, Jalisco, Tampico, Tejas, España, Valencia, Chapultepec, Popocatépetl, Roma, Madrid, Buenos Aires, Panamericano, etc. When not adopting national heroes' appellatives such as Colón, Cortés, Juárez, Zapata, Zaragoza, or Villa, exhibitors chose the more familiar names of Ramírez, Murillo, López, Chávez, Herrera, Vela, Monsivais, Roque, Guadalupe, Ramón, Victoria, or Yolanda. The list extends to theaters that appealed to ethnic sentiment: Azteca, Mayan, Anáhuac, El Charro, El Mexicano, and El Nacional. Finally, there were other venues with very descriptive names like Fiesta, Carpa, Hut, Tent, Open Air, El Grande, El Ratón, La Sandía, and one called simply El Cine.[18]

By the mid-forties, independent and circuit theater managers throughout the United States had fully realized the potential of Hispanic audiences, who wanted to see movies from Latin America. In order to book these attractions, exhibitors lined up at the doors of suppliers of Mexican films. The distribution companies barely met the demand, as an agent of Clasa-Mohme made plain: "To say that we have been busy these last weeks is to put it in the mildest possible form. We have literally been snowed-under with an avalanche of exhibitors, old and new, and the business is growing at a pace that seems fantastic. I'll admit that a lot of the new business represents small accounts but they help to build up our grosses. Some weeks we put on as many as four new accounts."[19]

The leading distributing companies, Clasa-Mohme and Azteca Films, accomplished a monumental task in bringing Spanish-language pictures to hundreds of theaters that were at the beginning reluctant to book them. In San Antonio, Texas, the manager of Clasa-Mohme, Gordon B. Dunlap, dutifully promoted these films. Judging from his correspondence, it is apparent that Dunlap took pride of the business he represented. Occasionally, he offered sincere comments about the nature of his job. "We find it very interesting to handle the fine pictures that the Mexican producers are now making," Dunlap wrote, "and in some ways we are doing a pioneer work, as we are opening up new theatres and territories for the product that we handle. It is surprising the great strides that the Mexican motion picture industry has made in the last three years.[20]

As thousands of contract laborers and other immigrants flooded the U.S., the demand for Mexican films began to exceed their supply. To compensate for this, many theater managers requested prints of old films that had proven popular in the past. Classic pictures from the thirties like *Allá en el Rancho Grande*, *¡Ora Ponciano!*, or *La Zandunga* played over and over as part of a double bill in small or big theaters until the prints wore out. According to scholar Alex M. Saragoza,

> [Movie houses] were forced to exhibit older movies in order to supplement newer releases. In Los Angeles, for example, in a two-month period in 1948, about 55 motion pictures were shown in theaters patronized by Spanish-speaking people. Yet, during that time, several of the motion pictures were repeated, often as second features, and in different movie-houses. Eighty seven percent of the films shown were made prior to 1947.[21]

Double feature programs constituted a sure-shot strategy for exhibitors, who knew that audiences would eagerly pay the cost of a ticket if this meant the treat of an extra picture. Theaters also implemented various marketing practices, such as personal appearances of singers, film stars and comedians. More often, though, they invited the public to be a part of the show. The "aficionado nights" or "noches del artista ignorado," welcomed anybody who cared enough to perform in front of an audience. San Antonio's Teatro Nacional had a "noche de ingenio" every Sunday night, giving away cash prizes to the most talented. At other times, there were raffles with all sorts of gifts. These commercial strategies worked towards one end: to bring more people into the theaters.

In general, a good picture with recognizable movie stars and an abundance of Mexican songs was the best formula to fill any theater. Stories that highlighted troubled romances or the struggle of the poor in a hostile environment, as well as the gripping family melodramas, were some of the subjects that audiences enjoyed more. For Mexicans living in the United States, watching a film about life in a bucolic hacienda or a drama of the slums was one of the most gratifying experiences. As a contemporary editorial suggested:

> It is truly amazing to observe the enthusiasm caused by a national film when shown to the spectators, especially if it includes Mexican artists. The fact of being outside of their country seems to infuse Mexican subjects with special interest. From the national point of view, each of these pictures brings forth new patriotic sentiments in the hearts of Mexicans. And among the public of Mexican origin that has not directly experienced our environment, one can notice the sparkle of curiosity in their minds regarding our social and historical themes. It is likewise satisfactory to note that a good number of foreigners derive pleasure from these national productions, favoring in particular those that contain musical scenes. These people go to the movies with yet another desire: to take practice in their learning of Spanish.[22]

The films of Jorge Negrete helped reinforce the myth of the *macho*. Original one-sheet poster for *El fanfarrón* (1938) (Agrasánchez Film Archive).

The Impact of Mexican Films

Beyond their basic merit as entertainment, films usually influenced people's values and customs in a varying degree. Regardless of the genre or type of story, a movie had the power of reinforcing the audience's commonly held attitudes and myths. The *charro* pictures, B-girl dramas, and urban comedies provided Hispanics with patterns of behavior and models close to their culture. The ritual of theater going exemplified a resolve by many to remain loyal to their roots. As author David Maciel has pointed out:

> The Mexican films of the Golden Age were films that appealed to everyone in the family. It was a cinema that you could take your entire family to see. It had tremendous social benefits for families. Everybody saw their own stories portrayed in the movies. There were heroes that they identified with. As with the Mexican Revolution itself, their relatives had fought in that upheaval, so it was fresh to them. And the Golden Age was a very patriotic cinema that was close to their heart. And then it became an institution, and it provided not only an escape as entertainment, but it provided cultural nourishment for survival. Because at the same time [the Mexicans] were being bombarded with the process of Americanization. And in order to maintain their "mexicanidad," the cinema turned out to be one of the few institutions around that could nurture this impulse.[23]

The impact of Mexican movies on audiences of the 1940s and 1950s, when television had not yet invaded people's homes, cannot be overstated. In its own way, motion pictures created a social context for the exploration of "mexicanidad," of what it meant to be Mexican. Jorge Negrete, for example, who through many of his songs inspired the pride of being a Mexican, remains an icon of national culture. His cinematic stance as the prototypical *macho* meant more to the adoring fans than the polished personalities of Hollywood's interpreters. Scholar Charles Ramírez Berg has explained: "There was a time when *machismo* was taken for granted and *el macho* was a pose that was unified, natural, and cheerfully unself-conscious. It was a time when a happy and self-assured Jorge Negrete could tilt his sombrero back on his head, smile directly into the camera, and sing about how happy he was to be a Mexican."[24]

With some exceptions, most south-of-the-border movies were designed for the consumption of people who were still illiterate, who resided in small towns, or who were currently moving from rural to urban areas. In this last case, people were caught in a process of assimilation to the new way of life in the cities. The traditions inherited from their ancestors seemed to contradict those of the urban society. Thus, movies of the period warned of the impeding dangers of progress and city life. For example, the 1941 comedy *Del rancho a la capital* told the story of a rural family who moves to the big city only to become the target of ridicule because of their straightforward and unsophisticated manners. Humiliated by the "modern and perverted" life in the capital, the family returns to the ranch, a place where they can live peacefully and take pride in being "rancheros."

Some of the most commercially successful movies in the forties glorified the land and re-invented the province. For example, *¡Qué lindo es Michoacán!*, *Guadalajara pues*, *Bajo el cielo de Sonora*, *¡Ay qué rechulo es Puebla!*, *Yo también soy de Jalisco*, *Sólo Veracruz es bello*, *¡Arriba el Norte!*, and *Como México no hay dos*. The movies brought to the fore an idealized country life, which was basically homogeneous throughout México with only distinctive brushstrokes according to the region. The local landscape, music, dances, costumes, and speech were enthroned and made more glamorous by the movies. These films provided the public with a sense of territorial pride and unrestricted fervor.

The 1941 movie *¡Ay Jalisco, no te rajes!* played over and over in large and small theaters. In Texas, it made close to $3,000 in one week at Houston's Palace Theater. In the

Rio Grande Valley, the picture broke all previous records for a Mexican production. *¡Ay Jalisco, no te rajes!* was reissued frequently many years after it premiered. "Its gross is just as big as ever," the film's distributor happily declared at the end of the forties. Part of the reason for its success was the freshness and vitality of the characters it portrayed. The film cemented the myth of the rural macho dressed up in his typical attire of a rancher from the state of Jalisco: a romantic hero who was equally brave and handsome and remarkably good at singing. Many things contributed to the charm of this movie, including its engaging plot, plain–Spanish dialogues, and likable cast that included the debut of child actress Evita Muñoz, nicknamed *Chachita*. Much of the appeal of *¡Ay Jalisco no te rajes!* involved its music, interpreted by Jorge Negrete, Lucha Reyes and the Trío Tariácuri. To this day, the theme song of the film remains a classic of the ranchero genre.

A lot of movies followed which echoed the title of the first hit: *Así se quiere en Jalisco, El tigre de Jalisco, Hasta que perdió Jalisco, Jalisco canta en Sevilla, La feria de Jalisco,* etc. Producers went to the expense of releasing *Así se quiere en Jalisco,* a 1942 film, in color and with added English subtitles. The picture became an instant hit, making one U.S. distributor comment: "We have never had a better film in the history of this company than *Así se quiere en Jalisco*; it is truly magnificent and will give your audience an idea of the beauty and colorfulness of Mexico and its friendly people."[25]

Audience Preferences

The success or failure of Mexican movies ultimately rested on the preferences of a varied Hispanic public. In Texas and California, the positive response to the national cinema was due to the proximity to the country where these stories originated and because patrons liked films "with Mexican flavor, with folklore and vernacular manners, but above all embellished by ranchero melodies and typical costumes." In those words a Los Angeles exhibitor, Frank Fouce, defined the appeal of Mexican cinema. He praised the public for their "extraordinary indulgence" toward anything that was produced south of the border. Fouce said that this virtue alone accounted for the success of many of the films shown at his theaters: "For these people there are no bad movies, and when a weak picture comes along, I release it with a vaudeville."[26]

Movies conjured up tears and rage, propelling viewers to applaud with passion the exploits of their idols. These pictures targeted a public that was eager and enthusiastic to the extreme. Confirming the overflowing response of Latin American moviegoers in New York, Oscar Godbout, a writer for the *New York Times,* commented:

> The patrons are a wonderfully emotional audience. They have been known to loudly urge the hero on to greater deeds, and the villain often gets an acerbic tongue-lashing. Musicals are the most popular with melodramas and dramas next in line. There is a reason for the similarity of basic structure in these particular films. One booker for a chain of Spanish theatres put it in this way: "If it is a musical, it's got to be a big one, with music all the time. An action picture has to have one player after another being knocked off, and it can't let up the action for a second. The same holds true for dramas; the audience must cry all the way through.[27]

Devotees of Mexican films were as varied as can be imagined, differing in tastes according to the region. In Texas, for instance, the majority of the movie-going public had little or no formal education at all. Immigration from México consisted mainly of rural groups and lower-income citizens. Having this in mind, a film distributor figured:

Y FUE BORRACHO, PARRANDERO Y JUGADOR...

Audiences liked films with Mexican flavor. *Juan Charrasqueado* (1947), a blockbuster that featured the virile Pedro Armendáriz playing the role of Scarface Juan (Agrasánchez Film Archive).

> It must be remembered that we have a vast population of only partially educated people. I think that this condition is perhaps more pronounced in Texas than in any other part of the country, for many Latin American people do not get enough education in English and virtually none at all in Spanish, and many of those who grow up in the country and in farming areas drop out of school before they finish the primary grades.[28]

This lack of sophistication on the part of viewers was perhaps more obvious when measuring the popularity of a few newsreels and short subjects. For example, producers in México City had their "Tele Revista" newsreel enhanced with a sprinkle of comedy. This special brand of humor, however, hardly convinced the general public in Texas. It was observed that "sometimes the little comedy skits go through the [projectors] so fast that lots of people, whose wits are not as sharp as they might be, fail to get the point of the comedy situations and, therefore, are unable to enjoy them."[29] Apparently, some of the newsreels were not popular with audiences. For instance, the manager of the Ritz Theater in Houston, Frank M. Fletcher, offered an interesting excuse for not wanting to show the short subject *Informe presidencial*, a news account of the State of the Union given by México's president in 1959.

> We advertised *Informe presidencial* good and I think it really hurt us, as I think the people liked [the feature] *Besos prohibidos*, but as the customers tell me: "We are Mexican Americans and if we were crazy about Mexico we would live there." Tell us how to end some of these strikes in Houston if you want to make us happy. We see better stuff free on Television than *Informe presidencial*.[30]

Although this sort of attitude was not representative of all patrons in Texas, it showed the fact that "the people of Mexican descent, who live in the Houston area, consider themselves very remote from Mexico and take pride in letting it be known all the time that they are Mexican Americans and don't much care what happens in their Fatherland."[31] The distributor of *Informe presidencial*, however, stated that in no other circumstance had the theater operators rejected this short subject.

Once again, audience preferences weighed heavily on the final selection of films that an exhibitor would make. The same manager of Houston's Teatro Ritz complained again for the lack of appeal of certain movies like *El Lobo solitario, Vuelve el Lobo,* and *La justicia del Lobo*, all featuring Dagoberto Rodríguez and singers Flor Silvestre and Rosa de Castilla. According to this exhibitor, such westerns were complete failures notwithstanding the fact that they had been commercial successes in the Lower Rio Grande Valley of Texas. In a rather colorful letter, he expressed:

> I said the people were tired of those Lobos... My people are no different than anywhere else, only maybe they talk a little more English than in the Valley. They like westerns too and so do I, as I was raised on a ranch. We're not highbrows; we don't like operas; just plain people. Don't you ever look at the American pictures I run with yours? Half of them are western Technicolor and the rest musical or action... Another thing you referred to was the "Pachucos." You know, the only time I let them in the theater is when I play Tin Tan, and I wish I didn't have them then [as] they go to the "Azteca" and have their fights there.[32]

At times, the opposition between Spanish-language movies and Hollywood entertainment was symbolic of the lifestyles of Hispanics in the United States. Very frequently, immigrants who wanted hard to fit into to their new social environment avoided theaters showing films in Spanish. Texas scholar and author, Alfonso Rodríguez, provided an interesting account of this attitude.

> Our home base was Crystal City, Texas, a small town of about 10,000 inhabitants, whose population in the fifties and sixties was about 85 percent Mexicano and almost 15 percent Anglo. There were a few Mexicanos, mostly members of the middle class, who could not identify with Mexican culture because it was offensive to the Anglo minority in town. They felt ashamed of their background... They never spoke Spanish. They only went to see American movies at the Guild Theater; never did they set foot in the Teatro Luna or Teatro Alameda, the barrio theaters which showed Mexican movies, exclusively.[33]

It was the contention of an exhibitor in the New York area that "as the educational level of Puerto Ricans rises and as they become more Americanized, they might not want to see Spanish-language films."[34] The same trend applied to Mexicans in Texas, California and elsewhere. This situation obviously troubled Spanish-language film distributors. In this context, the head of San Antonio's Clasa-Mohme Company ventured to say of audiences that "the less English they learn, the more they appreciate Mexican pictures."[35]

Charro Pictures and Dramas

In the 1930s, United Artists Corporation acquired the rights to distribute one of the first blockbusters of Mexican cinema, *Allá en el Rancho Grande.* It became obvious to UAC that this was an exceptional movie, as it harvested for the company an incredible $59,394 during its first two years of exhibition in Latin America. The company's records showed that, compared with the grosses of other UAC productions, the Mexican film's returns were "only surpassed by Chaplin's *Modern Times*, from which the UAC's royalties were $177,309, and by Selznick's *Garden of Allah*, with *$84,547. Rancho Grande* grossed more than Samuel Goldwyn's *Kid Millions*; Korda's *Scarlet Pimpernel;* 20th Century's *Clive of India* and Walter Wanger's *Algiers*."[36]

Many *charro* pictures were turned into box-office hits thanks to their musical themes. *Allá en el Rancho Grande* exploited the song of the same name made popular in the U.S. by Tito Guízar during the thirties. The 1941 blockbuster, *¡Ay Jalisco no te rajes!*, likewise took its title from a famous "ranchera" song. Another big picture was *Yo maté a Rosita Alvírez*, starring the singer and actor Luis Aguilar. It drew its title and theme from a well-known "corrido," a folk ballad that recounted the tragic story of a rancher who is blinded by jealousy, shooting his sweetheart to death. An article by the *Los Angeles Times* gave a snappy review of this *charro* picture.

> Sireening to end all sirening is that put over by María Luisa Zea in *Yo maté a Rosita Alvírez* ('I Killed Rosita Alvírez') on view at the California, Mason and Roosevelt theaters. Her vamping makes Theda Bara's, or anybody else's, look like a kindergarten effort... The siren works her wiles on two charros who labor on her uncle's ranch, one of said cowboys being engaged to the uncle's daughter. She plays them one against the other, then against a rich man who shows up and becomes enamored of her, precipitating various fights among the men. Finally one of them (Luis Aguilar), driven mad by her duplicity, shoots her. Various features of country life [add] a charming background, but it must be confessed a somewhat rough rodeo isn't pleasant to an American. Mexican music is lovely, as always.[37]

Distributors of Mexican pictures in Texas knew from experience that the most successful movies here were the westerns or *charro* films. According to the manager of Clasa-Mohme in San Antonio, "a picture like *Juan Charrasqueado*, which is of the type that means the most to the Texas territory, means a lot more to us than a sexy picture featuring somebody like María Antonieta Pons, or even one of those good musicals with people like Fernando Fernández and Meche Barba."[38] A variety of the popular movies were the urban melodramas that centered on a fallen woman transformed into a *cabaretera* or B-girl. Because of the abundance of musical interventions these films came to be known as "cine de rumberas," featuring hot female dancers of Caribbean rhythms such as María Antonieta Pons, Amalia Aguilar or Meche Barba. Audiences in Florida, for example, favored this genre above any other. Puerto Ricans as well as immigrants from Cuba and other Caribbean islands especially enjoyed the music and sultry atmosphere of these stories.

Frequently, the box-office pull of any film was measured in terms of the amount of music included in it. A Mexican producer, Alfredo Ripstein, Jr., once said that the distributor José U. Calderón of Azteca Films was hardly curious about the type of story or performers in a given movie. Rather, he only asked two questions when offered a film for distribution: "What is the title and how many songs there are in the picture?" According to Ripstein, the shrewdness of Calderón was even more noticeable when he added: "If you can crowd in nine songs in this movie, I will give you ten thousand dollars. While if you leave only seven, I give you seven thousand."[39]

Dramas came in second with a preference for tearjerkers. A typical hit was *Soledad*, starring a most famous duo of sentimental ladies: Libertad Lamarque and Marga López. *Soledad* was based on a popular radio serial from Argentina. The cinematic version, directed by Miguel Zacarías, became a classic of the melodramatic genre. In the story, Soledad is a poor and suffering mother, who relinquishes her baby daughter to a rich parent. After twenty years, Soledad sees her daughter again, but the encounter turns out to be degrading when the con-

Soledad (1947), an effective tearjerker that became a box-office hit. Above: Rubén Rojo opens his heart to Marga López (Agrasánchez Film Archive).

ceited daughter slaps her mother's face in a climatic moment of the film. Lamarque's performance included "many songs and three tangos."[40] An urban melodrama of the middle class, *Soledad* appealed typically to audiences in large cities. Film distributors in New York often said that any good picture with stars such as Libertad Lamarque, Arturo de Córdova, María Félix, or the Argentine Zully Moreno (all of them usually cast in urban dramas), would surely make money at the local theaters. One such picture from Argentina, *Dios se lo pague*, starring Zully Moreno and Arturo de Córdova, proved very effective at the New York box office.[41]

There were many top-notch dramas promoted by film companies. For example, Clasa-Mohme proudly presented *Río Escondido, Que Dios me perdone,* and *Enamorada;* all of them starring the stunning María Félix. Hailed by distributors as a strong, realistic drama, *Río Escondido* was awarded in México best picture of 1948, winning several "Ariel" prizes (equivalent to the Oscar) and later becoming an international classic. The story has María Félix playing a devoted schoolteacher sent by the Mexican President to "an obscure inland village to help raise the standard of living of the inhabitants, but she runs into heavy opposition in the person of the ruling tyrant." A newspaper in Los Angeles, California, had a word to say about this film that was called in English *Hidden River.*

> Peanut and popcorn noises gave way to sobs and sniffles yesterday at the California, Mason and Roosevelt theaters, when a genuinely excellent Mexican film, *Hidden River,* opened for a week's run. If you have just a smattering of Spanish at your command, or somebody else's sitting next to you, you can enjoy elegance and beauty painted at its best by writer-director

Emilio Fernández; Mexico's No. 1 photographer, Gabriel Figueroa, and the intensely arresting María Félix. And even if you don't understand "sí señor," it doesn't make much difference, since the idea comes across without any complications in a series of exquisite pictorial sequences. Only occasionally does the continuity burst forth in a verbal bombardment.[42]

In 1952, *El derecho de nacer* was released as the most successful melodrama of all times. The picture, starring Spanish actor Jorge Mistral, Gloria Marín and Martha Roth, took its title and story from a popular Cuban novel written by Félix B. Caignet. *El derecho de nacer* combined the essentials of a moralistic and overemotional account about a rich girl in Cuba who has a relationship with an unscrupulous man and becomes pregnant. Right after giving birth, her cruel father plots the killing of the child who is opportunely rescued and hidden by a devoted black nanny. *El derecho de nacer* played in more cities than any previous Mexican picture. In Texas alone, the film was exhibited in 170 theaters, grossing a staggering $143,600 at the box office during a period of two years.[43]

Comedies were very much favored by Spanish-speaking audiences, especially because adults and children and the whole family could go see them. The films featuring Mario Moreno *Cantinflas*, Germán Valdés *Tin Tan*, or Eulalio González *Piporro* were the staple of many exhibitors. As a rule, *Cantinflas*'s comedies attracted crowds that surpassed the seating capacity of all theaters. Some of the biggest box office receipts came from movies like *Soy un prófugo*, *A volar joven*, *El siete machos*, *El bolero de Raquel*, and *Sube y baja*, all featuring the humorous *Cantinflas*. Another exceptional comedian was Germán Valdés *Tin Tan*, star of *El rey del barrio*, and *¡No me defiendas compadre!* Audiences were delighted seeing him "as he rollicks and rolls" through extremely fast-moving comedies.

Perhaps the most successful melodrama of all times, *El derecho de nacer* (1951) played in 170 theaters in Texas (Agrasánchez Film Archive).

A *Cantinflas* movie always meant good business for theaters. Press sheet ad for *Abajo el telón* (1954) (Agrasánchez Film Archive).

Another very funny type was Eulalio González *Piporro*, who embodied the myth of the plainspoken "norteño," a rancher of northern México. The comedies with Piporro were regarded as "the bread and butter pictures for Texas, in that exhibitors are always willing to book them." Finally, pictures with the popular child actress Evita Muñoz *Chachita* were not to be missed by anyone who admired "the Shirley Temple of Mexican cinema." Some of her most enjoyable movies were *Morenita clara, La pequeña madrecita,* and *La hija del payaso*, in addition to the roles she played alongside idol Pedro Infante.

Non-theatrical Exhibition of Movies

Theaters were not the only places where Mexican films played. Although commercial venues represented the main channels of exhibition, other non-lucrative entities consumed south-of-the-border movies. Schools, hospitals, prisons, clubs, and churches

Several Mexican movies were also exhibited at academic institutions. Original one-sheet poster for *La casa colorada* (1947) (Agrasánchez Film Archive).

screened these films. The Clasa-Mohme distributor, for example, serviced 106 accounts of the academic type in 1949. Most of them requested movies in the 16 mm format. Generally, the flat rental price for a feature ranged between $40 and $50 dollars per screening.

Very few Mexican pictures had English sub-titles, and those that did were eagerly sought by educational institutions. Films like *María Candelaria, Flor Silvestre* and *Río Escondido* were quite popular among college teachers and students, as they portrayed stories of a dramatic nature with a strong social message. *Subida al cielo*, a film directed by Luis Buñuel, was also a favorite among avant-garde crowds. Other pictures shown at academic institutions included *Doña Bárbara, Pueblerina, Lluvia roja, Doña Perfecta, La casa colorada, Simón Bolívar, Angelitos negros* and *Memorias de un mexicano.*

San Antonio's Clasa-Mohme distributor eagerly proposed these films to institutions of higher learning. For instance, when referring to the movie *Flor Silvestre*, the manager of this company pointed out: "The acting of Dolores del Río is superlative and a real revelation; the story is gripping and is one which would greatly please women university students."[44] Another dramatic film that had been acclaimed in 1942, *Historia de un gran amor*, was amply recommended by the head of Clasa-Mohme: "This is a very romantic type picture and is just as pleasing to men as it is to women. I recently was told by a Catholic priest who during the summer months often shows pictures in Fort Collins, Colorado, to raise money for his parish, that this is the finest picture he has ever played, barring none."[45]

Movies became an excellent aid for instituting social programs at the local level. In Wichita Falls, for example, the Department of Parks and Recreation requested pictures in Spanish for a community project. The Clasa-Mohme film distributor always encouraged these efforts: "We feel that your project to start recreational facilities for the Spanish speaking young people of Wichita Falls is one that deserves high recommendation. Activities, which originate at your department of a nature that will keep young people off the streets and out of trouble, should be most useful in combating juvenile delinquency.[46]

Church community programs also took advantage of the availability of movies for Hispanic audiences. The list of churches, Catholic schools and convents that requested material in Spanish was very large. For example, Clasa-Mohme provided movies to the Oblate Brothers of Port Lavaca, Texas. During their summer retreats, the brothers showed a wide variety of films, like *¡Ay Jalisco no te rajes!, A toda máquina, ¡Esquina bajan!, Hay lugar para dos,* etc. They seemed to enjoy every picture, particularly *Cartas a Ufemia*, a comedy based on a popular "ranchera" song. The Discalced Carmelite Fathers, in Oklahoma City, were regular customers of the Mexican film distributors and they played many movies at their facilities. The same can be said of the Sisters of the Sacred Heart, from San Juan, Texas. The Catholic school where they taught asked the distributors for a list of pictures suitable for their use. *Los pobres van al cielo* was suggested, since the Catholic Legion of Decency had given it a preferred "A" rating. Also proposed to the Sisters was the movie *Un divorcio,* as it "has been given the highest possible recommendation by the Archbishop of Santa Fe, Edwin V. Byrne."[47]

Clasa-Mohme carried a catalog of about a hundred pictures for non-theatrical use, in the more compact 16 mm format. Many of these titles were appropriate for the whole family and could be programmed at schools and churches. However, the decision to show these movies depended upon the individual criteria of each religious group or institution. As stated by the distributor in a letter addressed to Sister Carmen, of the Sacred Heart Convent in Mathis, Texas: "Our pictures receive classification in Mexico according to the Catholic Legion of Decency and we have a list of such classifications." Clasa-Mohme acknowledged, "Very few pictures ever receive the high classification of 'A,' although there are some that merit this designation. Many films are classed as 'B-1' and 'B-2' and there are others which you would not want to sponsor, for they are occasionally classified as 'C' movies.[48]

A long roster of Mexican movies received the dreadful "C" classification, as a mater of fact. These were crime melodramas or stories with heroines of dubious moral qualities, as portrayed in the popular "cabaretera" genre. Most pictures featuring María Antonieta Pons had the stigma of a "C" category: *La mujer del Puerto, La reina del mambo, Konga roja, La insaciable,* etc. Many films with the Cuban dancer/actress Ninón Sevilla were considered anathema: *Amor y pecado, Perdida, Aventurera, Señora tentación, Mulata* and others. Under the strict censorship of the Catholic Church, films portraying adultery, sex or crime were not recommended. In fact, they were condemned as obscene and as having a negative influence on the public.

Several parishes in Texas regularly exhibited Mexican movies, as was the case in San Antonio, Beaumont, Martindale and San Elizario. The distributor Clasa-Mohme also supplied films to Our Lady of Guadalupe Church, in Amarillo. But it did so with certain difficulty because "we are beginning to have to scratch pretty hard to find acceptable pictures."

> Father A. Rodríguez of Amarillo refuses to take pictures from one company because he cannot be sure that he will be protected against films of questionable taste and bad rating. After all, he cannot exhibit under his own sponsorship, any films which the Legion of Decency classifies as C-1 or C-2, for that would be definitely contrary to his vows and he is usually very careful to stipulate that we do not give him any picture classified as B-3, since such films are catalogued as "para mayores con serios inconvenientes" [for adults; with serious objections].[49]

Still, religious establishments bent on raising funds demonstrated an interest in movies with suggestive titles and proven popular appeal. A few examples are *Amor vendido, Callejera, Amor de la calle,* and *No desearás la mujer de tu hijo,* which were classified as "C" films. The distributors were often amused to see "that an organization such as Sociedad de la Virgen de Guadalupe would want to sponsor pictures of this general type." They attributed this practice, nonetheless, to the fact that such institutions were "more interested in making money than anything else."[50]

Discrimination

Going to the movies in certain areas of the United States involved the challenge of racial discrimination against Mexicans. For many years, the majority of theater owners in Texas were very resistant to admitting Mexicans to their shows. In fact, some of these businessmen did not care much for dark-skinned people or worse; they did not see the value of exhibiting pictures in Spanish. According to the office reports of Clasa-Mohme, the management of certain theater in the aptly named town of White Face, near Lubbock, was regarded as "not interested in Mexican pictures, will not play them; the few Mexicans here would go to Levelland; exhibitor believes in segregation." Also, the town of Hamlin, in the vicinity of Abilene, had a reputation of being "anti–Mexican and Mexicans go around it."[51]

In Midland and Odessa, discrimination was the order of the day. The few movie houses for Mexicans and African-Americans were run very poorly and were kept in segregated

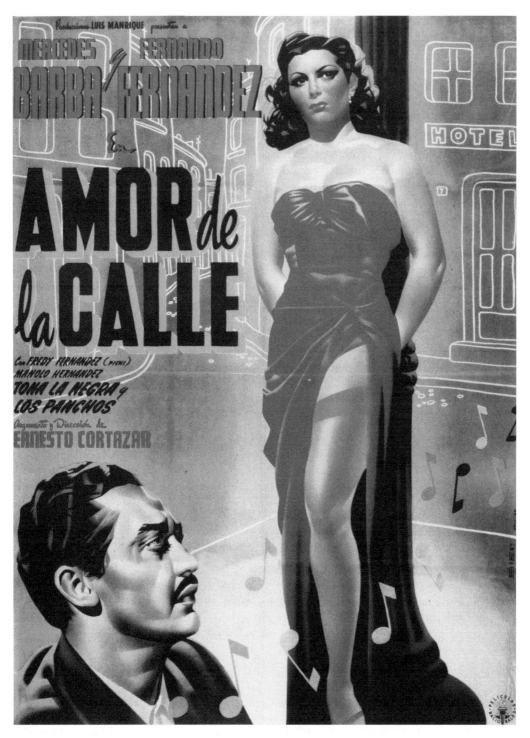

Amor de la calle (1949), one of the many "cabaretera" films that the Mexican Legion of Decency condemned (Agrasánchez Film Archive).

areas. When the agent of Clasa-Mohme went to the city of Odessa, he described the El Mexicano Theater in these terms: "Capacity 150–200 seats. Theater is a shack located in semi Mex-Negro neighborhood, removed from center of town and on a side street, about three blocks from Harlem Theater (a Negro house) that is also a shack." Another place visited by this agent was the Tropical Theater in Midland. He reported that this house "has a capacity of about 200 people, with no lobby, on the outskirts of town, en route to Big Springs. No seats, assorted benches, a poor house, meant to draw from immediate neighborhood only."[52]

Once more, it was clear to the Clasa-Mohme distributors that an exhibitor in Ropesville had decided not to play Mexican pictures because "he thinks his clientele (Americans) would not like the idea and he is doing O.K. with American pictures. Also thinks he gets most of the Mexicans to see these films, puts them in the balcony which seems to him is the policy here."[53] Furthermore, a 1942 official document of the Mexican Consulate in El Paso listed several incidents involving racial discrimination. The report said that in Pecos, theater managers segregated Mexicans and Negroes, who were sent to the balcony seats of these houses. But the worst case of discrimination took place in Morton, a town near Lubbock, where a policeman beat a Mexican and his wife "because they refused to sit in an area designated for blacks in a local theater."[54]

Mexican immigrant workers employed by the Texas and Pacific Railway at Monahans and Midland also complained of prejudiced treatment. Many of them "were denied entrance to public places of entertainment, were not permitted to sit at tables in refreshment parlors or to purchase items there except by using the service entrance, and could not patronize barbershops or other places of service except in areas almost inaccessible to them."[55]

This stringent attitude of racial segregation was prevalent in places like Galveston, Texas, where Mexicans were not allowed to go to the theater of their choice, but only to the one attended by blacks. Still, a concerned group of Mexicans fighting for social acceptance enlisted the help of the local consular agent, who was able to turn things around. "Since Saturday [September 7, 1935] they have started to exhibit Mexican pictures in the best theater in the city, which had not been achieved thus far," a newspaper commented.[56]

Also in a persuasive manner, the efforts of Mexican film distributors in the United States succeeded in making theater businesses open their doors to Hispanics. The process was not an easy one, especially since it involved the volatile issue of race relations. This dilemma is illustrated by the following incident. In 1944, Robert Jones complained that the Capitol Theater in Austin would only exhibit Mexican films after midnight, and that the Hispanic audience received very poor treatment from the theater staff. In a letter sent to the Clasa-Mohme film distributor, Robert Jones, who was also Secretary of the Hispanic American Club in Austin, expressed with bitterness the effect of these midnight shows.

> I have just seen *El peñón de las ánimas*, with Jorge Negrete. And if you only knew the anger I experience when I see what kind of treatment Mexicans receive here! And the way they sell tickets, open the doors to let the people in, and even the disdain and arrogance of the theatre employees towards the Mexicans. As if they were doing us a big favor in charging 40 cents to see only one picture in our Spanish language, and at those scandalous hours, up until two or three in the morning, in a theatre packed full to the second balcony, with so many people left standing. It's an injustice. The way of handling these exhibitions is an insult to the Mexican people. I will not allow them to treat me like an animal. And the Mexican colony is getting to dislike the way they carry on these exhibitions more and more... If this grave situation is not remedied soon, either by the opening of a theatre devoted solely to Mexican pictures, or else by playing Mexican pictures two

María Félix and Jorge Negrete: *El peñon de las ánimas* (1942) (Agrasánchez Film Archive).

or three days a week in some other theatre, *and at a decent hour*, I swear there will be a ruckus here among our people.[57]

The author of this letter also brought to the attention an editorial from the Spanish-language Austin paper *El Demócrata*. The same dissatisfaction was voiced in its article entitled "Midnight or Early Morning Show?" After listing several grievances, the paper concluded that the management of the Capitol Theater "has not found us worthy of getting these pictures during the day, at a time when families can attend; and therefore, they allow us only those hours of the night which they have no use for." In comparison, theaters in the nearby cities of Lockhart, New Braunfels and San Marcos allowed for the exhibition of Mexican pictures during the regular hours of the day.[58]

Censorship

In the United States, the censorship of movies was an issue that hinged on the laws of each state. While Texas had a more flexible attitude in overseeing the morals of pictures, in New York and Illinois this vigilance became an obsessive practice. The censors targeted all films: national and foreign. Examples of Mexican pictures that ran up against the New York and Chicago censorship codes were: *Mujeres de hoy, Profanación, Pecados de amor, El prisionero 13, Chucho el Roto* and *México lindo*. All of them were officially mutilated before their release in the 1930s. For example, the censors found the execution by firing squad in *El prisionero 13* excessively realistic. *Chucho el Roto* seemed to be an apology of thieves and was "revised" before its public showing. *Pecados de amor* also underwent some "eliminations" prior to screening, and *Mujeres de hoy* was not even allowed for exhibition by the Chicago Police Department. The musical *México lindo* presented several folkloric dances, one of them exposing a partially nude Indian woman. Only after wielding the scissors, was this film authorized.[59]

A different attitude prevailed in Los Angeles, California, where movies played almost unrestricted. In 1947, *Bailando en las nubes* was billed at three theaters. This musical melodrama featured the slender Canta Maya, a dancer with a heavy French accent. A newspaper review of the film warned: "Señorita Maya appears in one barbaric number which our censors probably would blue-pencil pronto." Although the musical sequence in question had Miss Maya embracing with an imposing half-naked black man, it apparently went unnoticed by the local censorship viewers.[60]

One of the states with dreadful censorship practices was Ohio. Distributors of Mexican films complained in private that several of their movies were not approved in this territory "until certain cuts were made in the pictures." When Clasa-Mohme was supplying more films to clubs and universities in the year 1950, the issue became a matter of concern for the distributors.

> Ohio has a very strict censorship law with a fine of $500 for each violation. We are trying to move very carefully and for the time being I am turning down all requests for bookings... The Censorship Board of Columbus, Ohio, demands above all things that the translation of the dialogue script be filed with the request of censorship, which is apparently what you [also] have to do in New York. This, however, would be a very difficult, involved, and costly procedure.[61]

Although the harsh attitude exercised by the official censorship was already diminishing in the mid-fifties, several groups felt it was their duty to keep the morals of public sentiment uncontaminated. Film distributors worried that the establishment of local censorship groups could seriously affect their business. One such "advisory board" was planned in San Antonio, Texas, in 1955. With the support of the Catholic Church, this group intended "to preview Mexican movies with the purpose of curbing the showing of immoral movies and movie displays." Immediately, the regional distributor of Clasa-Mohme asked its home office in Los Angeles for legal advise. A spontaneous reply came from California: "There is no reason why we should show all our pictures to these people. We could show them *El hombre que quiso ser pobre*, which is a good clean picture, or any other future release that you consider unobjectionable to the Church committee."[70]

The movie *Subida al cielo* provided yet another instance of censorship intimidation. Directed by Luis Buñuel and starring the exuberant Lilia Prado, the story followed a young man in a fishing village who is forced to leave his bride on their very wedding night. Once he gets on a crowded passenger bus, he is put face to face with the town's most provocative girl (Lilia Prado). An erotic adventure ensues, highlighted by some memorable surrealist scenes. The acting, the photography, and the direction of this picture were all finely executed. When *Subida al cielo* was released in the U.S. with English subtitles as *Mexican Bus Ride*, several people and institutions lined up to request a booking.[62] But in one particular case the distributor of the film had to reject a proposition for self-censorship.

> The booking that was requested, however, by Mr. Rodgers of Youngstown College, Youngstown, Ohio, is out the window as far as I am concerned, because I simply refuse to cut a print to accommodate some of those narrow-minded people, who, even though they might not be blue noses, are subject to the high handed control of the people in the censorship office.[63]

TIMELY and *Great* ENTERTAINMENT!

☆ **PROVOCATIVE!**
☆ **SHOCKING!**
☆ **GRIPPING!**

A Sensational Story Which No One Had Dared To Film Before!!

"LITTLE DARK ANGELS"

("ANGELITOS NEGROS")

PEDRO INFANTE, favorite singing actor of Latin America. RITA MONTANER, and EMILIA GUIU in the dramatic sensation LITTLE DARK ANGELS. Complete English titles. Distributed by Clasa-Mohme, Inc.

NOW AVAILABLE WITH COMPLETE ENGLISH TITLES

☆

YOU CAN

◀ **EXPLOIT IT!**
◀ **PUBLICIZE IT!**
◀ **PROMOTE IT!**

Successfully!

Released with English subtitles, *Angelitos negros* (1948) became even more popular and controversial in the United States (Agrasánchez Film Archive).

Very few pictures were as controversial as *Angelitos negros*, a 1948 film starring Pedro Infante and Emilia Guiú. The movie, which had several songs performed by Infante, touched the subject of inter-racial marriages and dealt with the common prejudices of whites toward blacks. In this popular tearjerker, a young white couple gives birth to a black child. The wife despises the baby, ignoring that she herself is in reality the daughter of a black woman, who in turn passes as her nanny. A lot of complications ensue, including the tragic death of the nanny. But in the end the black child regains her mother's love and a new life begins for the family.

Special prints with English subtitles were made available for the U.S. release of *Angelitos negros*. The lobby cards for the promotion of *Little Dark Angels*–as this version was called — gave some clues to the story: "A poignant film drama; Mother love at its purest; a symbol of tenderness and sacrifice. With beautiful Cuban songs." While the distributor worried that people in Texas "might object to the miscegenation theme and would walk out on the picture," it nonetheless showed confidence in broad-minded viewers.

> No doubt your audience was to some extent stirred by the controversial aspect of the theme of *Little Dark Angels*, although in our far Northern state of Vermont (this is from our point of view) probably there is less feeling aroused by a theme such as that treated in this film, as it is in the South where hot blood flows in people's veins and where tempers are easily frayed by the problem of miscegenation.[64]

Mexican cinema produced a few more stories dealing with racial conflict. Among these, another popular melodrama stands out: *Negro es mi color*, starring Marga López who plays "a girl with Negro blood but a white skin." The advertising proclaimed in typical fashion: "Not blood but deadly poison flowed through her veins; Ancestral hate; Turbulent passions!" Another film that caught the eye of the public was *La mulata de Córdoba*, which told the tragedy of "a mulatto girl divided between two societies." Although the New York censorship board opposed its exhibition, theaters in Los Angeles, California, unencumbered, offered the movie to its numerous clientele. A local newspaper gave an enlightening view of the story.

> The Mexican screen this week presents a controversial theme. Unlike Hollywood film fare, the Mexican screen is not subject to strict censorship. This may account in part for the success of many films seen here, permitting adult story treatment of underlying psychological factors. *The Mulatto Girl of Cordoba* is an intelligently handled story about a white plantation-owner who falls in love with a Negro girl. Despite the protests of his family, he marries her. They live in seclusion; ostracized by the villagers... The film has been given every care in human values. Its straight story presentation is commendable. As a production it has pictorial loveliness. The setting of the village with its background of native songs and dances; and the rich voice of Toña la Negra, famous Mexican singer...[65]

In the mid-fifties, Mexican cinema produced a series of films targeting adult audiences, some of the titles attesting to their content: *La fuerza del deseo*, *El seductor*, *Camino del mal*, and *La Adúltera*. All of these featured the beautiful Ana Luisa Peluffo, a young Mexican actress who inaugurated female nudity in the movies of the period. Every now and then, the pictures met with opposition from an exhibitor who was unwilling to show them. In San Antonio, Texas, for instance, the manager of the Alameda Theater did not want to exhibit Ana Luisa Peluffo's *Besos de arena*. He argued that this controversial actress was "not popular in San Antonio, as she has been typed as an exponent of sex to such an extent that some families will not go to a theater where one of her pictures is playing."[66] While this exhibitor oftentimes censored Miss Peluffo's film appearances, he did not mind to include in the program other comparable pictures like *Esposas infieles*, a film portraying sexy Kitty de Hoyos in audacious scenes and advertised through shocking posters. Theatergoers in San Antonio were aroused by this movie, which made "a pretty good business" at the Alameda during the opening day. The distributor of the film calculated: "Good weather no doubt has something to do with it, and perhaps the public is going to the theatre with the idea that they may be seeing something naughty."[67]

Certainly, the Catholic Church played an important role in film censorship, and any motion picture distributor with a degree of success had to abide by the standards of this dominant institution. The Church regularly issued a catalog of film titles that had been reviewed by the Mexican Legion of Decency. This catalog established a rating system by which distributors and exhibitors might be guided. Films were classified under the following categories: "A" for "Good for everyone"; "B-1" for "Adolescents and adults"; "B-2" for "Adults, with inconvenient content"; "B-3" for "Adults, with serious inconvenient content"; "C-1" for "Objectionable"; "C-2" for "Prohibited by Christian morals."

Although distributors of Mexican pictures in the United States did not expressly adhere to any creed's guidance, they had to follow a certain policy with respect to film censorship. Clasa-Mohme, for instance, distributed product regardless of the rating given to films by the Catholic Church. However, when dealing with specific "fussy exhibitors," the company cared enough not to offer certain movies that could be considered inappropriate. When the melodrama *La adúltera* (The Adulteress) was released, for example, Clasa-Mohme took precautions.

> Many customers of this office are highly conscious of ratings given to Spanish-language films by the Catholic Legion of Decency located in Mexico City.... In the Rio Grande Valley, where the influence of the Church is very great, exhibitors like Enrique Flores of the Rio Theatre, Mission, Mrs. E. R. Ruenes of the Ruenes Theatre, San Benito, and Mrs. E. R. Cuellar of the Mexico Theatre, McAllen, just to cite a few examples, are among those who work in close conjunction with the Church and will not accept pictures with bad ratings like *La adúltera*.[68]

In the Rio Grande Valley of Texas, there was a furious reaction on the part of Catholics when *Mulata* played. The movie that featured Ninón Sevilla contained scenes of erotic dances amid a Cuban pagan ritual called "Bembé." Naturally, the Church cautioned the public against patronizing theaters that showed *Mulata*. But the circuit belonging to exhibitor Miguel Benitez took full advantage of the unintended publicity, welcoming the impudent crowds that wanted to see the film.[69]

The Role of Exhibitors

In the 1940s, the number of Mexicans who came to the United States to find work increased substantially. The Bracero Program–established by the two neighboring countries after the U.S. entered World War II — allowed for many Mexicans to serve in the U.S. mainly as agricultural workers, but also as a maintenance force for the railways. When the war ended, this bi-national program had attracted some 300,000 laborers that took jobs in 25 different states. Because the Mexican government opposed the unfair treatment of migrant workers in Texas, the Bracero Program was excluded from this state. Instead, lots of Texas farmers turned to the hiring of illegal workers or "wetbacks." This clandestine labor force increased every year, to the point that, at the beginning of 1947, "the Mexican government secured the United States' consent to technical legalization of the estimated one hundred thousand wetbacks in Texas and the Southwest."[71]

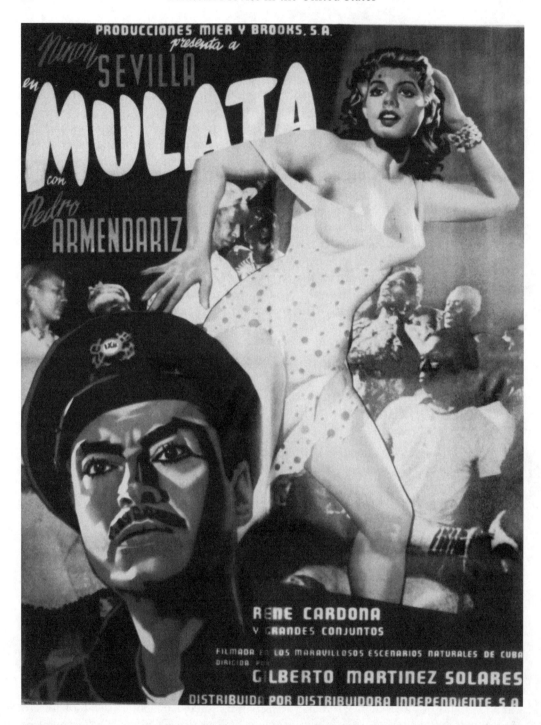

In spite of Catholic censorship, the impudent crowds went to see a very hot movie: *Mulata* (1953), starring Cuban dancer Ninón Sevilla (Agrasánchez Film Archive).

The sheer size of the immigrant movement had a profound impact on the entertainment business as well. Many movie theaters that were regularly showing English-language films turned their attention to this expanding audience and to the revenue that it represented. Small and large theaters alike experimented with pictures in Spanish, generally making good business. For example, the Globe Theater in Chicago tried a special premiere of *Juan Charrasqueado* in 1948. Encouraged by the success of this picture, the theater owner immediately asked Azteca Films distributors to provide him with more Mexican pictures. Powerful theatrical companies were also interested in acquiring "a few of the houses in the towns with the best income possibilities." Starting in the 1930s and 1940s, Interstate Circuit of Dallas bought or leased several venues in Texas for the exclusive use of Hispanic audiences. But a great number of Spanish-language theaters were in the hands of local impresarios, some of whom had a decisive advantage over big theater chains: the advantage of "race and blood." As suggested by the *Texas Spectator*, "a majority of the men who own and operate these little houses are part–Mexican or married to part–Mexicans." Local owners were also very resourceful:

> Independents managed to stay open through such devices as penny nights and vaudeville ... and they began to give their customers more. In addition to presenting, on the whole, better pictures than the English-language houses, they remodeled their theaters, put in good sound and projection machinery, installed air conditioning, and in general matched the English-language movies in the matter of comfort for the cash customers.[72]

Gordon B. Dunlap, head of San Antonio's Clasa-Mohme, emphasized the importance of theater entrepreneurs in the cultural life of the community. In a letter, this executive commented on the central role played by exhibitors:

> [The showing of] Mexican pictures is one of the most satisfactory business that there is and your audiences are so appreciative of what is done for them to the extent that a man really feels good in the thought that he is bringing them entertainment which is opening new worlds to most of them. You may have noticed that most Mexicans or Spanish-speaking people are not very talkative or demonstrative, but deep down inside they appreciate these things and you can feel that you are in a sense a benefactor when you give them these really outstanding attractions.[73]

In Miami, Florida, the Flagler Theater functioned as the main entertainment house exhibiting Spanish-language films in the mid-fifties. A few blocks away stood the Tívoli, which showed second-run Hollywood pictures and an occasional European or "art film." But, according to Clasa-Mohme, the business was a failure; its operator "soon discovered that about the only solution for the Tívoli Theatre would be Spanish-language pictures, since so many people had migrated from Cuba and other islands and countries around the Caribbean area, taking up residence near both of these houses."[74] The Flagler and Tívoli Theaters competed against each other for a share of the Spanish-language market, which was by all means substantial in the area. The supplier of films Clasa-Mohme conceded, "The total revenue from Miami is a most important part of our business."[75]

People from diverse regions in the U.S. wanted to gain access to the exhibition business. For many of them, the showing of pictures seemed to be the "quickest way to riches." An example could be drawn from Chicago resident Dr. Carlos Castro, who wrote an overly optimistic letter to the Clasa-Mohme film distributor. In it, he said he could open up a theater for Mexican movies in that city, with little or no difficulty at all. The distributor, however, cautioned Dr. Castro of the intricacies of the business, citing that the available product "is already greatly in demand and practically being fought over by the exhibitors" in the Chicago area. In 1952, Chicago had several Spanish-language shows. Some of the

The Clasa-Mohme exchange in San Antonio, Texas, distributed films as far away as Oklahoma, Louisiana and Florida. Photograph taken in 1944 (Agrasánchez Film Archive).

most important were the Teatro Villa, managed by Henry Erenberg, a devoted enthusiast of Mexican films; and the newly-opened Teatro Tampico, on Roosevelt and Paulina Streets, which was owned by Abraham Gómez.[76]

Several independents often met with obstacles in their efforts to establish a new movie business. The most common cause of concern was their failure to attract a steady audience. For instance, the Maxon Theater in Portageville, Missouri, had booked twelve Mexican pictures in 1949, of which only six grossed enough money to pay for rentals. The Maxon's and another exhibitor from the town of Risco (the Algerian Theater) had to quit their experiment with Spanish-language films because "the receipts were not very good."[77] Also, an impediment to success came from the competitors in the same area. A man from Cotulla, Texas, for example, bought an old theater in this city and remodeled it "to a first class theater." He was very enthusiastic about showing Spanish-language films but the established theaters in the locality made it impossible for him to start a business.

> Finally I got it completed but the other theatres booked every film that they could get hold of. They left me out completely. In despair, I bought another local theatre (the Victory), hoping to get the film contract with [the distributors]; but Ramírez Theatre went to Azteca Film Exchange and bought the contract for $265 to freeze me out and he did. [Then] I opened the theatre with few old pictures from Republic, but I had no success. The Majestic and Ramírez booked the pictures of every company in the United States and Mexico. I have a $20,000 theatre, modern and beautiful, and it is a shame to keep it closed. I didn't know that competition was so keen in this field to be almost barbaric.[78]

A regular policy of Clasa-Mohme with respect to first-time exhibitors was to help the new business achieve some degree of stability. It was to the advantage of both parties to keep running the theater, even if this meant sacrificing high returns on the part of the film distributor. As described by an employee of Clasa-Mohme: "I have heard Mr. Mohme say that it is better to get more pictures played at a fair price, thereby increasing our distribution, than to restrict our bookings to very few engagements at high prices." This philosophy helped build strong business ties between theater operators and the supplier of films.[79] When an important exhibitor from Florida, Joe Chamoun, complained that his theater was not making enough money with Mexican pictures, the executives of Clasa-Mohme suggested that the theater owner should make available his accounting books, "and if they showed that we were charging too much, we would be very happy to make a contract for a lesser price." This gesture motivated Chamoun to the degree that he remained a loyal customer of Clasa-Mohme for many years, operating two houses in Florida, the Teatro Casino in Ybor City, and the Royal Theater in West Tampa.[80]

Oscar D. Ramírez, owner of the Flagler Theater in Miami, likewise asked the film distributors for help, as his business was not doing very good. He readily accepted the proposal to make available a breakdown of his theater expenses. The Flagler's gross income for eight months was calculated at $39,689. This figure included income from box office receipts, candy sales, vending machines, and paid advertising. Total operating expenses of this theater amounted to $40,587, where film rental and salaries alone took the lion's share of $23,067. The Clasa-Mohme film suppliers understood that "Mr. Ramírez isn't making too much from the business." Thus, in order to improve the situation of the Flagler Theater, a new contract with better terms for the exhibitor was implemented.[81]

Frictions between the distributor and the operator of a movie house were unavoidable though. In New Orleans, for example, a Miss Wellington acquired the lease of the Garden Theater, which exhibited Clasa-Mohme product. She and an associate of hers had rented the property thinking that this would be a good business.

> It proved to be anything but a gold mine and these people lost heavily, to such an extent that they have run out on their indebtedness and cannot be located. I don't think that we will ever discover the whereabouts of Miss Wellington... Our chances to obtain box office receipts and percentage rentals for three pictures that we served to this theatre during the summer are absolutely nil.[82]

Business was getting tougher for distributors and exhibitors in 1960, a year in which many small-town theaters were forced to shut down their doors. This situation derived principally from the widespread acceptance of television entertainment. "It is astonishing to look back into the records of business of ten years ago, or even as late as five years ago, to see how many theatres have disappeared entirely," commented Clasa-Mohme's Gordon B. Dunlap. He also was anxious because a considerable number of exhibitors, "including several of importance are somewhat delinquent in the reporting of percentage pictures and in the payment of service." Dunlap's patience was nearing an end when he expressed:

> Eddie Joseph of Austin, one of the prominent exhibitors of Texas, continually gives us a bad time. Mr. Ratcliff of Epsom drive-in theatre, Houston, is another man who thinks we should help finance his operations during the bad winter months. Leon Bernstein of the Trail drive-in theatre, El Paso, is one of the worst with whom I have dealt. He refuses to answer letters and won't send box office reports and money... I am not going to take any more bookings from this man. Some months ago he started a business of selling coins to collectors... I am convinced that he has been using our money to his own purposes, figuring he can get away with it. The credit situation here in Texas has gone from bad to worse and I see very little chance for improvement. J. G. Long of Long Theatres, which controls

many towns, is way behind and I doubt that he will ever catch up... This get-tough policy that I am instituting may cost us some customers. Eventually they will all come back, for pictures prove to be magic magnet and we are fortunate in having lots of films.[83]

It has been said that one of the factors adversely affecting theater attendance in the sixties was the enormous competition from television. But another issue refers to the changing attitudes of the new generation, as people of Hispanic background began to identify more with Hollywood's movies and American popular culture in general. This trend made young audiences avoid the Spanish-language spectacle and the theaters that offered it. Furthermore, theaters were losing a substantial number of their seasonal patrons when agricultural mechanization and the enforcement of new immigration laws in the decade reduced the influx of *braceros* and "wetbacks."

Prints, Short Subjects and Advertising

Proper exploitation of a movie required distributors to have the adequate number of prints, trailers, short subjects and publicity accessories at hand. In Texas, for example, Clasa-Mohme distributors normally called for a minimum of three 35mm prints for every feature to be released commercially. This standard also applied to the other major distributor, Azteca Films. Both companies' subsidiaries in San Antonio had to look after the large territory of Texas. Clasa-Mohme, in addition, handled many theater accounts outside this area, including Oklahoma, Louisiana and Florida. The film stock of this exchange was always very tight as far as available prints of popular movies. During World War II, the rationing of celluloid by the United States government made the supply of prints to be cut down from three to two. Therefore, distributors had to manage their product in the most efficient and careful manner. Sometimes, prints got damaged by a theater's projector or by an unexpected fire in the booth, complicating matters for the distributors. In order to discipline theater managers, Clasa-Mohme often levied extra charges for any spoiled reels, warning the operators: "We simply cannot get positive prints from Mexico any longer for replacement."[84]

During normal times, the number of release prints for a territory like Texas could increase to four or even five, as was the case of several smash hits like *Juan Charrasqueado*, *El derecho de nacer*, and *La Cucaracha*. One of the most successful Mexican features was *La Cucaracha*, which played in scores of U.S. theaters in 1960. The Clasa-Mohme distributor in Texas ordered five prints and six trailers of this popular color picture. Having such material available made it possible for the distributor to book the movie more efficiently, obtaining maximum profits from its initial run in the summer of that year. The life duration of a 35mm print depended ultimately on its careful handling by distributors and exhibitors. Some popular films, like those featuring Pedro Infante, were booked continuously yielding an average of one hundred screenings per print. Although highly flammable, a print on nitrate stock was more durable than the newer "safety film," which replaced nitrate celluloid in the 1950s. The exchanges also carried prints of certain titles in 16mm, a more compact format that was preferred by clubs and universities. For this specific market, Clasa-Mohme made available English subtitled versions of a few selected films.

Both distributors of Mexican pictures in the United States promoted the use of short subjects in every theater. Azteca Films and Clasa-Mohme carried their own distinctive brand of newsreels in Spanish: *Noticiario Mexicano*, carried by the former and *Revista Mexicana*, put out by the latter. These subjects were issued weekly. According to the publicity of Azteca Films, they were "Produced in Mexico; Up to the minute; Gives our people welcome news of home and country; Vital for the goodwill of your patrons; A must in every theatre." The reels contained the latest information about Mexican boxing, racing, swimming, soccer, baseball, polo, athletic events, bullfights, football, aviation, civic and government events, etc. As ephemeral as they might have been, the importance of these short features lay in their potential to reinforce the national sentiment and cultural values of many Mexican immigrants, as well as a large group of Mexican-Americans who still saw themselves as *mexicanos*.

The best way to advertise a film was by playing a trailer, a five-minute reel previewing the picture. Exhibitors could rent these trailers from the distributor for a five-dollar fee, to be run in the theater a week before the release of the feature. They also had at their disposal an assortment of movie posters, lobby cards, and still photographs. Handbills advertising the movies were quite popular and inexpensive items. The circulation of these fliers constituted an effective way of attracting a large audience. Handbills usually had a printed black & white illustration, with the name of the movie, its cast, and the date and place of showing. When radio or newspaper advertising was unaffordable, the spreading of handbills achieved almost the same goal. One distributor recommended its use: "I have always considered the handbills as being very effective and as carrying a permanent message to the public. These people usually save such programs as of great interest for they receive very little literature in their own language, and they are great savers of anything of this nature, even going so far as to decorate their homes with them."[85]

Some exhibitors had their own pick-up truck–plastered with posters of the current attractions— which traveled all around the city to advertise a film. Many times, the driver carried a loudspeaker to spread the spectacle's sensations. Loud music also forced nearby people to take notice. More elaborate means of promoting a picture included the use of radio, television, and newspapers announcements. For those willing to pay for a radio spot, the distributor made available recorded material for the advertising of movies. The tapes and disks, which became available in the late fifties, contained a segment of a song and the most important or dramatic dialogues from the film. Apparently, theaters in small towns did not favor this method of promotion. According to a distributor, "most exhibitors in Texas just won't be bothered with radio tapes. Some exhibitors say that we give too much dialogue to the public and it spoils attendance at the theatre. Others allege that the high cost of radio time makes it almost prohibitive for them to use the tapes."[86]

Besides the standard supply of one-sheet posters, lobby cards and B&W photographs, Clasa-Mohme provided theater managers with yet another advertising tool: the "Box Office Tonic." These 8 × 10 bilingual publicity pages reproduced photographs and poster artwork from the film, as well as including an assortment of catchy phrases meant to attract audiences. A salient characteristic of the "Tonic" was that it often quoted newspaper articles with reviews about the movie. Curiously, these reviews were copied unedited and no effort was made by the distributor to hide the critic's typically poignant or even adverse opinion of a film.

For example, the "Box Office Tonic" for the 1945 boxing melodrama *Campeón sin corona* included a review by critic Marie Mesmer, who wrote: "This is the same old stuff. David Silva doesn't look at all comfortable in the role of a prizefighter. He tries hard for the burly part, but it just doesn't come off. His mannerisms aren't natural. If the lifelike treatment had been maintained throughout, the film might have succeeded as a serious study of a poor Mexican boy who has a chance at success." To advertise Pedro Infante's best remembered film *Nosotros los pobres*, Clasa-Mohme's "Tonic" selected a commentary

FERNANDO SOTO, AMANDA DEL LLANO, y DAVID SILVA en una escena emocionante de "CAMPEON SIN CORONA." una superproducción de Raúl de Anda, distribuida por Clasa-Mohme, Inc.

A publicity tool, the "Box Office Tonic" contained an assortment of catchy phrases in English and Spanish. *Campeón sin corona* (1945) (Agrasánchez Film Archive).

from the *Los Angeles Times*, which read: "The trouble with *Nosotros los pobres* (We, the Poor) is that which afflicts many Mexican pictures. It crowds in too many dramatic doings to be a tightly integrated story. No tear-jerking situation is too old or corny to be used. However, there are redeeming qualities. The acting is superb. Also there are emotionally arresting moments." Shockingly, some very negative film reviews found ample space in the "Box Office Tonic" pages. This was obvious in the publicity for the movie *Ya tengo a mi hijo*, a drama about "a famous kidnapping case, reenacted on the screen by the kidnapped child himself!" The critic's thundering comment read: "The very emotional impact the film attempts to convey is lost in a maze of undramatic detail and unconvincing direction. Unfortunately, as it stands, the production neither takes full advantage of the opportunity offered nor furnishes good entertainment."[87]

Cinema and the Press

Printed sources with information about Mexican movies were available in most areas of the United States. Newspapers, in particular the Spanish-language editions, advertised the release of pictures and promoted local theaters. Exhibitors who could afford this medium placed ads as frequently as each change of program required. *La Opinión* of Los Angeles, *La Prensa* of San Antonio, *El Continental* of El Paso, and several others were the main papers preferred by Hispanics. Even small communities, like the Pomona Valley in California or the Texas town of San Diego, had their own periodicals in Spanish. These publications were important vehicles for the promotion of Mexican films. Besides their regular theater ad column, newspapers carried a section dedicated to Mexican and Hollywood cinema. In the 1930s and 1940s, *La Prensa*'s Sunday edition contained a page full of information about the Spanish-language film industry, its stars, directors, etc. San Antonio theaters, like the Zaragoza, Nacional, Guadalupe, and Alameda advertised continuously using very attractive ad displays and poster illustrations of the films. *La Opinión* equally announced the theaters in Los Angeles, giving preference to the California, Mason, Roosevelt, Mayan, and Million Dollar Theaters.

Some English-language newspapers also advertised and gave reviews of Mexican movies. The *Los Angeles Times* and the *Daily News* appraised the Mexican films shown in Los Angeles during the forties, while *The New York Times* offered commentary on all foreign pictures released by local theaters in the 1930s and 1940s. The monthly magazine *Cine Mundial*, which was issued in New York, also provided information about Spanish and Latin American film stars working for the Hollywood studios, like Antonio Moreno, Lupe Vélez, Dolores del Río, Tito Guízar, etc. A column dedicated to Mexican movies, called "El cine en Méjico," and another section with interviews of famous Hispanic actors, made this a popular publication. The pages of *Cine Mundial* carried excellent illustrations and many good photographs.

Widely read by New York's Puerto Ricans and other Spanish speakers were *Cine Variedades*, a publication devoted to film fans, and the community-oriented magazine *Revista de Artes y Letras*. Their articles contributed to the dissemination of news about films from Hollywood, México and the rest of Latin America. Other New York journals, like *Gráfico*, frequently advertised current movies and reported on personalities of the Latin American silver screen. Even Masonic-style journals, like *Alianza* of Tucson, Arizona, carried information about Mexican cinema.[88]

Printed in Los Angeles, *La Novela Cinegráfica* became the leading source of information for the Hispanic film buff. The ten-cent monthly magazine began circulating in October of 1947 with the aim of "familiarizing the public with the stories, the songs, and the dialogues of the Spanish-language films." This was the first magazine "addressing specifically the Spanish-speaking audiences of the United States, the Philippines, Puerto Rico, and the North of Mexico." Its director, Armando del Moral, enthusiastically announced that the 10,000 copies of the first issue had been insufficient, therefore increasing the subsequent runs of the magazine to 30,000 copies. The pages of *La Novela* contained a "novelización," a dramatic narration of a popular Mexican movie. The stories of *Pepita Jiménez, Soy un prófugo, Los tres huastecos, Nosotros los pobres* and many others were the meat of this publication. It also offered a "cancionero fílmico" with the lyrics of famous songs, a section on Hollywood stars, and a "correo íntimo" answering letters from the public or even analyzing personal handwriting. A section advertising upcoming movies, and a page recounting the development of Mexican cinema were likewise included.

The editors of *La Novela Cinegráfica* received hundreds of letters from movie fans. Many of them requested photographs of their idols, while the majority just wanted to get in touch with other fans of Mexican stars. A few placed personal ads in order "to have written correspondence with *señoritas* from anywhere in the continent." Even university Spanish teachers found this publication useful. A Mrs. Gray, from San José State College, planned on taking a group of fifty faculty members to see a *Cantinflas* movie; she ordered copies of the magazine's story of *Soy un prófugo*, so that the group could better understand and enjoy this comedy.

Another feature of *La Novela Cinegráfica* was the section called "El barómetro de la fama," which functioned as a thermometer measuring the popularity of movie stars. Readers were invited to vote for their favorite screen idols. The four-category poll cast the following results in an issue of 1950. Male singers: Pedro Infante (4,589 votes), Jorge Negrete (1,455), Luis Aguilar (900), and Antonio Badú (798). Female singers: Libertad Lamarque (855 votes), María Antonieta Pons (800), Sofía Álvarez (475), and Amanda del Llano (315). Actors: Pedro Armendáriz (821 votes), Arturo de Córdova (756), Gustavo Rojo (400), and Ricardo Montalbán (384). Actresses: María Félix (976 votes), Rosita Quintana (544), Dolores del Río (454), and Esther Fernández (357).[89]

Publications such as *La Novela Cinegráfica* illustrate the importance given to the Mexican star system during the forties and fifties. The contents of this periodical reflected the trends and preferences of contemporary moviegoers. Furthermore, its popularity demonstrates that a cinematic culture–in which audiences were able to exchange experiences and opinions on the movies— was in the making. Besides *La Novela Cinegráfica,* several magazines printed in México also circulated in the United States. The weekly issues of *Cinema reporter, Novelas de la pantalla, Álbum de oro,* and *México cinema,* were widely read by movie fans and could be bought at almost any city with a substantial Hispanic population north of the Rio Grande.

Distribution of Films

The distribution of Mexican motion pictures in the United States had its beginnings in the early twenties. In 1922, the International Amusement Company with offices in El Paso, Texas, and México City began to negotiate for films made by Mexican producers. This company, for example, acquired the rights of *El caporal* and *El hombre sin patria,* two silent movies produced and directed by Miguel Contreras Torres. For the first picture, the distributor paid $800 that included the cost of a 35mm print of the movie. According to Contreras Torres, the distribution company made a profitable deal with *El caporal,* which he said grossed more than $15,000 at the box office. *El hombre sin patria* (aka *Los braceros mexicanos*) was later sold to the same firm by Contreras Torres in a much better deal of $1,800. Other producers engaged in similar transactions with the International Amusement

Logo of Azteca Films, Inc., pioneer distributor of Mexican movies in the U.S. (Agrasánchez Film Archive).

Co. Among them was Germán Camus, who had made *En la hacienda, Alas abiertas, Hasta después de la muerte,* and the 12-chapter serial *La banda del automóvil* (aka *La dama enlutada*). Camus, aware of the commercial worth of his film stock, pressed the distributors and obtained $5,000 for each contract.[90]

A group of enterprising businessmen residing in the border cities of El Paso, Texas, and Ciudad Juárez, Chihuahua, took part in the establishment of the International Amusement Co. They were: Rafael Calderón, José U. Calderón, and Juan Salas Porras. These entrepreneurs owned and operated several movie theaters in the area and, starting in 1932, established the Azteca Films distribution company. The extent of their influence became manifest five years later when they opened a film laboratory and studio in México City, in partnership with pioneer cinematographer and inventor Gabriel García Moreno.

As early as 1933, an entrepreneur from México, José J. Jiménez, began to distribute Spanish-language films in San Antonio, Texas. His business, known as the Latin American Film Exchange, operated in accord with Azteca Films of El Paso. As a result, ninety-nine percent of the Mexican movies distributed by the Latin American Film Exchange were supplied by Azteca. In 1939 Azteca took over this exchange completely, as the enterprise of Calderón and Salas Porras had already grown to include distribution offices in several major U.S. cities, like Los Angeles, Denver, Chicago and New York, in addition to the exchange in El Paso.

From its beginnings, Azteca Films acquired pictures for distribution on a perpetual and outright basis from the independent Mexican film producers. This practice continued until Azteca Films was purchased in 1954 by CIMEX, the Mexican Producers cooperative. Azteca Films represented an important source of income for producers, who generally obtained "anticipos" or money up front for their movie projects. This financing method became an indispensable tool for the development of the local motion picture industry.

Mention should be made here of Carabaza Films of Laredo, Texas. José Carabaza, who had been active in the distribution business since 1934, headed the company which later became a subsidiary of Azteca Films. Other small enterprises handling Spanish-language pictures in the 1940s were Coppel Amusement Co., with offices in Denver, Colorado, and Trans-Oceanic Films, operating out of New York City.

Clasa-Mohme, Inc., a pivotal film distributor, came on the scene in 1942. This firm was led by Gustav Mohme, who coordinated the release of Spanish-language films from his main office in Los Angeles, California. Clasa-Mohme opened its own exchanges in San Antonio, New York, Denver, and Chicago. Mohme's credentials included a very interesting career in the movie business. In 1926, he began working as a representative of United Artists Corporation in Lima, Perú. Then, in 1937, Mohme became manager of the Universal Pictures's distribution office in México City. He later took the management of 20th Century Fox in the same city. Finally, at the start of 1942, Mohme opened an exchange in Los Angeles for the exclusive distribution of Mexican movies. For a brief period, his business partner was the influential Mexican movie producer Jesús Grovas, from where the company derived the initial name of "Grovas-Mohme, Inc." At the time, this producer had a participation in Clasa Films Mundiales, one of the largest Mexican film-producing corporations. When Clasa Films bought out Jesús Grovas, a year later, it automatically replaced Grovas as the business partner of Mohme.

The San Antonio branch of Clasa-Mohme, located on 501 Soledad Street, had Salvador Osio as its first manager. Beginnig in 1944, this office was headed by Gordon B. Dunlap, a man with a long career in the film business. He had lived in México for many years, working for Paramount Pictures, United Artists, and Mexicana de Aviación. For a brief time, Dunlap joined Pan American Airways in México City before taking over as manager of Clasa-Mohme in San Antonio. Under his management, the exchange expanded significantly. By 1951, the number of employees working for this Texas film exchange had grown to 29 (compared to a staff of five that had started in 1942). While the main office in Los Angeles hired a workforce of 28 people, the much smaller exchanges in Denver, Colorado, and New York City had four employees each.[91]

Clasa-Mohme's business deals throughout the United States were successful in widening the influence of films made in México. To a certain degree, it set an example for its competitor Azteca Films. A memorandum written by Richard H. Dunlap, son of Gordon B. Dunlap and legal advisor to Clasa-Mohme, explained in detail the strategy followed by this company:

> Most of the pictures distributed by Clasa-Mohme were secured through a Mexican motion picture financing corporation, Exportadora de Películas, S.A. Clasa-Mohme distributed [these] pictures on a basis of a percentage of the gross earnings on a picture by picture basis. Clasa-Mohme was the more active distribution company insofar as opening up new territories for Mexican pictures is concerned. Its method of doing business was to have salesmen contact posible exhibition outlets for Mexican pictures from each distribution office and to work out a contract with the theatre concerned for the service of a substantial number of pictures–usually a year's product. In the earlier years of its operation Clasa-Mohme released 26 pictures per year in each territory but increased this to 52 pictures per year as the number of pictures produced in Mexico was increased. Its film salesmen would attempt to place as many of these pictures with the theatres as could be negotiated. Terms agreements, rarely for over a one-year period, were common because every exhibitor who changed the theatre policy from English-language pictures to Spanish-language pictures desired to be protected with a term agreement for his immediate neighborhood or small town in order to be assured of a steady supply of the Spanish-language product over a substantial period of time.[92]

Another major effort by Clasa-Mohme involved the adoption of more favorable terms for the distribution of Mexican films, demanding from exhibitors a percentage of the box-office earnings instead of the traditional flat price rental. This proposal was at the beginning opposed by theater owners, but the percentage method prevailed as the most convenient and practical way of doing business. Finally, this company managed to convince the exhibitors to show Mexican movies on Sundays and at regular hours. This prime showtime had so far been reserved for Hollywood product. Mexican pictures were initially booked for a day or two during weekdays, sometimes getting a Saturday midnight function. But gradually the theaters stayed open for Spanish-language entertainment seven days a week.

During a period of twelve years, from 1942 to 1954, Clasa-Mohme acquired the distribution rights of approximately 600 Mexican films. Its catalog also included several pictures made in Spain and Argentina. The number of movie theaters in the United States that had an account with this company in 1955 amounted to approximately 450. In Texas, the company had been quite successful in securing at least one outlet for Mexican pictures in every major town. For example, when Clasa-Mohme released in 1952 *El derecho de nacer*, the number of Texas theaters it had contracts with was 170.

Notwithstanding the strong competition from Azteca Films distributors, Clasa-Mohme reported excellent box-office results within a few years after its establishment in 1942. During the forties, both companies seemed to be engaged in an amicable and fruitful race. Thus, Clasa-Mohme adhered to a division of equal playing time in all theaters supplied by both exchanges. A system of alternate bookings allowed each company to show their movies every other week at the first-run theaters. Gordon B. Dunlap and Jewel Truex, the heads of the two San Antonio exchanges, were generally on good terms. In fact, before becoming manager of Azteca Films, Truex had occupied a position in San Antonio's Clasa-Mohme, which made him a close acquaintance and co-worker of Dunlap.

For a long time, a high degree of diplomacy existed between these two distributors. One incident seems to confirm this attitude. When a theater operator who was being supplied exclusively by Azteca Films asked Clasa-Mohme to be his substitute provider of movies, this operator was immediately cautioned:

> I would be very reluctant to take any of their [Azteca Films] playing time, especially as they have worked with you presumably over a period of years, and while we are competitors in every sense of the word, I do not like to be a party to taking business from them which they have exclusively developed, for by so doing this could easily prove detrimental to us in other situations where they could do the same to us if given the opportunity.[93]

A third distributor, Columbia Pictures, Inc., had shown interest in Mexican films since the 1930s. The company acquired some of the earliest "talkies" for distribution in the U.S., such as the popular *Cruz Diablo, María Elena, ¡Ora Ponciano!*, and *Tierra Brava*. A few other pictures made in the forties were also commercialized by Columbia. But it was not until 1957 that this distributor began an aggressive campaign to penetrate the U.S. Spanish-language market. Once Columbia began to reap significant economic benefits, the other two distributors reacted with alarm. In San Antonio, the Azteca Films exchange was "very conscious of the entrance of Columbia Pictures into the market and on occasions apparently made it difficult for a theater to acquire its product if the theater exhibited Columbia Pictures product."[94] This attitude led to friction among the three distribution companies and also several exhibitors, sometimes to the point of legal suits.[95]

By the late fifties, competition was already entrenched. Although Columbia had only a small number of Mexican movies, their exploitation proved as effective as the most popular releases of any competitor. Films were promoted through well-planned ad campaigns that included newspaper announcements, radio spots, and the distribution of hundreds of posters targeting Hispanic neighborhoods. Top pictures featuring the comedian Mario Moreno *Cantinflas* gave enormous leverage to this company. Columbia released some of the biggest hits of this performer, like *Entrega inmediata, El bolero de Raquel*, and *Sube y baja*. Knowing the cash value of these movies, Columbia gradually acquired the rights to all of the films starring *Cantinflas*.

Since 1957, Columbia Pictures began in earnest to compete for a share of the Spanish-language film market (Agrasánchez Film Archive).

This distributor had offices in New York, Los Angeles, San Antonio, Chicago, Denver, Dallas, and San Francisco. The Columbia Pictures catalog of Spanish-language movies issued in the late sixties contained 120 titles. Most of these pictures were produced in México, but there were also a number of Argentine titles and a few Spanish films. The catalog included a group of 28 *Cantinflas* pictures, the firm's most valuable assets. Fernando J.

Clasa-Mohme, Inc., came into the scene in 1942 as a powerful distributor of Mexican films in the U.S. (Agrasánchez Film Archive).

Obledo, manager of Columbia's San Antonio branch, was very successful in opening up new accounts throughout the region. His strategy was to travel every Sunday to cities where Spanish-language theaters operated, and meet with the house managers to discuss the release of Columbia's product.[96]

Before Columbia's incursion into the Spanish-language market in the fifties, all movie theaters catering to Hispanics had contracts with Azteca Films and Clasa-Mohme. These contracts generally extended for periods of one year. A typical 1945 contract between the film distributor Clasa-Mohme and a first-run theater, stipulated that 30% of the picture's gross receipts was to be paid to the distributor. When the total gross exceeded $900, a 50–50 split was agreed upon. This split applied automatically to any movie starring *Cantinflas*. In the same way, when the star of the film was Jorge Negrete, a 40% of the gross was to be paid to the distributor regardless of the net receipts. Certainly, the popularity of these two stars guaranteed a full house every time their movies were played.

In 1954, a majority of the Mexican producers backed by the government-financed Film Bank organized a cooperative, Cinematográfica Mexicana Exportadora (CIMEX), to distribute their own pictures in the United States and other parts of the world. This corporation agreed to pay the sum of $1,700,000 for the acquisition of all the stock of Azteca Films, Inc.[97] Then, in August 1958, Gustav Mohme sold his 53% majority interest in Clasa-Mohme to Mexfilms, Inc., a Delaware corporation controlled by the CIMEX cooperative. The purchase of Clasa-Mohme included a payment of $484,250 made by CIMEX. A new general manager, Juan Bueno, was appointed to head Clasa-Mohme from the main offices in Los Angeles. Gordon B. Dunlap, San Antonio's branch manager, remained in his post offering valuable advise to the recently-arrived Bueno.

Azteca Films and Clasa-Mohme continued as distributors of Mexican films on behalf of the Mexican motion picture producers. In 1961, Clasa-Mohme ceased operating as an autonomous company; its large inventory of movies came under the direct control of Azteca Films. During the seventies and eighties, the powerful Azteca Films faced not only the competition from Columbia Pictures but also from other entities like American General Film Distribution, Inc., and Mexcinema Corp, both of which handled Spanish-language movies in the United States. Opportunely, Mexcinema expanded its business by joining the emergent video-home culture of the eighties, a phenomenon that affected movie theaters adversely. Finally, as a result of the decline in filmmaking in México, the pioneer distributor Azteca Films went out of business in 1990. By this time, virtually all Spanish-language theaters in the U.S. closed; the few that remained open screened subsequent-run American movies or, as a last resort, X-rated fare. An era of imported Spanish-language family entertainment concluded, after nearly seventy years of continuous patronage in large and small cities throughout the United States.

2

Los Angeles, California

One of the appalling traits of American society in the 1920s was its aversion to ethnic minorities. Poles, Italians, Blacks, Mexicans; every person looking strange or talking differently was a "suspect." Nativism was the order of the day, perhaps as a consequence of the First World War. Many people, who wanted to keep America "pure," saw Mexicans as a menace. The press, the politics, and even the movies fed this perception. Although immigrant Mexican labor had been recognized as indispensable by agricultural business in the Southwest, federal lawmakers insisted on restricting the flow of nationals from south of the border. The Depression, more than anything else, was responsible for the massive deportation of Mexicans. As a consequence of the economic slow down, more than 50,000 nationals living in California were repatriated in 1931.[1]

Notwithstanding the exodus caused by the Depression, the Hispanic population in Los Angeles remained substantial. Of the city's 1,238,000 people in 1930, nearly ten percent were Mexicans. Because of the need for cheap labor, California's economic growth depended largely on immigrants from Mexico. This "humble and silent" workforce was employed in almost every type of wage job. Besides farming, Mexicans labored in stores, laundries, barber shops, printing presses, and restaurants; they were hired as chauffeurs, trash collectors, gardeners, shoe shiners, butchers, ranchers, carpenters, factory hands and more. Those who had achieved a measure of success and were educated enlarged the ranks of pharmacists, lawyers, priests, teachers, reporters, and government servants.[2] This huge pool of Mexicans represented an integral part of the economy of Los Angeles. Their presence lent a strong Latin American flavor to the city as well. In Hollywood, an assortment of artists, writers, translators and technicians from across the border made their living. Most noticeable among them were the film actors, like Ramón Novarro, Dolores del Río, Gilbert Roland, and Lupe Vélez, who over the years joined the pantheon of Hollywood screen celebrities.

Audiences in Los Angeles were exposed to an enriching mixture of movie entertainment. While American theaters ostentatiously celebrated the release of movies starring Charlie Chaplin, Greta Garbo, or Rudolph Valentino, local Spanish shows modestly announced a "función de cine mexicano," complemented by several stage performances. The Hispanic clientele had the option of patronizing a spectacle that was more akin to their lore and customs. Movie going not only served as a temporary relieve from the hardships of daily life, but, more importantly, it offered vital nourishment that strengthened the Hispanics view of themselves. To those who felt severed from their roots, Mexican cinema provided an opportunity to grow closer to the homeland. Through its compelling array of images and sounds that included sentimental tunes, this mass spectacle was able to furnish both a momentary distraction and a lasting inspiration. The depiction of the Mexican landscape, its traditions, and the sparkling humor in the movies constantly fed the immigrant's state of mind. In the midst of a different culture, people could momentarily "feel at home" by simply attending a Spanish-language theater. It is no wonder that these imported films were appreciated to a greater degree in Los Angeles than back home.

"Something So Intimately National"

Since the 1920s, a variety of establishments offered live and filmed entertainment to the Spanish speaking community of Los Angeles. For those folks desiring to spend a few hours of diversion, the Teatro Principal and the Teatro Hidalgo featured moving pictures and "variedades," which were live shows. Sometimes, these theaters would publicize movies made by local people. On November 30, 1926, for example, the Teatro Principal announced the premiere of *El que a hierro mata*, a Mexican film produced in Los Angeles by the Compañía Cinematográfica Cuautla. As a prologue to the screening, a live performance introducing the stars of the movie took place. Actress Amparo Ramos and Fernando Parra were presented along the rest of the cast. The Teatro Hidalgo announced *El pasado* (*Her Sacrifice*), a Hollywood production starring Ligia di Golconda but advertised as a Mexican film. It played in January of 1927, and for the opening night, a forty-man band performed at the door of the old Hidalgo Theater.[2]

In the vicinity of Belvedere and Maravilla Park, Hispanics could attend several amusement centers. The Teatro Bonito, as its name indicated, had a pleasant atmosphere and was "built according to the modern needs." Another favorite of the local people, the Sala Chapultepec, featured a small auditorium but "clean and with a stage that is quite acceptable." The new Teatro Azteca, on Carmelita Street, became the pride of the "México chiquito," the Little México, as the community of Mexican immigrants living in Los Angeles was called. The "decent and comfortable," 350-seat Azteca Theater was hailed as an example of progress. Its architecture highlighted the decorative motifs of Aztec art. For its opening night, the Azteca presented a musical stage show followed by the silent movie *The Phantom of the Opera*.[3]

Two of the most popular entertainment venues for Hispanics of Los Angeles were the Teatro México and the Teatro Hidalgo, both on Main Street near La Placita and the old Post Office, the hub of Mexican middle- and working-class life. Besides offering live performances, these theaters showed movies regularly. In March of 1928, the Mexican film *Sol de gloria* played at the Teatro México, preceded by an impressive advertising campaign. A number of Hollywood luminaries assisted to the premiere: Lita Grey Chaplin, Roy D'Arcy, William Duncan, Edith Johnson and Barry Norton. Also in attendance were the film's director and leading actor, Guillermo Calles, and the actress Carmen La Roux. *Sol de gloria* was hailed as the "Non Plus Ultra; The best Mexican picture, having as central themes love, suspense, mystery, ferocious animals, execution by firing squad, thrilling and sensational scenes." Romualdo Tirado's Stage Company set up an opening act as a prologue to the film. A crowd of two hundred waited in vain to get a ticket for the premiere, as the management regretfully said that the size of the theater could not accommodate more people.[4]

The Teatro México engaged *Sol de gloria* for a full week, with attendance at an estimated 10,000 people. Since there were not enough seats, many residents watched the picture only after it was brought back a month later. A stream of Mexican attractions followed

A traditional gathering place for Hispanics in L.A., the Teatro México occupied the building of the Grand Theater (demolished in 1936) (Agrasánchez Film Archive).

at this theater; *El vuelo de Lindbergh a México* showed the historical reception of Charles Lindbergh by the people in México City, and *Un drama en la aristocracia* featured the famous caricaturist and artist Ernesto García Cabral. At the same time, the Teatro Hidalgo offered a documentary about México's miraculous folk healer, *El prodigioso Niño Fidencio*. This film was later shown with English subtitles in an American theater, but some in the audience reacted angrily saying that it denigrated Mexicans, because it gave too much emphasis to the poverty and sickness of the dispossessed. Throughout the year, these theaters announced the latest documentary reels from across the border, expediting in one occasion a newsreel brought to Los Angeles by plane.[5]

In December of 1929, the Teatro México publicized the release of *Sombras habaneras*, purportedly the first Spanish-language "talkie." Cuban-born René Cardona, a pioneer filmmaker who later went to perform in over a hundred Mexican movies, produced and acted in this five-reel picture shot in Hollywood. Cardona run into a lot of problems trying to finish his film. First, a fire destroyed the original negative kept in the laboratory, leaving only a print of the film. During its premiere, the sound did not function properly and the engagement flopped. But five months later, the Teatro Hidalgo booked a new and improved version of *Sombras habaneras*.[6]

With the advent of sound in the late twenties, American motion picture producers lost no time and set out to conquer the domestic and international Spanish-language market.

Most of the films that they made were Spanish-dialogue versions of movies originally shot in English. Their cast included a wide array of actors and actresses from Spain, México, Argentina, Cuba and other Latin American countries. For example, the classic horror picture made by Universal Studios, *Dracula*, had its Spanish-language equivalent. In this version, Carlos Villarías interpreted Count Dracula, a character originally played by Bela Lugosi, while the beautiful Mexican actress Lupita Tovar imparted a sexy feel to the character played by Helen Chandler in the English version. Among the list of Spanish-language productions made in Hollywood in the early thirties were: *Resurrección*, with Lupe Vélez; *La fruta amarga*, starring Virginia Fábregas; *La señorita de Chicago*, with Mona Rico; *Carne de cabaret*, which brought together Lupita Tovar, Ramón Pereda, Carmen Guerrero, and René Cardona. By 1935, the studios had produced about 160 Spanish "talkies" that included both feature-length and short subjects. All of them played in Los Angeles at the Fox Criterion, Million Dollar, Fox Palace, Warner Brothers, Hidalgo, and California Theaters.[7]

Seventh-art amateurs in Los Angeles took advantage of the opportunity offered by sound movies and started shooting their own films with much enthusiasm. The Mexican brothers, José and Roberto Rodríguez, were intent on developing an original movie recording system. After endless experimentation, they came up with a lightweight, portable optical sound system. Their first effort consisted of a short feature called *Sangre mexicana*, in which the fearless Celia Montalván sang a melody in the company of a lion inside a cage. Also, *Charros, gauchos y manolas*, a film made by the popular musician Xavier Cugat, attempted to mix the folklore of various nationalities in a musical extravaganza. Both pictures were exhibited in 1930, a year that saw the release of many Hollywood productions in the Spanish language. As the decade progressed, however, the studios slowed down their output of Spanish "talkies." Their poor reception by Latin American audiences was the cause of this decline.

While the production of Spanish-dialogue movies in Hollywood decreased, the opposite occurred south of the border. During the Depression, Hollywood studios cut back on their employment of immigrant labor. Many artists who had been serving the industry returned to their home countries in the early thirties. In México, a group of enthusiasts backed by local capitalists decided to try their luck at filming sound pictures. Talented people like the Rodríguez brothers and other artists and technicians with Hollywood experience contributed to the success of this national cinematography. At the beginning, Mexican pictures obtained only a few theaters for its domestic exhibition, as U.S. film companies monopolized the majority of entertainment venues. Notwithstanding, the output of this emergent industry jumped from 2 pictures filmed in 1931 to 23 made in 1934. With the construction of more studios, the industry was able to make 57 features in 1938. In the end, Mexican cinema got the better part of the Spanish-language market that Hollywood had originally intended to conquer.

The newly refurbished Teatro California reopened on May 20, 1932, for the Los Angeles premier of México's first sound picture, *Santa*. This gripping drama, based on Federico Gamboa's widely read novel of the same name, had sprouted many stage adaptations and even a silent film. The new version, starring Lupita Tovar and directed by Antonio Moreno, met with enormous success in México City and was applauded by audiences in San Antonio and El Paso, Texas.

On its first public screening in Los Angeles, the film attracted multitudes. Among the artists attending the Teatro California were Lupita Tovar, José Mojica, the comedians Laurel and Hardy, Ramón Pereda, Luana Alcániz, Julio Peña, Juan Torena, Paul Ellis, Carlos Villarías, etc. Also presiding at the event were: Rafael Calderón, distributor of the film;

Lupita Tovar starred in several Spanish-Language movies made in Hollywood in the early thirties. *Carne de cabaret* (1931) (Agrasánchez Film Archive).

Frank Fouce, local exhibitor; Juan de la C. Alarcón, producer of *Santa*; and the film critics Gabriel Navarro and Esteban V. Escalante. The Hispanic community of Los Angeles, aware of the importance of this premiere, turned the Teatro California into a celebration of México's cinematic efforts. The entrance to the theater sparkled with bright lights as the crowds surrounded their film idols to chat with them or get their autograph. Huge portraits of Lupita Tovar, Antonio Moreno and Carlos Orellana hung from the marquee. "It doesn't

The Teatro California in 1932, on the night of the opening of *Santa* (Agrasánchez Film Archive).

seem like we're talking about a movie," said Rafael Calderón, "but rather of something that forms part of the very life of México; something so intimately national as its own artistic banner."[8]

The movie was pretentiously billed as "El excelso drama del dolor sacrificado por el amor en el triste calvario de la vida" ("The sublime drama of suffering; sacrificed by love in the sad ordeal of life"). Tinted by realistic details, *Santa* drew much praise for being an effective tearjerker. According to a reporter, the movie was applauded more for its sentimental power than for its technical correctness. The measure of its success, therefore, lay in its capacity to stir the public. This reporter observed that near the end of the story, "we became aware of many ladies that were silently crying in their seats." With such evidence, the journalist came to the conclusion that "the Hispanic public enjoys the crying more than the laughing."[9]

The "Empresa Francisco Fouce"

Located near the corner of Main and Eighth Streets, the Teatro California supplied Spanish-language movies to the Los Angeles community for many years. In 1932 the impresario Francisco (Frank) Fouce leased this 1,900-seat house and operated it continuously for sixteen years, before it was transferred to new management. Fouce had been an enthusiast of Mexican cinema since the early 1920s, when he toured the United States exhibiting a silent picture, *Alas abiertas*. Born in Hawaii of Spanish parents, he came to California and established himself as the manager of the Teatro Hidalgo. Always striving to offer the Hispanic community the best in entertainment, he added in 1934 a third theater to his enterprise: the Electric. Between the modest Hidalgo Theater and the more elegant Teatro California, the Electric stood middle ground. Compared to the Hidalgo that had a capacity for 750 people, the Electric accommodated only 345, but it successfully reprised the films already shown at the California and Hidalgo. In this way, Frank Fouce intended to reach a wide-ranging audience: from the more affluent to the less prosperous families. Whether it was a live or filmed show, a new release or a re-run, Fouce's theaters drew customers from all economic and social levels.

When Fouce traveled to México in 1934 to negotiate the exhibition of films, he told the press, "The success of Mexican movies in California has been outstanding, and nearly all of them have been received favorably." He also said that he intended to acquire the majority of the new productions for his theaters. Fouce used this trip to engage some of the most popular artists for presentations and live performances in California.[10] Upon returning to Los Angeles, the active impresario immediately announced 14 new movies in Spanish to be released in his theater circuit. Among the films advertised were *Pecados de amor, Profanación, El héroe de Nacozari, Tiburón, Águilas de América,* and a rural drama set during the Mexican revolution, *El compadre Mendoza.*

The Empresa Fouce brought a change of program every week, sometimes adding to the films a vaudeville act. The Hidalgo, whose motto was "El teatro de la raza," catered mainly to the working class and charged very low admission prices. On a typical night, it offered a Spanish-language movie, like *La buenaventura*, and a live show featuring Don Catarino and the troupe of Los Pirríns. On Fridays, it promoted a "Día de vajilla," with the management giving away a dishware to every ticket-holder. To encourage assistance, an ad suggested: "350 Mexican families are putting together their sets of dishes." The Teatro California showed *¡Viva México!*, a patriotic film directed by Miguel Contreras Torres. It opened on September 14, 1934, a day before its México City premiere. To celebrate Mexican Independence, consuls and representatives of 12 Latin American countries were invited to take the honor seats at the California Theater that night. *¡Viva México!* turned out to be so popular that it was held at the California for two straight weeks, a rather long engagement for a Spanish-language movie.[11]

The theater organization established by Fouce was so powerful that it kept potential competitors in the area from entering the business. For example, in 1935 the impresario Dan Sherman reopened the old Teatro México, which had been the main outlet for south-of-the-border silent films, and changed its name to the Teatro Grand. Its amenities included a staff of "beautiful Mexican employees catering to customers." The courtesies extended to allowing patrons to remain in the theater as long as they wish, or until the doors were shut. Unfortunately, the Grand failed to attract enough people in the first week, and was forced to close again. Fouce, calculating the potential of this centrally located theater, took over its lease. He immediately got rid of the sign that read "Grand," reinstating its more patriotic name. The México had 700 seats and boasted "the best stage facilities available for Spanish-language entertainment." At the end of 1935, the film *Martín Garatuza* played simultaneously in the México and California Theaters. This swash-buckling story featuring the popular comedian *Chato* Ortín was a hit, giving its director, Gabriel Soria, enough publicity to become the first Mexican to be invited by Hollywood to direct a movie; the 1939 Spanish-language comedy *Los hijos mandan.*

Mexican melodramas had universal appeal for Hispanic audiences, but were especially liked by the female part of the public. In 1936, a stream of pictures depicting motherly love and exalting the Latin American woman flooded the screens of Los Angeles. The film *Sor Juana Inés de la Cruz*, playing at the Electric Theater, portrayed the life of the illustrious nun and poet of Colonial México, while other movies paid tribute to ordinary women. The most famous of them was *Madre querida*, a tearjerker honoring the virtues of a long-suffering mother. *Madre querida* unleashed the sentiment of the masses, and gave way to a string of melodramas that included *Madres del mundo, El calvario de una esposa, Mater nostra,* and *Eterna mártir.* All of them were advertised as "intensely dramatic" and prescribed as "a glorious anthem to maternity." When Andrea Palma's *Ave sin rumbo* appeared at the Teatro Electric, a newspaper ad put it in a nutshell: "A new genre in Mexican cinema. Without crime, loudness, deaths, or violence. But intensely saturated with salty tears." The Electric Theater complemented this drama with the American musical *Ready, Willing and Able,* charging only 20 cents for adults and 5 cents for children.

Frank Fouce's enterprise acquired the Teatro Roosevelt (842 S. Main St.) in 1937, after the old México Theater was demolished a year before. The California and Roosevelt announced a "Fiesta de la Raza" commemorating Columbus Day. The movie *¡Ora Ponciano!* played simultaneously at both theaters and Carlos Villarías, one of the film's actors, managed to appear in person at each screening. Attending the special function at the California were Rosita Moreno, Agustín Lara and Anthony Quinn, as well as representatives of the consulates of Mexico and other Latin American countries. To enliven the occasion, the Teatro California presented a stage play of one act and an orchestral performance of Lara's popular theme "Noche de ronda." The folkloric picture, celebrity presentations, and musical interludes all added up to a very nationalistic outpouring. Thus, this theater provided not only a place for everyday entertainment but, more significantly, it became an occasional shrine for ethnic celebration and a bastion of national pride.

The movie that defined Mexican cinema locally and abroad was the 1936 folkloric comedy *Allá en el Rancho Grande.* Featuring the popular tenor Tito Guízar, Esther Fernández, René Cardona and Carlos López *Chaflán,* the picture became a symbol of rural México and its people, portraying their virtues and character, glorifying their music, and dignifying their charros. The film was one of the most successful releases of the period. In order to lure a wider audience, the film's distributor in Los Angeles added English subtitles to the picture. It played simultaneously at the California, Electric and Roosevelt. The publicity campaign recommended: "Bring your American friends too!" Apparently, the ads worked effectively, as more than 2,000 non–Hispanics were drawn to the California Theater to see *Rancho Grande.* The popularity of Tito Guízar with the American public was a result of his radio programs in which he performed many Latin American songs, including the contagious tune of *Allá en el Rancho Grande.*[12]

A string of pictures in the style of *Allá en el Rancho Grande* appeared on the screens of the local theaters. *Las cuatro milpas, Jalisco nunca pierde,* and *Así es mi tierra* were some of the most visible titles with folkloric themes in 1937. Frank Fouce's theaters advertised the rural comedy *Amapola del camino,* bringing Tito Guízar, Pedro Armendáriz and *Chato* Ortín together for the first time. Romantic songs as well as cheerful melodies were the key ingredients found in these films. Music helped reinforce nationalist sentiment in the audience. A curious song called "El viejo procedimiento," which was performed in *Amapola del camino* by Tito Guízar, satirized the Yankees' invention of test-tube babies while praising the Mexicans' wiser reliance on nature's old mating procedure.

Lydia Mendoza, the young singer from Texas popularly known as "La Alondra de la Frontera" (The Meadowlark of the Border) and "La Cancionera de los Pobres" (The

Songstress of the Poor), performed for the first time in Los Angeles at the end of 1937, drawing large crowds "from nearby towns, from the fields, from the most out-of-the-way neighborhoods." Her charismatic voice and personality made her an undisputed idol of the working-class. Frank Fouce, who had recently purchased the Mason Theater, brought Lydia Mendoza and her show to perform at this venue. Located on Broadway Avenue, between First and Second Streets, the Mason was a perfect place for live shows. The singer herself later appraised the importance of this theater:

> Señor Fouce had just acquired the Mason Theater, formerly an opera house, which when added to the three movie theaters he already owned, really put the icing on the cake. Unlike the other three theaters, the Mason had been designed from the beginning for the presentation of live performances and really added an element of class to his operation. Señor Fouce, whose family was from Galicia, Spain, was sincerely committed to furthering Hispanic culture in Los Angeles, and had already taken the unprecedented step of devoting all three of his big, downtown theaters to exhibiting Spanish language films on a full-time basis.[13]

A carefully-planned advertising campaign greatly aided the success of any live show or movie presentation. Frank Fouce made it a habit of promoting the coming attractions by having a full-page advance advertising in the Spanish-language newspaper *La Opinión*. A new movie coming to the screen was usually announced a week before the opening. Eye-catching posters were displayed outside theaters and in the streets, while radio spots publicizing a film reached a larger number of theater-going public. For all listeners, particularly illiterates, the radio functioned as their prime source of information. Word-of-mouth gave the theater attractions an extra haul. In the 1930's, the local KMTR radio station ran the ads for the Fouce theater organization. Tony Zane, David Orozco, Ramón Arnaiz and Rodolfo Salinas hosted some of the most popular broadcasts in Spanish. According to Frank Fouce Jr., these programs were transmitted directly from the theaters.

> We had an early morning radio show from the stage of the California Theater every morning at dawn... It was free. Anyone could just walk in off the street... There were always a few dozen people around watching the show. And, in those days, the radio programs not only sold advertising, but they also sold requests. Well, 'This is a request by Juanito for María.' And [people] would pay a quarter to have their song played on the radio.[14]

Mexican Cinema During World War II

Important developments stemming from World War II contributed to the advancement of Mexican cinema. In May 1942, after German submarines torpedoed two Mexican tankers, President Ávila Camacho declared war on the Axis, formally enlisting the country as an ally of the United States. To further this alliance, Washington took its Good Neighbor policy one step ahead by devising a plan to aid the film industry in México. It was calculated that this national cinema could be quite an effective medium at carrying the message of hemispheric solidarity throughout Latin America. With little competition from European countries and contending mainly against Hollywood studios, which churned out too many war propaganda films, Mexican cinema successfully found an audience nationally and internationally.

The astonishing growth of the film industry in México was due to the demand for movies in Spanish. This trend was reflected in the construction of more studios. Besides the already established Clasa, Azteca, México, and Tepeyac, the new Churubusco Studios opened in 1945 as the largest film facilities in all of Latin America. Hundreds of artists, writers, technicians, and directors worked for seventy-five production companies. Exhibitors expanded or renovated their theaters to provide the public with better service and to stay ahead of the competition. Producers, too, increased their investment in the manufacture of films. Compared to the $30,000 dollars required to make a standard movie in 1940, the cost for a first-class movie in 1946 increased fourfold. It is no surprise then, that some of the best films in the Spanish language came out of the Mexican studios at this time.

The period's crafted production served as a backdrop for the great performances of México's stars. Dolores del Río, Pedro Armendáriz, the Soler brothers, Joaquín Pardavé, Sara García, *Cantinflas*, and many others were acclaimed for their talent and charisma. Movies became an ideal medium to promote the image of a country and its culture. The "comedia ranchera" genre, for instance, with its singing *charros* and colorful rural settings, remained popular for decades. People saw the quintessential Mexican male in idols like Pedro Armendáriz, Jorge Negrete, Pedro Infante, Raúl de Anda, and Luis Aguilar. And the selected romantic songs incorporated into these movies made Mexican cinema the most appealing form of entertainment for Hispanics.

With the advent of World War II, the United States sought to unite the Latin American countries on the side of the Allied Powers. To give form to this impulse, a policy of hemispheric solidarity known as Pan-Americanism was implemented by the State Department. Its head, Nelson D. Rockefeller, created the Office of the Coordinator for Inter-American Affairs (CIAA), which had a Motion Pictures Division. Francis Alstock and Frank Fouce represented the CIAA in México. Accompanied by a group of cinema technicians, Fouce traveled to the neighboring country in 1942 to develop a plan to modernize the Mexican film industry. The experts made recommendations for the improvement of motion picture studios and laboratories. New equipment coming from the United States would be sold to the studios through a convenient method of payment by installments.[15] Another important measure involved the creation of a Film Bank, established with the cooperation of the Mexican government.

Within a few years, the result of these policies became tangible: movie production rose from 29 pictures made in 1940 to an unprecedented 82 features in 1945. Many of these movies observed high quality standards and at the same time attained significant commercial success, locally and abroad. Frequently, the Mexican fare was able to compete advantageously at the box office with the pictures made in Hollywood. This became evident to some U.S. diplomats when they said in 1944: "We understand that the Mexican producers' income from the United States [market], proportionately to their total investment, is much greater than the income obtained by U.S. producers from the distribution of their films in Mexico."[16]

Infused with the spirit of Pan-Americanism, movie stars of both countries united in a common cause. Frank Fouce was commissioned by the CIAA to organize a group of Hollywood luminaries bound for México to take part in a 'Festival of Good Will.' A reciprocal event took place in Los Angeles almost coinciding with Mexican Independence Day. At a gala performance at the Philharmonic Auditorium on September 11, 1943, Mexican singer Tito Guízar, wearing a *charro* costume and clutching his guitar, alternated with Hollywood's Ann Sheridan, outfitted in the traditional Mexican "China Poblana" dress.

Entertainment was heralded as the healthiest antidote to the fears and preoccupations of World War II. The movie industry, more than anything else, offered such a relief. Opportunely, a newspaper ad campaign set out by the local Azteca Films distributor recommended:

Even when momentarily, casting into oblivion the enormous tragedy that drains the blood of Humanity invigorates our spirit. The cinema, which is not only artistic expression but also an educational tool and a powerful vehicle to disseminate and strengthen doctrines, will always offer you hours of recreation, encouragement and enthusiasm. Patronize the theatres that exhibit movies in your own language, and stop worrying—at least for a while—about the anxiety of the present moment.[17]

During the war, a number of Mexican films stirred by the official ideology sought to reinforce themes of patriotism and regional solidarity. *Soy puro mexicano, Tres hermanos, Espionaje en el Golfo,* and *Escuadrón 201* were some of the movies that portrayed Mexicans as the heroes battling the evil forces represented by Nazis and Japanese spies. *Cadetes de la naval,* for instance, imitated the war adventure incidents characteristic of contemporary Hollywood stories, incorporating footage of a German submarine attack. In a subtler way, though, *La virgen que forjó una patria* carried the message of "the love of freedom under the flag that is always sacred, the flag of a free land." This religious-patriotic film played at the California and Mason Theaters in September of 1943. That same month, Frank Fouce opened a new outlet for movies on South Main Street. As if reaffirming the ideals of freedom and democracy, the theater was called Teatro Liberty. And indeed, it started to function very democratically: "Strictly with programs petitioned by the public," so a person could simply ask for the movie that he or she wanted to see, in writing or by going directly to the box office. This 280-seat theater was opened in part because "many people have the habit of going to the other theaters of the Empresa Fouce to solicit some movie that has already been shown."[18]

Patriotic films such as *Escuadrón 201* reinforced the official ideology of hemispheric solidarity during World War II (Agrasánchez Film Archive).

Frank Fouce had established a practical method of film exhibition at his four theaters. A new feature and a filler (reprise picture) were usually programmed at the California and Mason Theaters simultaneously. After a week, the same program transferred to the Roosevelt Theater, ending the round at the Liberty. On the whole, the circuit engaged a movie for about a month. Afterwards, the same picture could be re-released by other local exhibitors, like James C. Quinn, who operated the Monterey and Unique Theaters. One more house offering "películas de México" was the Teatro Barbara, on 147 E. Santa Barbara Avenue, which began to screen Spanish-language films in 1942.

In addition to its pro-war film production, Hollywood designed some movies to promote the new spirit of continental cooperation in Latin America. Walt Disney, above all, contributed to this effort with the musical fantasy in color *The Three Caballeros*. Donald Duck, José Carioca the parrot, and Panchito the rooster, the three feathered characters portrayed in this story, represented the United States, Brazil, and México respectively. The movie was a big success in the U.S. and Latin America. It played at the California and Mason Theaters in Los Angeles, as part of a program that included two Mexican feature films: *Rosa de las nieves* and *La virgen morena (Emperatriz de América)*. This last movie about the Virgin of Guadalupe contained a message that echoed World War II propaganda. "The miracle that united the Mexicans will likewise unite all the peoples of America," proclaimed the film's ad. In their own special way, *The Three Caballeros* and *La virgen morena* helped reinforce the ideal of cooperation between the United States and the Latin American nations.

The popularity of Mexican films reached an all-time high during the war. Immigrants came north by the thousands to work in agricultural fields. Throughout California, exhibitors were willing to offer their Hispanic clientele the movies they craved and understood. By 1943, sixty-two cities in the state were showing Spanish-language pictures. Because of the unprecedented demand, a new film distributor, Clasa-Mohme, entered the business and began to compete effectively with pioneer supplier Azteca Films. This resulted in the opening of more release houses for Mexican pictures. Thanks to a healthy competition, 81 movie theaters catering to Hispanics were active in the state. Independent exhibitors operated the majority of these houses, with approximately 25 theaters belonging to circuit companies, like Fox West Coast, Warner Bros, Redwood Midland, Golden State, Feldstein & Dietrich, and B. Aranda Jr. At last, exhibitors were waking up to the drawing power of Spanish-language pictures, taking this opportunity to increase their sales.[19]

In 1946, Frank Fouce became president of the Latin American Division of the Democratic Committee in California. He concentrated on the political organization of the vast numbers of Mexican-born who were U.S. citizens. This organization, under the Democratic leadership, promised to fulfill "the dream of equality, to end all racial prejudices that trouble us and humiliate us." Fouce saw the unification of minority groups in California as necessary in order to endow these groups with "a civic power, with electoral force." The call reminded Hispanics to defend their right to vote in the coming elections by registering as Democrats. One convenient spot where Mexicans could obtain a voting card was at the door of the Teatro California.[20]

During an interview in his office, located above the Roosevelt Theater, Frank Fouce talked about the Hispanics in Los Angeles and their preference for Mexican-filmed entertainment. He pointed out that there were approximately half a million people of Latin American origin in California, representing an enormous potential for Mexican cinema.

The California and Mason Theaters were first-run houses for Mexican films. Newspaper ad published in *La Opinión*, 1945 (Agrasánchez Film Archive).

> The Latin colony of California is the noblest audience that exists. Their extraordinary contentment, which shows equally in all circumstances, has helped greatly in the implantation of Mexican cinema in this region. For me and for them, there are no bad Mexican pictures. When we get one that is rather weak, I release it with vaudeville. The local public likes things with Mexican flavor; folkloric, vernacular, depicting their customs. But above all, that which comes saturated with *ranchera* songs and typical dresses.[21]

The dynamic impresario strove to give to the masses the best entertainment available. His theaters offered movies and live shows at a price within the reach of anyone. Admission rates were always guided by the principle of a seat for every wallet. For those who could afford it, a first-run release house was provided in the circuit. Still, people may choose to attend either a middle-priced theater or a subsequent-run house that only charged a few cents. What's more, a variety of programs were available for the vast spectrum of movie fans. In appreciation of his endeavors for this cinema, the Mexican government gave Frank Fouce in 1948 the "Águila Azteca," the highest official medal extended to a foreigner for services to the nation.

The Mayan and Million Dollar Theaters

After sixteen years operating the Teatro California, Frank Fouce left his cherished theater. He transferred this house to Alejandro Lapiner, who continued to screen Spanish-language films. Fouce programmed a pair of tearjerkers as a farewell: the Mexican melodrama *Soledad*, featuring the queen of the tango Libertad Lamarque, and the Argentine feature *Claro de luna*, starring the twin sisters Mirtha and Silvia Legrand. This program played at the California during the last week of 1948. As a gesture of thankfulness to the local audiences, Fouce confided:

> [The California Theater] was a friend that we found twenty years ago alone and abandoned by the English speaking public. With no lights, its auditorium deserted and covered with dust, a great house that had aged prematurely; we picked it up fifteen years ago by chance. We gave it life, moved by our dream of providing a Mexican theater to Los Angeles... The industry of Mexican cinema had just taken its first steps. And we served as intermediaries in making the Mexican of California one of the industry's principal sources of income and strength.[22]

Spanish-dialogue movies continued to be shown at the Teatro California under the management of Alejandro Lapiner. This popular locale weathered a series of managements until the mid 1980s. At the end of that decade and after seventy years of existence, the old California Theater of 810 S. Main Street was finally demolished.

Frank Fouce had intended to replace the Teatro California since 1948 with a more modern facility, which led him to acquire the Mayan Theater. The impressive Mayan, at 1044 South Hill Street, offered a better setting for the exhibition of motion pictures and the presentation of live shows. Fouce invested approximately $500,000 dollars in the 1,700-seat movie house that was flamboyantly advertised as "El teatro máximo de la raza." Besides this considerable expenditure on the Mayan, the impresario ordered substantial renovation work for his other three theaters. For instance, he spent $154,000 to reform the Mason, $34,000 to renew the Liberty, and $30,000 to fix the Roosevelt. An enterprising businessman, Frank Fouce relied not only on the loyalty of the public and the efficiency of his many employees, but on the support of his wife, Anita Fouce, and the work of his son Frank Jr., who assiduously helped in the operation of the theaters.[23]

The profusely ornamented Mayan, originally built in the twenties for Hollywood pictures,

The beautifully ornamented Mayan Theater in the 1950s (Agrasánchez Film Archive).

reopened on March 3, 1949, solely for Spanish-language entertainment. Movie star and singer Libertad Lamarque performed for the inauguration, followed by several other artists. The theater's programming during its first month featured *Que Dios se lo pague*, an Argentinean film starring Arturo de Córdova and gorgeous Zully Moreno, *El gendarme desconocido*, a hilarious farce featuring *Cantinflas*, and the urban drama of the slums *Nosotros los pobres*, with Pedro Infante. The Mayan was frequently visited by famous singers and performing artists from Latin America. The Trio Los Panchos, for example, attracted thousands of people in 1950, making the musicians extend their commitment for a full month.

Spanish-language theater business in Los Angeles peaked at the beginning of 1949. In January, the Mason Theater announced a personal appearance by Luis Aguilar, the singing *charro* and film star also known as "El gallo giro." Another virile singer, Jorge Negrete, appeared in the movie *Tierra de pasiones*, playing at the Roosevelt Theater. At the Liberty, people could have a laugh with the *Cantinflas* picture *Soy un prófugo* and also pick up a free photo of this popular comedian. One more film with *Cantinflas* played at the American Theater, located on the corner of Broadway and 48th Street. Under the management of Alejandro Lapiner, the American had just started a new policy of Spanish-language pictures three days a week. To attract its clientele, this house also offered a jackpot lottery with $100 in prizes. Finally, the Victor Theater, on 1718 South Main, advertised a double bill: *Misión blanca*, and the comedy *Padre de más de cuatro*. Admission tickets for the Victor were 44 cents for adults, and 14 cents for children. All of these movie houses played regularly a Mexican newsreel and an American cartoon. Charity events often took place at the theaters, as when the Teatro Mason organized a live show to raise money for the victims of a flood in the state of Sonora, México.

During the fifties, television programming competed effectively with the theaters. In Los Angeles, "little by little we are having shows on T.V. for the Hispanic public," said a show business reporter in 1952. The musical program "Momentos Alegres" was broadcast every Saturday, under the direction of Eddie Rodríguez and the orchestra of Don Tosti. Even the commercials of the Acme Brewing Co. were in Spanish. Movie star and singer Tito Guízar performed in yet another popular program. Despite the competition, live shows at local theaters continued to draw audiences, demonstrating that people were willing to spend their money in exchange for an evening with their favorite idols.

With that in mind, Frank Fouce decided to acquire the imposing Million Dollar Theater, an elegant locale with a capacity for two thousand people, located on Broadway and Third Street. It automatically became the number-one entertainment house in the circuit owned by Fouce. At the beginning of 1952, screen idol and singer Pedro Infante made a personal appearance at the Million Dollar, accompanied by the Trio Los Compadres and a variety show. On the night of his presentation, the theater exhibited *Los tres huastecos*, an amusing rural comedy with Infante playing three different roles: a priest, an army officer and a tough saloonkeeper. Charming child actress, María Eugenia Llamas, portrayed a tomboy whose pets were a tarantula and a poisonous snake. As expected, the Million Dollar did proverbial box office business thanks to Infante's movie exploits and live performance. Meanwhile, other theaters were offering some of the finest films of the year. For example, Luis Buñuel's masterpiece of juvenile delinquency, *Los olvidados*, played at the California. Competing with this film, the Mayan and Mason Theaters exhibited Alejandro Galindo's *Una familia de tantas*, a classic melodrama that revealed the generational clash of an old-fashioned, authoritarian father and a modern, assertive teenage daughter.

One of the biggest films presented in Los Angeles was *Dos tipos de cuidado*, which brought together, for the first and only time, two superb legends of Mexican cinema: Pedro Infante and Jorge Negrete. This explosive movie, directed by Ismael Rodríguez, paired the two famed machos in an upbeat story of rivalry, gorgeous women and top-notch singing. The movie humorously played off the antithetical characters of the two stars: Negrete is the wealthy macho, petulant, aggressive and good-looking; Infante, on the other hand, is the humble, stoic, sentimental and noble guy. In real life the actors' personalities seemed to mirror these stereotypes. For this and other reasons, *Dos tipos de cuidado* remains a delightful anecdotic tale, showcasing two of the greatest idols of Latin American popular culture. The film was released following the untimely death of Jorge Negrete, which occurred in Los Angeles in 1953.

That year, ironically, Jorge Negrete had been brought to Los Angeles by Frank Fouce to perform at the Million Dollar Theater. The show had been announced for November 26, but Negrete fell ill upon arriving in Los Angeles. A victim of a chronic liver disease, he was taken to the local Cedars of Lebanon Hospital. Unable to leave his room, the star wrote a letter in which he apologized to the public for not being present at the theater for his engagement. A photographic enlargement of the letter was posted at the door of the Million Dollar and the show proceeded as scheduled without Negrete. A week later, after a painful struggle to save his life, the idol of Mexican cinema died. The reaction of the public was moving. A congregation of more than ten thousand fans in Los Angeles passed in front of Jorge Negrete's coffin to express their sorrow. The funeral continued in México City, where the multitudes took to the streets in a sign of mourning and prostration.[24]

At the height of his career, singing star Jorge Negrete died in Los Angeles in 1953. Scene from *Un gallo en corral ajeno* (1951) (Agrasánchez Film Archive).

Decline In Theater Attendance

Over the years, the Million Dollar Theater became the top stage in California; it brought the most popular stars to Los Angeles. Marga López, Amalia Aguilar, Elsa Aguirre, Amanda del Llano, Emilia Guiú, Armando Soto *El Chicote*, ventriloquist Paco Miller and his pal Don Roque were some of the artists who performed for audiences in the early fifties. Not all of them did well at the box office, though. It was disappointing, for instance, when the 1952 shows of Toña la Negra and Imperio Argentina failed to meet expenses for the Million Dollar. In comparison, a commentator said that Pedro Armendáriz had been invited to San Antonio, Texas, for a "Fiesta de Simpatía." The movie star collected for himself almost $2,000 dollars worth of "sympathy" during this event at the Alameda Theater. It was unclear why both the movie business and live performances had been doing so poorly in Los Angeles at this time.

> Although the movies are better than ever, there is a crisis in the theatres of Los Angeles. There are first-run theatres that are making only 300 or 400 dollars during weekdays. And in neighborhood theatres, receipts are 50 or 60 dollars. The regional business of Los Angeles is today the worst of all the country. Perhaps we are too close to the [movie] industry, or perhaps they are not marketing the pictures the way they should be exploited. To be

The Million Dollar Theater screened films and staged the shows of the most popular Latin American performers. Early 1950s photograph (Agrasánchez Film Archive).

honest, pictures in other languages are also suffering from the same illness that affects the trade.[25]

It took imagination and a tested will to prevail in the competitive business. Frank Fouce's Mayan Theater, for instance, announced in 1954 a new booking strategy by promoting three changes of program per week. Since a regular program consisted of the main attraction followed by a filler or secondary film, the Mayan's total consumption in a week was six pictures, plus a good amount of short subjects. By offering an assortment of movies, the management expected to lure more people into the shows. At any given time, seven or eight local theaters were exhibiting Mexican films, which signified an average of sixteen pictures advertised daily. This variety represented an attractive offer for the theater-going public, as well as a tough competition for the Mayan Theater.

Without a doubt, the most radical development affecting the movie business was television. The new medium gained popularity rapidly, and it prospered at the expense of theater patronage. Some of the films' titles reflected the wide acceptance of aired shows, as exemplified in a series of Mexican comedies: *Del rancho a la televisión, Sindicato de telemirones, Locos por la televisión,* and *Te vi en T.V.* Because television entertainment represented an innovative medium with a promissory future, Frank Fouce himself became actively involved in its establishment. He and other investors, like Emilio Azcárraga and Julián Kaufman, created the Spanish International Broadcasting Company, which operated the KMEX-TV station of Los Angeles. Not until 1962, however, did the pioneer station begin airing programs on channel 34.[26]

In spite of the challenge from television, the exhibition of Mexican movies in Los Angeles continued to be a profitable business during the fifties. Proof of this is that the Mexican entertainment industry generated an average of one hundred pictures per year. Theaters continued sprouting everywhere. In Los Angeles, many businesses competed for

Poster advertising the comedy *Sindicato de telemirones* (1953) (Agrasánchez Film Archive).

a share of the Hispanic market. But in 1952, as a result of this saturation, Frank Fouce declared that the movie business was approaching a disaster. Of his five theaters in Los Angeles, two were shut down. The Million Dollar Theater was presenting live shows as the only way to attract an effective audience. Fouce said that if the other two movie houses, the Mayan and Mason, did not make enough money to pay for their rent, they would inevitably be converted to English-language theaters. The degree of financial losses had become

Espaldas mojadas (1953), a film about the exploitation of illegal immigrants in the U.S., appealed to a large segment of Mexicans (Agrasánchez Film Archive).

unbearable for these two houses. Obviously alarmed, the impresario cited the decline of theater attendance as the main reason for adopting stringent measures.

> When business goes bad, one should appeal to an extreme course of action. I would call it desperate moves. The situation is such that, besides launching intense publicity campaigns that include all resources –from television to flashy street parades—, today I have undertaken the most expensive and unusual advertising strategy. Every Tuesday, we give out in my theatres $1,000 in raffles, while every third Tuesday of the month we give a brand new car in a lottery. Besides, there are a variety of prizes given daily. Now, do you know the result of all these efforts? Painful: the public does not bother to find out if the movie is worth it. Thus, we pay the price for the bad reputation created by defective Mexican films, which affects in no small way the better pictures. I used to make $1,700 a week in some of the theatres, but things have changed and now the company owes me $68,000.[27]

The salvation of the Mexican film industry, as Fouce went on to suggest, rested on the right decisions of producers and cinematographic authorities south of the border. He warned of impeding chaos if the industry was left to the improvised, non-professional elements. Mexican filmmakers should do well imitating the policies of Hollywood, which only hired experts in every field, Fouce said. This meant that producers needed to look around for talented people, inside and outside of the country, without prejudice toward foreigners. Lastly, the impresario demanded an end to films of low morals.

> We've had enough of cabarets, bawdy houses, treacherous gangs, and lowlife in Mexican movies. Let's raise our standards; let's make it morally better. Because, what would be the

consequences if we don't? Real simple: the families and their children will be scared away from the theatres exhibiting these pictures. We are talking about the opposition of the Church, the negative reaction of the people that have a lot of respect and consideration for México, where many things noble and beautiful happen.[28]

No matter its shortcomings, the public continued to patronize this national cinema. Above all, going to the movies was a ritual and a communal experience. Families flocked to the neighborhood theaters on Sundays to watch the latest *Cantinflas* comedy, or the *charro* pictures with singer Tony Aguilar, or perhaps a funny movie with the popular Lalo González *Piporro*. There was always a recognizable name advertised on the marquee of the Teatro California, a place that remained a favorite among Spanish-speaking audiences for many years. Its owner, Alejandro Lapiner, was able to establish new records at the box office. The exhibiton of *Espaldas mojadas*, a film denouncing the exploitation of Mexican illegal workers in the United States, reaped $13,210 during its release in 1956. Following the success of *Espaldas mojadas*, a color production with Pedro Infante and Libertad Lamarque, *Escuela de música*, grossed $10,660 at the same theater. Aided by a special advertising campaign, the mystery drama *La bruja* was able to bring $8,403 in ticket sales. Lapiner proved that promotional expenses, which were usually avoided by producers and distributors of Mexican pictures, could actually pay off in the long run. Publicity efforts, Lapiner said, should include a well-planned campaign to promote the film's stars and the new performers that were little known to the public. He placed great emphasis on the role of movie magazines published in México, and also suggested the use of radio advertising prior to the release of films.[29]

Last Decades of the Movie Business

Assiduously, the Mayan and Million Dollar Theaters continued to offer the usual attractions: screening Mexican films and occasionally announcing a "variedad." One of the most successful movies in 1960 was *La Cucaracha*, a superb production in color starring María Félix, Dolores del Río, Pedro Armendáriz, and Emilio Fernández. It played simultaneously at both theaters. According to Frank Fouce, box office receipts during the first two weeks of exhibition were in excess of $59,000. In 1959, the Spanish-made film *Marcelino, pan y vino* played for five straight weeks at the Mayan Theater, harvesting $35,620. *Cantinflas* was the absolute champion of box office hits, and the release of his comedy *Sube y baja* confirmed this opinion by making $71,000 during its four-week run at the Million Dollar Theater.[30]

Frank Fouce's Million Dollar Theater prevailed as the top-rated venue for Mexican movies and live entertainment in Los Angeles. It welcomed scores of artists from México and Latin America. In the mid-sixties, an average of fifty performers came to the United States every month to work on the stages of theaters. The majority of these artists were brought to Los Angeles for an appearance at the Million Dollar. Frank Fouce also arranged for them to continue their presentation at several other spots in California. Mexican artists were applauded everywhere they went, collecting salaries that often surpassed those earned at home. Usually, a touring company or "caravana artística" traveled throughout the state after an initial debut in Los Angeles. In 1964, one such "caravana" headed by the actress and singer Irma Dorantes "and her beautiful horses Gatillo de Oro and Justiciero" took the stage of the Million Dollar Theater. Plenty of songs and folklore performed by Los Panchos, Ángel Infante, Rudy Frudy, and the Mariachi Águila, highlighted the main attraction. A double bill rounded up the program with the movies *Los apuros de dos gallos* and *¿Con* *quién andan nuestras hijas?*[31] Another big event that year for the Million Dollar was the appearance of María Félix and Agustín Lara, together for the first time in Los Angeles.

Two subsequent-run theaters offering Mexican films, the Monterey and the Unique, although lacking in live entertainment, managed to stay open in the 1960s thanks to a loyal clientele. The Vagabond Theater, on Wilshire Boulevard, and the Starland Theater, on North Broadway, similarly maintained their program of Mexican pictures. Other movie spots catering to Hispanics in Los Angeles at this time were the Broadway, Globe, Granada, Down Town, Floral Drive-In, and the Alameda Theater in East L.A.

By the mid–1970s, radical changes took place in the cinema of México. The so-called "Nuevo Cine," which was sponsored by the government of President Luis Echeverría and championed by a younger generation of filmmakers, sought "to produce a worthy cinema that may reflect the historic and actual way of living [of a] country in process of development."[32] Some of the films produced under the new system were: *Reed México insurgente, El cambio, Mecánica Nacional, El rincón de las vírgenes, Aquellos años, El principio,* etc. Although several pictures traveled to international film festivals, the majority of them unfortunately failed to win local audiences. The bold experiment represented the efforts of an educated middle class that wanted to break away from the traditional commercial films. The new cinema explored themes of historical and social significance, but the poor box-office performance of many of these movies made the exhibitors extremely cautious about programming the Nuevo Cine. Instead, theaters continued to favor run-of-the-mill pictures with recognizable names. In this way, the singers Vicente Fernández and Tony Aguilar, or the popular comedians *Cantinflas* and María Elena Velázco, better known as *La India María,* came to stand as the box office favorites.

Traditional Mexican producers continued supplying theaters with plenty of sure-shot pictures for the masses. This can be seen, for example, in the June 1, 1977 issue of *La Opinión,* which carried the ads of more than twenty Spanish-language attractions offered in Los Angeles. While the Million Dollar presented a variedad with Vicente Fernández, Estrellita and Los Bribones; the Teatro United Artists screened *María,* with Taryn Power and Fernando Allende, supplemented by *El moro de Cumpas,* with Tony Aguilar and Flor Silvestre. The Panorama exhibited *Los desarraigados* and *Los hijos de Satanás*; the Teatro El Monte also announced a double bill, *El imponente* and *La isla de los hombres solos*; the Globe Theater showed *El padrino es mi compadre* and *Carne de horca*; the Broadway likewise offered two movies, *México México ra ra ra* and *La amante*; the Teatro Olympic played *La comadrita,* starring *La India María,* and *Soy chicano y mexicano,* with singer Cornelio Reyna; *Canoa* and *Tacos al carbón* were paired at the Whittier Theater; while the Pacific, Floral, and Sundown Drive-Ins offered films that were playing at the other theaters. Finally, the California, Rialto, Alameda, and Westlake Theaters also billed Spanish-dialogue films.

After more than six decades of incessantly offering Mexican films to the locals, exhibitors finally reached the end of a cycle in the late 1980s. Once the center of Spanish-language popular culture, the theaters in Los Angeles shifted to American movies or closed for good. This was the result, among other things, of the widespread usage of VCRs and movie rentals. When films began to be marketed directly to the consumer as convenient videotapes, the cinema industry as a whole fell into a crisis. The main U.S. distributor of Spanish-language movies, Azteca Films, went out of business in 1988. Subsequently, important theaters like the California, Mayan, and Million Dollar became vacant or were torn down. At the same time, the new generation of Hispanics appeared to be finally assimilated into the American popular culture, showing little interest in Spanish-language films. Until this time, scores of viewers had regarded Mexican movies as a fitting way of connecting to the land that stretches south of the border. Thus, the period from the 1920s to the 1980s remains as a significant episode in the history of movie entertainment for Hispanics in the United States.

3

Pomona Valley, California

The farming communities of Pomona, Chino and Ontario, located near Los Angeles, provide us with an opportunity to observe the peculiarities of movie-going and race relations in California during the 1930s and 1940s. Segregation in public places such as theaters, although not unique to this area, was an issue that came up regularly to the awareness of the locals. Through this confrontational stance that involved theater clients and exhibitors, an example of the bold attitude of Mexicans and Mexican-Americans in the region can be drawn.

Agriculture in this bountiful Californian land attracted waves of migrant workers from the rest of the country and from México since the early 1920s. The large majority of newcomers were poor and uneducated. Living conditions, in the main, continued to be deplorable for these individuals, even after the Farm Security Administration constructed labor camps in 1935. For Mexicans, it was a toiling experience, especially since they were unable or not permitted to unionize, as most American workers had done in an effort to improve their situation. At the start of World War II, American migrant workers fled for the factories in the cities, while cultivation of the land was relegated to Mexicans' hands. For a majority of the large farmers, this meant that they could keep wages low for a long time. Instantly, "California's agri-industrialists were provided with the cheap and undemanding labor force they had come to view as their natural right."[1]

Author Rob Hughes gives a description of the living conditions of the Mexican laborers in the Pomona Valley. This "Valley of the Goddess of Fruit," as Hughes appropriately called the region, was a place full of activity.

> The freight trains did stop in the Pomona Valley. They stopped at the packing houses where thousands of oranges and lemons and grapefruits were packed in wooden crates that carried the labels of the various packers... Just beyond the railroad tracks and the train station was a tiny village of Mexican-Americans who worked the groves and fields. The village was an early foothold for those immigrants from below the border who had returned to their rightful land. They cultivated the land and harvested its fruits... But they were poor and they could only hope for a better life. Their families were close. They were religious. They fought among themselves, but they were fiercely united and protective of threats from outsiders.[2]

Mexicans living in the Pomona Valley also went to the movies. About six theaters offering Hollywood films on a regular basis were advertised in the pages of Pomona's Spanish-language weekly, *El Espectador*. The old Teatro Woods of Chino had offered filmed entertainment in Spanish since 1934, when its management put aside one day of the week to show Mexican movies. Already, the importance of the Hispanic population in the Pomona Valley was reflected in the locally published *El Espectador*. Its editor, Ignacio I. López, was an ardent defender of the rights of the working class, denouncing with frequency the narrow-mindedness of racial segregation and the abuses that it encouraged. The paper helped cement a feeling of communal identity, while at the same time becoming a reputable agent of publicity for an array of thriving businesses in the area.

The Woods Theater

Among the most active enterprises in the Valley were the theaters. Ashley L. Woods, owner of the Woods Theater, renovated and enlarged this movie house in 1937 to adapt to the increasing influx of Mexican laborers. The Woods, located on 328 Sixth Street, re-opened its doors to the public on November 23, boasting a 500-seat capacity. The new theater was equipped with an elegant stage and decorated in a modernist fashion. A "special substance on the interior walls for the perfection of acoustics" made its Preddy High Fidelity sound system work to its optimum potential. The Woods had two separate rooms in the auditorium, "where the ladies can attend their sons while watching the movie and without bothering the rest of the public." Another room with a view to the screen was provided, so that "the gentlemen can smoke at ease." Mr. Woods' inaugural campaign highlighted the popularity of his theater, which was "due to a great extent to the excellent programs and to the good treatment given to Mexicans."[3]

Besides offering the Mexican swashbuckler drama *Don Juan Tenorio*, the opening program of the Woods included a talent show. In order to attract more public, the Woods proclaimed: "Oiga, vea y admire a los Aficionados del Valle." Amateur artists from Chino, and the nearby towns of Ontario, Pomona, La Verne, and Upland performed that night in front of a varied audience composed of children, adults and the elderly. Measuring the favorable box-office results, the management adopted the aficionado nights every so often giving cash prizes to the winners of these contest. Typical programs at the Teatro Woods incorporated a double bill; for example, *Jalisco nunca pierde* and *Shadows of Chinatown* played on the screen complemented by a vaudeville attraction. The nearby Teatro México, in the town of Cucamonga, also offered Mexican films, with the added appeal of an American cowboy picture and an episode of *The Clutching Hand*. Both the Woods and the México charged 25 cents for adults and ten cents for children. The size of Cucamonga's Teatro México was small, with a capacity of 250 seats, just enough for the town's two thousand inhabitants.

In Ontario, the 325-seat Forum Theater played English-language movies only. But this larger town also had a boxing arena announcing every Wednesday a succession of fights, or "Pleitos sensacionales," for an admission price similar to that of the movie places. If entertainment was inexpensive, so were the basic attire items; for example, a pair of used shoes bought at an army outlet cost one dollar and fifty cents. "La Simpatía," a Mexican restaurant in Ontario, charged only 25 pennies for a full meal and ten cents for a cold beer. A ticket for a dance at the Downtown Ballroom in San Bernardino –which featured the Orquesta Moderna playing "the latest musical creations currently in vogue in México"— cost one dollar for the gentlemen and 70 cents for the ladies. Schools and churches also brought live and filmed shows to the locals. The Salón Parroquial of the Catholic Church in La Verne, for instance, advertised a combination of amateur vaudeville with the screening of the picture *No te engañes corazón*.[4]

The Teatro California of Pomona brought to its clientele the latest hits of the Mexican screen. *El Espectador* newspaper ad (1947) (Agrasáncez Film Archive).

Recreation for Hispanics was not limited to films, plays or ballroom dances; quite a few male adults also patronized cantinas. These popular taverns attracted a steady flow of Mexicans. In Ontario, the local saloon was under the management of a man named Hanna, an Anglo that was famous for his bad treatment of non-whites. Voicing the demands of the locals, the editor of *El Espectador* called for the support of a group of Mexicans that had declared a boycott to Hanna's cantina. Endorsing this strategy against prejudice, the paper counseled: "Boycott is the most efficient weapon to stalemate those people that try to seize us, living off the money obtained from Mexicans." It did not take long to see the results of this boycott, as Hanna's place saw its clientele diminished significantly in the following days.[5]

Owners of commercial establishments in the Pomona Valley knew that the weight of Hispanic patronage determined to a great extent the well being of their businesses. At almost every occasion, the astute vendors tried to lure this copious ethnic group to their camp. Sometimes the merchants appealed to the Mexican's desire for, not only good prices, but also dignified and fair treatment. With this in mind, the opening of the Teatro California in Pomona was announced. An advertisement informed: "On Sunday 25, [1938,] Christmas day, the Teatro California of Pomona will open, with two first-class pictures: *Alexander's Ragtime Band* and *The Texan.* General admission will be 15 cents and it will be given special consideration to the Mexican clientele, according to Mr. Sidney Pink, manager of the California."[6] This special consideration meant, of course, that Spanish speakers could sit anywhere they wanted and that segregation would not rule in this business. Its seating capacity (1,275) and large stage made the theater apt for live presentations. Mexican stars performing in Los Angeles could conveniently make an appearance at this spot drawing a crowd from the nearby towns in the Valley. The charismatic child actress, Evita Muñoz *Chachita*, for instance, came to Pomona's California Theater in 1945, at the height of her popularity. One of her most memorable movies, *¡Ay Jalisco, no te rajes!*, was shown here to accompany *Chachita*'s personal presentation.

The Teatro California of Pomona endeavored to bring to its clientele the latest hits of the Mexican screen. Starting in 1946, the management of this house advertised a Spanish-dialogue picture every Wednesday. A good combination program that played in April consisted of *La fuga*, a film starring charming Esther Fernández and handsome Ricardo Montalbán, complemented by an episode of Pedro Armendáriz' action serial *Calaveras del terror* and a Hollywood cartoon in color. The California had three different admission categories this year: children 16 cents, adults 50 cents, and soldiers 30 cents.

Mexicans Belong in the Front-Row Seats

Racial segregation at public places continued to be an issue for Mexicans. *El Espectador* reported on February 17, 1939, that a Mexican couple went to the Upland Theater and were humiliated by the assistant manager when they tried to take the seats in the middle of the auditorium. The manager ordered a young Mexican-American, Pedro Tucker, and his girl friend to move to the front-row seats. But Pedro complained to the man in charge, arguing that if the seats they first wanted cost more, he was ready to pay for them. The employee answered swiftly: "either you two sit where I assign you, or out you go." The paper's editor added that the Mexicans were poorly treated "not because they were dressed untidy or because of bad discipline but, worse, for belonging to the Mexican race."[7]

According to the editor of *El Espectador*, the state of California did not have any law prohibiting segregation. Moreover, the Upland Theater's racial policy seemed to stretch back many years, and the Mexican public had grown accustomed to this shameful practice. Exposing the nature of the abuses, the paper rebuked: "Notwithstanding, the Mexicans continue patronizing day after day [the Upland]; going to this place and spending their well-earned money only to be shamed and separated, as if they had leprosy, forcing them to sit down so close to the screen that, besides [experiencing] the deformities of the images, it will hurt their eye sight sooner or later." A reporter from this newspaper later met with the assistant manager of the Upland Theater, Charles Adams, who only reinstated the official posture: "The Mexicans that come to this theater will have to occupy the seats of the first fifteen rows or they will not be admitted, regardless of who they were or what they wore."[8]

The insistent fight of *El Espectador* did not stop here. It immediately called for the Comisión Honorífica Mexicana de Upland to defend the rights of the people, or at least the rights of *most* of them: "We do not ask that all the Mexicans be treated the same way, for unfortunately there are many of our people that because of their bad behavior and their sloppy dressing and cleanliness, do not deserve any consideration." The paper's strategy to fight racial prejudice in public places consisted basically in implementing a boycott: "We have an arm and we ought to use it, and make it stand for what it is; this arm is to abstain from patronizing the theater in question [and] all the commercial establishments and companies that have ties with the place referred to."[9]

Less than two weeks later, surprisingly, the owner of the Upland Theater, B. G. Meyers, apologized formally to the people of the Comisión Honorífica that had gathered at the playgrounds of the Frontón Martínez. A group of more than a hundred persons attended the meeting. Meyers acknowledged that his theater's personnel had offended some of the patrons and declared, "the Mexicans and persons of Hispanic descent will receive equal consideration like the rest of the public at our theater."[10] Later, in 1944, the Upland began to advertise Spanish-language movies in an effort to attract this larger segment of the populace. One of the first pictures shown here was *María Candelaria*, a drama of peasant life starring Dolores del Río and Pedro Armendáriz.

The exhibition of Mexican movies in the Pomona Valley reached a climax in 1945, at the height of WWII. In fact, people seemed to be enjoying this popular pastime more than ever. The continuous stream of pictures from México made it easier for theater operators to build up an audience, with Hispanics as the most loyal moviegoers. Two Los Angeles-based film exchanges, Azteca and Clasa-Mohme, assured these exhibitors of a steady supply of Spanish-language pictures. During the forties, competition between these companies resulted in the opening of more outlets for their product. To the already established shows in the area (Woods, México, California, Upland), other businesses announcing films in Spanish followed quickly. The Golden State Theater, in Riverside, the Salón Iturbide of Ontario, the Fremont Auditorium of Pomona, and the Patio Misión of San Bernardino were among the most conspicuous spots showing imported pictures at this time. The Golden State Theater offered one of the most attractive programs in 1945, as it announced in April a personal appearance by the youthful film star Pedro Infante. Ads for the occasion invited the public: "Meet the most noble, the most friendly, the most gentleman and humble of the national cinema's stars." The crowds saw Infante perform several romantic melodies accompanied by the Trío de la Victoria.

Another incident involving racial segregation occurred in 1943, this time in the nearby community of Azusa. The Mexican people of this town decided to put an end to the discriminatory policies of the State Theater. A group of concerned residents proposed a boycott against the theater, calling for the support of other Mexicans living in the neighboring towns of Glendora and Irwindale. Since the State was the only theater in Azusa, a boycott from the discontent alliance almost certainly guaranteed a blow to this business.[11]

Segregation affected all public facilities, of which theaters were only the most conspicuous examples. In the San Bernardino School District, children were separated according to their skin color; Blacks and Mexicans went to La Ramona School, while Anglos attended Mt. Vernon. A 1946 proposal to allow the Mexican and Anglo children to share both facilities met with stern opposition on the part of the Board of Education. Even in cemeteries a strict division for the deceased of each ethnic group existed. *El Espectador*'s editor, Ignacio I. López, exposed the nature of this problem saying that in San Bernardino, "the so-called Friendly City," racial prejudices did not end with death. As a proof, he referred that the local Mountain View Cemetery continued to assign burials of Blacks and Mexicans in a separate section of the grounds. In an effort to be more objective, López met with the owners of this cemetery, Wilmex N. Glasscock and Robert Mack Light, ready to hear their argument in favor of such practice. On the one hand, they politely acknowledged their prejudice but insisted that segregation was the social custom. Glasscock and Light, furthermore, understood that this represented "anti–Christian and anti-democratic behavior," something they so deplored but had absolutely no control of.[12]

Some theaters objected to Mexicans sitting near the Anglo Americans because of their improper behavior and dressing habits. This observance was no different here than in other places, such as the Chicago-Gary region where Hispanics were told by a theater management that "the distinction was made because the Mexicans hugged the girls; the movie man also said Mexicans come in their overalls, [and they] are partly to blame for this discrimination. Many of them are dirty and wear old clothes to a movie." Bad manners could become intolerable in some cases. Estela S. De la Fuente, a Texas resident, referred how the locals there reprimanded a typical male behavior at the movies. According to De la Fuente, "My grandmother would take her teenage daughters to the Grande Theater. To ensure that none of the [Mexican] men took liberties with the girls, by sitting too close to them or even by pressing up against them in line, my grandmother would take a large hat pin with her and as she led the girls to their seats, she would wield the hat pin right and left, stabbing the men in the legs surreptitiously, to make them jump out of the way."[13]

Luring the Mexican Public

Theater owners in the vicinity of the Pomona Valley recognized that without the patronage of the Mexican population their business risked failure. Thus, luring this large part of the audience became one of their prime objectives. Newspaper ads for the Woods Theater, for example, announced the *Cantinflas* comedy *Ahí está el detalle* prompting the public: "*Haga Patria!* Be patriotic! Come and make your children see these beautiful shows in their own language!" At the Upland, people could also feel good by watching a spirited Pedro Infante perform in *Mexicanos al grito de Guerra*. Riverside's Arena Theater presented "Vistas todas las noches," movies every night, in an unbeatable programming like the one that billed five attractions in a row: *Adios Mariquita Linda, Rin Tin Tin, Fangs of the Wild,* a newsreel and a cartoon.[14] Woods, Upland and Arena, all three theaters competed to attract the Hispanic populace by appealing to nationalist sentiments and by offering the best in movie programming.

Local Mexican audiences generally consumed a mixture of Spanish and English-language movies, with a strong tendency in the younger generation to assimilate into the

Theater owners in the Pomona Valley tried hard to lure the Hispanic public to their business. *El Espectador* newspaper ad (1947) (Agrasánchez Film Archive).

Anglo-American cinematic culture. In Pomona, parents rewarded their children with a mid-day offering of Walt Disney's *Pinocchio*, in Technicolor, at the State Theater. Later in the day, the whole family could go to the Teatro California for an evening with *La monja alférez*, starring María Félix, followed by the permanently in vogue action serial *Calaveras del terror*. At Riverside's Arena Theater, the quintessential Mexican feature *Allá en el Rancho Grande* played back to back with *Island Captives*. This dual offering of filmed entertainment coexisted for several decades in the theaters catering to Hispanics.

Even the local newspaper, *El Espectador*, grew more sophisticated over the years while targeting the changing tastes of Mexican-Americans. Since 1945, it included regularly news and information about Hollywood as well as Mexican movie stars. The periodical contained a section graphically showcasing beautiful actresses from both countries dressed in the latest fashion. There was a column called "Bocadillos" (Snacks), condensing film trivia, and another one with biographies of the stars. Photographs of María Félix and Joan Crawford, Sofía Álvarez and Cyd Charisse, the comedians *Cantinflas* and Abbott and Costello among others, shared the pages of this Pomona weekly.

Such a bicultural trend in the entertainment field was not unique to this region. Being exposed to the cinema of both countries became the norm for many Mexican-Americans. Just south of the Pomona Valley, in the town of Corona, the Hispanic community patronized simultaneously the Corona Theater and the Teatro Chapultepec. Viola Rodríguez, a local resident, once described the movie going habits of youngsters: "The Mexican American children weren't always eager to go to Corona Theater because they had to sit by themselves in a segregated section. The Spanish theater [Teatro Chapultepec], on the other hand,

Crowd inside the Teatro Chapultepec, in Corona, California (1930s) (courtesy W.D. Addison Room, Corona Public Library, Corona, CA).

had movies in both languages, as well as the vaudeville entertainment, so it was well patronized. The highlight of the week was the Saturday matinee at which an English-language serial such as *Flash Gordon* or *Captain Midnight*, was shown." Rodríguez also said she learned at an early age that "the Mexican films were more realistic than American films; they weren't based on fantasy, they were more realistic and down to earth."[15]

Spanish-language movies alternated with Hollywood productions throughout the fifties. For example, in Pomona, the Sunkist Theater announced a double bill for one of its 1952 Sunday programs: Pat O'Brien's *Okinawa* and the Mexican comedy *La tienda de la esquina*. Similarly, the United Artists Theater played *Singing in the Rain* followed by *Como tú ninguna*, a Mexican-Cuban production. This movie house also promoted Sunday evenings as "Noches de aficionados," giving cash prizes to the winners of these popular amateur shows.

The Teatro Chapultepec "had movies in both languages, as well as the vaudeville entertainment, so it was well patronized" (courtesy W.D. Addison Room, Corona Public Library, Corona, CA).

By the mid-fifties, television had become a major contender for theaters. Pomona's newspaper *El Espectador* carried multiple ads that offered new and used T.V. sets, priced anywhere from $25 to $150. It also included a column reviewing the programming of two local channels. After twenty-four years of being published in Spanish only, *El Espectador* added a section in English, as "many of the third and fourth generation of Mexican descent find it difficult to read the Spanish language: Your writer is among this group."[16] But while reading skills were in fact necessary to fully understand a Spanish-language publication, being illiterate in no way impaired people from enjoying a movie in that language. As the number of residents in the Pomona Valley increased, so did the theaters catering to Mexicans. In 1956 the Woods Theater of Chino was still in business, while the State and Fontana Theaters in Pomona began to include pictures in Spanish. Some of the new Mexican releases could be seen at the State: *Escuela de vagabundos*, with Pedro Infante; *El hombre inquieto*, starring Tin

Tan; and *Caballero a la medida*, featuring *Cantinflas*. For those who wanted to see a Hollywood film, the Mission Drive-In Theater offered *Blood of the Vampire* in Eastman color, while at the United Artists the program included *Hell Squad* and *Tank Battalion*, which was billed as "Raging inferno of war! Where kids learned to kill or be killed!"[17]

The case of the Californian Valley of Pomona serves to illustrate the conditions under which Mexicans went to the movies. A popular pastime, theatergoing did not escape the issue of race segregation for a minority of the populace. Throughout the 1930s, Mexicans in the region were separated at American movie houses. But when the Woods Theater of Chino began to include in its program Spanish-language films in 1934, local audiences enjoyed an option in entertainment without having to be discriminated against. Other theaters followed this example, often pressured by vocal groups in the Pomona Valley. During WWII, a significant increase in the business of many theaters developed. Luring the important segment of Hispanic residents to these venues was obtained by programming Mexican movies, but also by securing a special treatment to all patrons.

At one time, the movies constituted a family habit that cut across age groups. However, a shift in the public's preference occurred at a time when the new generation was assimilated to mainstream American culture, doing away with its ancestor's natural longing for the homeland. Hollywood films aggressively targeted the public, providing plenty of fare that was enhanced with the latest technological gadgets, like color films, panoramic screens, and stereo sound. For most of the youngsters, the offer seemed irresistible. Meanwhile, the movies from México continued to entice the adult portion of the audience, who would remain loyal customers of the Spanish-language theaters until their demise in the 1980s. A fashionable, more modern culture of VCRs and movie rentals substituted the traditional outing with the family.

4

New York City

A diverse mix of ethnic groups from Spain and Latin America made the city of New York the hub of Hispanic culture in the northern part of the United States. According to a 1930 census, some 100,000 residents in this urban center spoke Spanish as a first language. Forty percent of them came from Puerto Rico, following in number other groups: Spaniards, Central and South Americans, Cubans and Mexicans. The number of Mexican-born citizens accounted for only 3,405 of the total Hispanic population. However, the films imported from that country quickly became a staple for most local Spanish-language theaters. Beginning in 1934 and until the end of the decade, a yearly average of 23 first-run Mexican pictures were exhibited in New York City. Comparatively, Argentine product accounted for six releases per year, while Spanish "talkies" made in the U. S. followed with five films, leaving only three movies imported from Spain. The result was that local Hispanics, whether by force of habit or sincere preference, grew accustomed and developed a taste for the ubiquitous Mexican fare.[1]

In the heart of Spanish Harlem, the Teatro Campoamor was a favorite place for live and filmed attractions. Located on the corner of Fifth Avenue and 116th Street, the Campoamor had a capacity of about 1,500 seats. People flocked to this amusement center the night of its inauguration, on August 10, 1934. A personal appearance by Argentine singer Carlos Gardel was announced, accompanied by a variety show and the premiere of a movie, *Cuesta abajo*. A Paramount Pictures film shot in New York, it starred Gardel himself, Mona Maris and Anita Campillo. This was one of the many Spanish "talkies" made in the United States during the first half of the thirties. The program of the Campoamor made for a full house that night, as a large crowd remained standing in line outside of the theater. Just before the show, the police was called in to contain the excitement of the masses that were waiting for the arrival of Gardel.[2]

The Teatro Campoamor became known for a brief time in 1936 as the Teatro Cervantes. After a year, its new management renamed it the Teatro Hispano. Then, at the beginning of 1940, this house was upgraded receiving the name of Radio Teatro Hispano. Another place of entertainment in Harlem showing Mexican films was the Teatro Latino, on Fifth Avenue and 110th Street. This theater had been in business since 1924, when Cuban impresario Fernando Luis opened it under the name of Teatro San José.[3]

New York City's growing Hispanic population motivated some of the area's exhibitors to offer Spanish-language movies, either as an added attraction to the American films or as an alternative to live performances. The first pictures with Spanish dialogue came from

Hollywood and New York studios, following since 1932 a variety of other films produced in México, Argentina, and Spain. Some theaters like the Belmont, on Broadway, exhibited European imports from Italy or France, which were quite popular among Hispanics. In all, local audiences had a chance to enjoy a rich and tempting sample of filmed entertainment. People in general preferred real-life dramas and tragedies. Hollywood musicals and adventure stories were acceptable to a certain degree. But according to some viewers, Spanish-language movies were perceived as being "more sincere in their passion and in the details of the everyday-life that they describe." Mexican pictures held the public's attention so much because "they are like a whirlwind, with all the complexities, all the colors, all the flavors; but mainly because they get inside the reality of life, even when it is cruel and difficult, manifesting sometimes the scourge and blemishes of civilization."[4]

Mexican Films: A Gold Mine

For those assiduous film commentators who attended the screenings of Hispanic theaters, appraising a film became an exercise in balancing the virtues and shortcomings of each reel. On the occasion of the release of *Corazones en derrota*, for instance, a reviewer said: "When Mexican motion-picture makers set out to produce a soul-searching film demanding a tragic ending, they have the courage of their convictions and stick to them until the fade-out. Evidence of this logical development of a morbid tale may be found at the Teatro Campoamor in *Corazones en derrota*."[5] The picture had a malevolent crippled young woman interfere in the happiness of a newly wedded pair. In one repulsive scene, the crippled girl is seen rejoicing at the torturing and killing of a caged bird.

Another Mexican tragedy arrived at the Campoamor Theater at the end of 1934. *El compadre Mendoza*'s "highly intriguing scenes of ranch life and revolutionary activities" stirred the emotions of viewers. A rich hacienda owner befriends a *zapatista* leader and makes him his *compadre*, but later accepts a secret deal to turn over the revolutionary leader to his enemies, who assassinate him. The fine performance of the beautiful actress Carmen Guerrero, as well as the work of other actors in the film, was credited to director Fernando de Fuentes, "who allowed no superfluous histrionics." The picture's photography and sound reproduction left nothing to be desired. In short, *El compadre Mendoza* satisfied critics and public alike during its run at the Campoamor. Tragedies seemed to follow one another at this theater, as the movie *Dos monjes* opened in January of 1935. This "fatal romance" recounted the death of a "rather attractive heroine," and a mortal enmity between two friends. In a powerful ending, the friends expunge their sins in a gloomy monastery while one of them loses his mind. The film's expressionistic atmosphere emphasized the sentiment of betrayal and madness that permeated the story.

Melodramas scored highly on the public's taste for sentimental movies. Such was the case of *Madre querida*, a typical film of motherly love which prompted a critic to issue a warning: "Patrons of the Teatro Campoamor who have tears may prepare to shed them now, if they have not become inured to the hardships so lavishly inflicted upon film heroes by Mexican directors." The picture attracted a large audience during its release. A follow-up to this tearjerker was *Eterna mártir*, a sad tale about a woman "who sacrifices herself for the happiness of her child and its father." Another recent import, *Abnegación*, was greeted as "a rather depressing picture" that made spectators weep a little over "the unsolved triangle and the long-delayed outburst of mother love." A Mexican melodrama was not complete without Sara García, an excellent actress that became a symbol of motherhood throughout hundreds of films. One of them, *Mi madrecita*, played at the Teatro Latino in 1940. A *New York Times* critic, who attended the release of this picture, had no problem in admitting: "From a cold-blooded, critical point of view the waste of acting talent in *Mi madrecita* is something fearful. But judging from the way Harlem audiences are weeping through most of this highly sentimental film and cheering and laughing at the happy ending, it is just what they like."[6]

One of the first Mexican box-office hits at the Teatro Campoamor was *Cruz Diablo*. It broke all previous admission records, even though it rained for two straight days during its exhibition. This swashbuckling story performed so well that it was contracted for a reprise. No other Spanish-language picture had attained such popularity yet. *Cruz Diablo* was reviewed as "a dashing romantic motion picture based on the more or less legendary exploits of a Mexican Robin Hood of the seventeenth century, who had the habit of putting a cross on the foreheads of his enemies with his sword and who was popularly believed to be in league with the devil."[7] Several mystery and adventure pictures shown at this time were *El fantasma del convento*, *La Llorona*, *Los muertos hablan*, and *La isla maldita*. (This last movie appeared boring to some.) A local film critic said of this last movie that, while "it is fairly good from the technical side, the action is slow and the attempt to create an atmosphere of suspense and horror falls flat."

Harlem's Teatro Hispano featured variety shows and movies regularly. In 1938, it exhibited several Mexican films like *Marihuana el monstruo verde*, which was an entertain-

New York City's Teatro Hispano, in Harlem, was a favorite place for live and filmed attractions (Chata Noloesca Collection, San Antonio Conservation Society).

ing thriller about a wicked drug gang. Perhaps in order to avoid confusion with the American-made *Marihuana, the Devil's Weed*, the Mexican film's title was changed in the U.S. for the more innocuous *El traidor*. A disgruntled reviewer, who went to the Teatro Hispano to watch the movie, said of its director: "José Bohr has pitched all the familiar ingredients with astoundingly unamusing results. Among the actors whose abilities are wasted in this mix-up of traitors, smugglers and cops are René Cardona, Lupita Tovar, Barry Norton, Sara García, Manuel Noriega and señor Bohr himself. Perhaps as penance, the management is also showing *Vida, passion y muerte de Nuestro Señor Jesucristo*, a Holly Week film."[8]

Folkloric movies of ranch life, with plenty of music and regional dances were shown at theaters with excellent cash results. In her first Mexican feature, Lupe Vélez paired with Arturo de Córdova in the tropical romance *La Zandunga*. Another hit, *Huapango*, also featured an abundance of folk dances from Veracruz. Smoothly directed by Juan Bustillo Oro, this last film contained "so many enjoyable incidents that the audience hardly realizes that it runs for two hours." The Teatro Latino played *La Adelita* in October of 1938. A famous *corrido* (folk ballad) of the same title served as an inspiration to this anecdotic story, in which the beautiful Esther Fernández plays the courageous heroine of the Mexican Revolution. Efforts like *La Adelita* signaled a new preference for countryside films with upbeat themes, instead of the melancholic and morose fare that had been prevalent in earlier Mexican cinema. An observer said of this movie: "The tragic part of the action is held down to a minimum; there are no real villains, and during most of the time the audiences at the Teatro Latino are being convulsed by witty sallies and comic situations." A few days later, the clientele of Teatro Latino witnessed a personal appearance by some of the most popular Mexican folklore musicians: composer and film actor Lorenzo Barcelata, his wife, María Teresa, and the Trío Los Calaveras. All of them were featured in the film *Tierra brava*, which also played on the screen of the Latino.

The arresting spectacle of bullfighting could be seen in several Mexican features. Famous matador Lorenzo Garza, for example, played himself in the movie *Un domingo en la tarde*. A commentator exaggerated somewhat the reaction of the public to the climatic scenes of this film: "When the grand finale is reached in the bullring in Mexico City," he said, "the applause in the Teatro Hispano is so vociferous that one expects to see hats and silver dollars flying through the air." The same year, Lorenzo Garza returned to the screen in *Novillero*, the first all-color film produced in México. It opened at the Teatro Hispano on March 4, 1939, to the delight of bullfighting aficionados. Another sample of what someone called "the usual Spanish manner of dispatching the unfortunate animals," was offered in the picture *El Gavilán*. Even comedian Mario Moreno *Cantinflas* had his antics tested in front of a bull in *Así es mi tierra*, presented at the Teatro Latino.

Jorge Negrete, the Mexican baritone and virile screen actor, made a personal appearance at the Teatro Hispano when his film *Juntos pero no revueltos* played here at the end of 1939. An entertaining musical comedy, the picture had "lots of funny incidents in and around a México City tenement house peopled by all sorts of strange types." The story had Negrete in the role of a novice opera singer looking for a job at several radio programs, only to be turned down because of his obsolete repertoire and antiquated style. In real life, ironically, the baritone had encountered a similar opposition to his operatic fervor from the producers of Mexican cinema. When Negrete renounced to singing arias and accepted to perform simple but powerful *ranchera* songs, his fame was assured. This came about with the popular success of folkloric movie *¡Ay Jalisco no te rajes!*, which played on the screen of New York's Belmont Theater (West 48th Street), in the spring of 1943.

La Zandunga (1937), a moneymaker starring Lupe Vélez. She made a second film in México in 1944 before committing suicide (Agrasánchez Film Archive).

> A newly refurbished Belmont Theatre was reopened yesterday as the projected midtown
> outlet for Mexican films with the musical *¡Ay Jalisco no te rajes!* Apparently this was a
> move in the right direction, judging by the reaction of yesterday's packed house. The audi-
> ence chuckled loudly and often, and even hummed an accompaniment to some of the
> film's tunes. Jorge Negrete is a handsome, quick-shooting south-of-the-border Gene
> Autrey.[9]

A local theater operator, Gilbert Josephson, took a three-year lease of the Belmont with the specific purpose of bringing "the cream of Mexican-made pictures right into the heart of the theatrical district." Mr. Josephson also managed the World Theater, "the latter-day Mecca of French films," for which he planed a policy of Spanish-language movies alternating with "films from any land." This exhibitor seemed well equipped for the business, as he had contracted sufficient product from the leading U.S. distributors of Mexican movies, Clasa-Mohme and Azteca Films. Moreover, his contacts with the Office of the Coordinator for Inter-American Affairs helped him establish the Maya Films Distributing Corporation, an exchange that handled locally the movie catalog of Azteca Films.[10]

Blessed with a steady supply of first-run pictures, the Belmont Theater continued to offer very attractive programs. A new Jorge Negrete picture, *Así se quiere en Jalisco*, became the first all-color Mexican musical shown here. The young and attractive María Elena Marqués adorned the story as the heroine of this comedy set in a blossoming Mexican ranch. *Así se quiere en Jalisco* was released in the United States with English subtitles. People attending the premiere commented: "The new film is quite a riotous display of gay fiestas, stunning señoritas and equally stunning cowboy pants." Another Jorge Negrete vehicle with English subtitles shown at the Belmont the following year was *Tierra de pasiones*. The star's popularity seemed to increase with the passing of time. Movies with Negrete were a sureshot for exhibitors everywhere. When the local Teatro Hispano screened *Una carta de amor*, in March of 1945, the public gave a standing ovation to the spectacle. "Very few times have we seen an audience so enthralled with a cinematographic production," an observer declared.[11] A romantic story, *Una carta de amor* benefited from a polished script and a superb mise-en-scène written and directed by Miguel Zacarías. But the pull came naturally from the familiar names on the theater's marquee: Jorge Negrete and Gloria Marín, the star couple of the moment.

All sorts of Mexican-made pictures reached the theaters in New York City. While many of them were quite successful with local audiences, a few turned out to be total flops. The Belmont Theater, for example, screened *Por un amor* and *Su gran ilusión* in 1947. Marta Elba, an actress and writer visiting the United States, reported that *Su gran ilusión* was a "churro" (i.e., a poor movie). Even though its cast included more than thirty actors and it had plenty of romantic songs, the lack of coherence in the plot made audiences yawn. Fortunately, the reporter said, this movie was followed by *San Francisco de Asís*, a production of religious significance, and *Soy un prófugo*, a funny comedy with *Cantinflas*, "who is an idol over here."[12]

Pictures that featured music from the Caribbean became potent magnets for theaters. *Embrujo antillano*, a film produced in México and Cuba, was the most successful engagement of the year in New York. Released at the beginning of 1947, the movie featured Cuban-born María Antonieta Pons, the singer Ramón Armengod, and Blanquita Amaro. Although most critics in México City dismissed *Embrujo antillano* as one of the worst pictures ever made, its mass appeal demonstrated that people knew what they wanted in the form of movies: authentic ambience, recognizable music and tasty dances. Distributors found a gold mine in the exploitation of similar pictures with ethnic flavor. Referring to the widespread

appeal of this kind of cinema, Puerto Rican Fernando Ferrer has recently said: "Before Spanish-language television arrived, Spanish-language movies were the primary form of entertainment for Puerto Ricans and overall Hispanics in New York. It was common to see lines of people around the block waiting to get into local theaters, to watch the films and live performance interludes that made them feel closer to home."[13]

The World Theater, on 153 W. 49th Street (near 7th Avenue), started programming Spanish-language pictures in 1943. Its successful release of *Seda, sangre y sol*, featuring Jorge Negrete and Gloria Marín once again, made everyone feel optimistic about the business of Mexican pictures. The movie played here for a record-breaking eight weeks. This first-class house not only exhibited Spanish-language fare, but continued offering other foreign-language films as well. Judging from the success of Mexican screenings at New York's World Theater, a contemporary magazine suggested: "The theaters that exhibit these movies are in fact very few, compared to the total number of Latin people which are addicted to Spanish-language cinema. Therefore, it is necessary the modification or construction of other theaters."[14]

Steady Faith in the Show Business

The demand for Spanish-dialogue movie houses encouraged local investors to enter this lucrative business. In 1944 an enterprising woman, Jeane Ansell, opened several theaters for the Hispanic

Embrujo antillano (1945) had a tremendous mass appeal in New York (Agrasánchez Film Archive).

public. She started out with the Manhattan Theater (W. 109th St. and Manhattan Ave.), later adding the Heights Theater (159 Washington St., in Brooklin), the Art Theater (1077 Southern Blvd., in the Bronx) and the Tiffany (1007 Tiffany St., in the Bronx), which became known as the Teatro Isla. Each house had an average capacity of 600 seats. Ansell and her financial advisor, Irving Rosenblum, were quite interested in opening more theaters in some of the trendy zones. Her theater chain grew to include the Belmont, which had been one of Gilbert Josephson's movie houses, and the Forum, located in the South Bronx. The Forum's large locale (the building used to house a boxing arena) permitted the accommodation of 2,200 people. This theater was renamed Teatro Puerto Rico, becoming one of the liveliest places of entertainment for Hispanics during the early fifties. Jeane Ansell had invested heavily in renovating the Teatro Puerto Rico. Other theaters also managed by this exhibitor were: the Teatro Azteca, in East Harlem, the Borinquen (formerly the Jackson), in the Bronx, and the Amor Theater, located in Brooklyn; Ansell had refurbished these three in 1948 and 1949.[15]

In an interview for a movie magazine, Ansell made it known that she had a steady faith in the show business, expressing that "the Spanish-language pictures have already secured a permanent place in the exhibition world in the United States." Her opinion was based on the assumption that México had reached a point where its star system guaranteed the success of almost any picture. As proof of this she mentioned some familiar names: Dolores del Río, Jorge Negrete, María Félix, Arturo de Córdova, *Cantinflas* and Puerto Rican Mapy Cortés, all of whom were favorites among local theatergoers. Also, stars from Argentina such as Libertad Lamarque, Luis Sandrini, and Zully Moreno supplemented the list of artists that were most popular among Hispanics in New York.[16]

María Antonieta Pons, a gorgeous Cuban dancer and competent actress, achieved popularity thanks to her Mexican movies. The Teatro Puerto Rico announced a personal appearance of this artist in December of 1948. María Antonieta Pons, "con sus rumberos y

The Forum was later called Teatro Puerto Rico. Photograph taken in 1948 (Agrasánchez Film Archive).

Cuban-born María Antonieta Pons achieved fame as a "rumbera." Her "well-rounded and snow-white legs" caused commotion in the 1950s (Agrasánchez Film Archive).

bongoceros," performed side by side with the musician Óscar López. During the first week, the theater grossed more than $35,000 dollars, drawing a daily crowd of 2,200 that filled the seats of the Puerto Rico, plus an extra 500 that stood up throughout each show. This engagement established a box-office record and served as an example of the unique appeal of Latin American artists in New York. After the second week, the Cuban star shared the stage with Sara García, a veteran actress whose roles as an authoritarian grandmother or "abuelita" turned her into a symbol of Mexican melodramas.[17]

Two of the best theaters in the Ansell Circuit were dedicated to the presentation of live shows: the Puerto Rico and the Belmont. A parade of Latin American artists performed at the Teatro Puerto Rico during the years 1948–1949. Emilio Tuero, Antonio Badú, María Luisa Zea, Mapy Cortés, Agustín Lara, Ramón Armengod and the Lecuona Cuban Boys were among the most famous personalities entertaining theatergoers. The greatest star appearing on the stage of the Teatro Puerto Rico was Libertad Lamarque. Cash receipts during one week amounted to $45,000, of which Lamarque received approximately $17,000. The show of Jorge Negrete attracted many people too, bringing in $28,000 to the box office. Comparatively, the appearance of María Félix at the imposing Teatro Del Mar was able to draw $24,000 in one week. Finally, Hugo del Carril, a star from Argentina, visited the same theater with cash results of $23,000.[18]

At the end of 1949, however, live shows were getting too expensive for audiences and theater owners alike. Jeane Ansell's enterprise, for example, had lost more than $60,000 in the operation of the Teatro Puerto Rico. Apparently, not all shows produced enough money to pay for salaries, publicity and other expenses. In one important case, Agustín Lara's performance turned out to be a flop at the box office. Faced with this prospect, the Puerto Rico and another venue called the Teatro San Juan began to favor the exhibition of movies as a way to minimize losses. The reasons for the economic failure of some live shows were complicated and varied. But one observer was able to pinpoint the root of the problem:

> The public that attends the Hispanic theaters in New York is one that is generally poor. They are working people that live long distance from where the theaters are located. Therefore, it becomes too difficult for them to go to a show. Besides, these workingmen have their families and they have to carry four sons and a wife with them. The admission price is one dollar and fifteen cents, and with all the family the entire week's salary is spent. That is why these people prefer to go to the smaller barrio theaters. They are only fourteen or fifteen cents a ticket, and they are located just around the corner.[19]

A few theaters that relied on live performances became entangled with monetary problems at the beginning of 1950. For instance, the Triboro showed signs of weak finances when its manager was unable to hand payments for the appearance of Mexican actress Elsa Aguirre and comedian Angel Garasa. At the last minute, the good-looking Aguirre received a bad check from the theater, while Garasa was told abruptly that his salary would have to wait. Aware of the irregularities, other stars immediately cancelled their contract with the Triboro. But Amalia Aguilar, a forthright Cuban dancer, took a decisive step when she openly threatened to sue the theater's manager for breach of contract. At this point, the local actors union resorted to closing the doors of the Triboro, an entertainment center located on the corner of 125th Street and Third Avenue.[20]

Meanwhile, the Teatro Puerto Rico established itself as the hub of Hispanic entertainment. When the movie *Hipócrita* was released, its leading stars appeared in person at the Puerto Rico drawing thousands of people. Besides leading artists, Antonio Badú and Leticia Palma, *Hipócrita* featured the admired musicians Trío Los Panchos. The movie told the misfortunes of a cabaret dancer who has a scar on her face. After undergoing surgery, she becomes a beautiful and successful star, attracting at the same time gangsters, corruption and vice. The film played simultaneously at the Puerto Rico and San Juan Theaters, breaking all records for a Mexican movie. The management of the Teatro Puerto Rico even agreed to lower the admission prices in order to allow more people to see the show. Other pictures exhibited simultaneously at the Puerto Rico and San Juan Theaters were *La vorágine* and *Las puertas del presidio*. Blanca Estela Pavón, who had recently died in an airplane accident, starred in the latter film. When the Teatro Del Mar exhibited her last appearance in *Ladronzuela*, a throng of admirers waited in line to get inside the theater, a gesture that proved the extent of Blanca Estela's popularity.

Exotic dancers, commonly known as "rumberas," like María Antonieta Pons and Ninón Sevilla, enjoyed wide appeal whether in films or on the stage. Miss Pons, for instance, typically aroused male audiences in the movie *La mujer del puerto*, a new version of the 1933 classic, while the spirited Sevilla alternated with legendary composer Agustín Lara in *Coqueta*. Both films were shown in 1950 to packed houses in New York. The Puerto Rico Theater shrewdly advertised the debut of another famous Cuban dancer, Amalia Aguilar. Teasing the public, an ad suggested an imaginary match between Aguilar and Pons: "Something never done before was accomplished by Chucho Montalbán's Teatro Puerto Rico. At the same time that María Antonieta danced two rumbas and two mambos in the picture *La hija del penal*, showing on the screen, Amalia Aguilar stormed the stage with a very hot rumba and two fiery mambos, to the point of awakening a dead person."[21] Other famed hip-swingers that took the stage of the Puerto Rico this year were Meche Barba and the always-polemical Yolanda Montez *Tongolele*.

The influence of this type of films on the younger generations was best described by one of the regulars to Spanish-language theaters in New York City. Looking back to his adolescent years, Carl J. Mora, an author and film historian, candidly said:

> I also vaguely recall seeing at the Belmont Theater, a bullfighting movie with María Antonieta Pons, a voluptuous Cuban rumbera... Many films liberally used Cuban music (rumbas, congas, cha cha, mambo) and Cuban rumberas like the aforementioned María Antonieta Pons, the fabulous Ninón Sevilla, Rosa Carmina, and Amalia Aguilar among others. It was these actresses along with the Mexican sexpots like Lilia Prado, Elsa Aguirre, and many others that helped jumpstart me into puberty. Oddly, the two great beauties of Mexican cinema, Dolores del Río and María Félix, did not have the same effect on me. They were too icy and inaccessible, too perfect. Beautiful yes. But a sort of idealized beauty that placed them beyond mere sexuality. The others were earthy and fun, girls that a young man could see himself trying to date (as I often fantasized).[22]

Although television had just begun to air a diversity of programs that included old films, theaters continued to command the attention of a good part of the people looking for entertainment. In the spring of 1950, the city of New York was given the world premiere of a film with Mario Moreno *Cantinflas*. A 2,250-seat movie house, the Teatro Del Mar (Broadway and 138th Street), announced the release of *Puerta joven*. In this comedy, *Cantinflas* played a poor neighborhood's apartment caretaker who falls in love with the sweet and innocent Silvia Pinal. As with other films featuring the popular comedian, *Puerta joven* became a box-office success and was considered among the best Mexican pictures of the year exhibited in New York. Also included in the top categories were *Doña Diabla*, starring María Félix, and *Al son del mambo*, a musical film with the impetuous Amalia Aguilar. The classic picture from Spain, *Locura de amor*, and the Argentine production *Santa y pecadora* completed the list of the best Spanish-dialogue movies screened in New York in 1950.[23]

The popularity of Mexican movies and the good works of the motion picture distributor Clasa-Mohme prompted the English-language Star Theater, on Lexington Avenue and 107th Street, to adopt a new policy and a new name. It re-opened as the Boricua, proudly displaying at the door Puerto Rican flags. Starting in 1952 its program consisted of second-run Mexican features, at lower admission prices. For its kick-off in January, two powerful dramas were shown: *Negro es mi color*, a story of racial conflict starring Marga López, and the already popular *Doña Diabla*. Receipts from the opening of the Boricua surprisingly beat the box-office records of first-run houses, a fact that signaled the preference of the public for economic, barrio-oriented cinema entertainment.[24]

A Competitive Environment

Jeanne Ansell was by no means without competitors in the exhibition business. Harry Harris established another theater circuit converting several English-language movie places into outlets for Mexican films. The chain included: the Teatro Boricua (formerly the Star), the Caribe (formerly the Arden), the San Juan (formerly the Audubon), the Del Mar (formerly the Gotham) and the Atlantic, which was advertised as "El gran teatro hispano de Brooklyn." Harris later added to his circuit the Antillas Theater, the Strand, also in Brooklyn, and the Colón Theater. This last one stood on the West side of Manhattan (Columbus Avenue and 84th Street).[25]

Doña Diabla, a 1949 powerful drama with a top-notch leading actress (Agrasánchez Film Archive).

Theaters catering to Hispanics sprung up everwhere in New York City. Opening of Teatro Boricua in 1952 (Agrasánchez Film Archive).

Another exhibitor targeting New York's Spanish speakers was Max Cohen, whose Cinema Circuit of eleven English-language theaters had been in business since 1946. He first got the lease of the Teatro Hispano in 1949. Subsequently, the Cinema Circuit opened the following theaters for the exclusive showing of Spanish-dialogue pictures: the Studio, on Broadway and 65th Street, the Edison, in Manhattan, the Marcy, in Brooklyn, the Metropolitan, on 14th Street, the Aster, in Greenpoint, and the Prospect, located in the Bronx, near Jeanne Ansell's Teatro Puerto Rico.[26]

With the expansion of theater chains and the brewing of competitive business, some frictions among the leading film distributors and exhibitors were bound to arise. In 1953, while the demand for Spanish-language films in New York reached a high point, a dispute developed between Max Cohen's Cinema Circuit and the Clasa-Mohme distributor, which was supplying movies to the Harry Harris theater chain. Problems also piled up for the powerful Ansell Circuit. In an unprecedented disclosure, the company of Jeanne Ansell and Irving Rosenblum was charged with tax evasion. The court manifested that the theaters' accounting records had omitted the tax payment on ticket sales in 210 occasions. Ansell and Rosenblum had "filed hundreds of false admission tax returns between 1946 and 1949; and on each of the returns, the amount of admission taxes collected was understated by 50 per cent or more," according to information gathered by U.S. Attorney Dennis C. Mahoney. In short, the Ansell Circuit had committed a fraud amounting to $372,000. Besides this accusation, the U.S. Attorney was holding 17 other charges against Ansell and Rosenblum.[27]

Jeanne Ansell and his business advisor, Irving Rosenblum, were liable to a maximum of five years in prison and a fine of $10,000 on each of the 210 counts. Whether the sentence was carried out is not ascertained, but a Columbia Pictures employee, Fernando Obledo, recently said that Jeanne Ansell "did not put a foot in the jail."[28] However, the problems for this embattled exhibitor did not stop here. While these legal matters perspired, the competitors Harry Harris and Max Cohen took advantage and acquired the lease to most of the theaters in the Ansell Circuit. In 1959, Ansell filed a suit against both exhibitors and also against Azteca and Clasa-Mohme. The complaint alleged "conspiracy and discrimination by exhibitors and distributors" in an effort to squash Miss Ansell out of business.[29]

The Triboro Theater also presented Spanish-language movies and vaudeville in the forties. Other places for Mexican films were the Municipal Theater, the President Theater, and the Boro Hall. This last one belonged to the Ansell circuit. Perhaps the largest locale for movies was the Teatro Del Mar, with its 2,500 seats. The distributor Clasa-Mohme was vigorously supplying films to this and other houses in 1948, a year that signaled the height of the motion picture business, with sixteen theaters for Mexican movies in New York City. Still, the number of screens for imported pictures was not enough, considering that the Spanish-speaking population living in the area at the end of the decade had reached 600,000. As more movie places were opened, the increase in business naturally followed. In October of 1951, producer Felipe Mier visited New York and told the press that receipts from "the thirty-three theaters exhibiting Mexican pictures here could be said to surpass the box-office records obtained in Los Angeles, California, during its Golden Age."[30]

In 1957, Columbia Pictures, Inc. became the third major distributor of Spanish-language movies in the United States. Five influential Mexican producers joined efforts to initiate business with Columbia: Mario Moreno *Cantinflas*, Jacques Gelman, the brothers Santiago and Manuel Reachi (all four of them representing Posa Films), and Sergio Kogan (head of Internacional Cinematográfica and Alfa Films). Among the first movies they gave to Columbia for distribution were *El bolero de Raquel*, starring *Cantinflas*, and *La Escondida*, with María Félix and Pedro Armendáriz. Both movies ranked at the top of current Mexican productions of high commercial value. *La Escondida* was considered one of the most expensive films ever made.

Columbia Pictures established an effective system of distribution whereby theaters were supplied with Mexican and Hollywood product under very attractive terms. This company, for example, helped pay for the advertising on most first-run movies. A decidedly good deal, exhibitors found an opportunity to add to their business every time they booked a Columbia movie. Also, this distributor provided theaters in the U.S. with American pictures subtitled in Spanish. In every instance, the company knew exactly how to win the favor of exhibitors.

Besides the regular Mexican fare, Columbia Pictures offered an assortment of movies from Spain and Argentina. The distributor's catalog was enriched during the 1960s with many new productions, some of them billing renowned performing stars. To its basic list of 28 films featuring the comedian *Cantinflas*, the film company added other attractions starring famous singers such as Raphael, Sandro, Massiel, Julissa and César Costa. Two celebrated erotic symbols from Argentina, Libertad Leblanc and Isabel Sarli, were likewise part of Columbia's stock. Movies with performers Palito Ortega, Angélica María, Joselito, Miguel Ángel Álvarez, and Jorge Salcedo engrossed the list of hits. Later on, *La india María*, and even the masked superhero *El Santo* helped reinforce Columbia's catalog.[31]

Columbia's competitors meanwhile continued to release the best Mexican films available. Clasa-Mohme, for instance, announced in May of 1960 the color picture *Yo pecador*, which played at five local theaters and made $30,000 during one week. This film contained scenes of New York City, Chicago, and Lima, Perú, a fact that accounted for its wide appeal among Latin American audiences. The cast of *Yo pecador* included some famous names: Pedro Geraldo, Libertad Lamarque, Pedro Armendáriz, and Christiane Martel. But its main draw was the story, based on the autobiography of José Mojica, a Mexican opera singer and Hollywood star of the 1920s that later became a Catholic priest.

Mexican film production in the mid-fifties resented the effects of Hollywood's newest invention: the Cinemascope. As movies in the wide screen drew most of the crowds to theaters, the cinema from south of the border sought to integrate the folklore of as many Latin American countries as possible with the aim of retaining its habitual audiences. Movies such as *Las canciones unidas, Música en la noche, Llamas contra el viento,* or *Escuela de música* were designed specifically to blend the landscape and traditional customs of Central and South America, as well as the Caribbean, in a marathon of musical performances. Spain was also invoked in films like *La Faraona, El gran espectáculo,* and *Sueños de oro,* all of them starring the well-known Flamenco dancer Lola Flores. The melodrama *Llamas contra el viento,* for example, was actually filmed in México, Cuba, Panamá, Colombia, and Venezuela, with the explicit intention of promoting the local folklore of each region.

These efforts by the Mexican film industry illustrate the shrewdness of its promoters, who had plainly understood that the survival of their business depended on giving the public a well-rounded spectacle. This included the fabrication of a cinema that sometimes appeared artificial in its mixing of assorted elements drawn from so many different countries. It could be argued here that the popularity of Mexican films was based on the illusion of a unified Latin American culture. The common assumption that Hispanics represented a homogeneous group can indeed be challenged. But perhaps the issue of artificiality may gain in perspective when taking into account the competitive environment prevalent at that time. México's cinema last effort to counter Hollywood and European dominance was to integrate the folklore of Latin America into a filmic narrative with plenty of musical performances; precisely the kind of show that appealed to the masses.

Many of the movies produced south of the border were clearly designed to take advantage of the cultural similarities found among the Latin American people; and they did so by appealing to their instinctive love for music. One of the reasons why Mexican cinema was still accepted by Latin American audiences outside of México is because it provided cultural nourishment via the songs and dances that were indigenous to the region. The

New York public carried on patronizing Spanish-language theaters throughout the sixties, perhaps as a gesture of loyalty to their Latin American roots. Mexican filmed entertainment gave them just the right amount of sustenance with its romantic, passionate tales amidst a background of tropical melodies.

5

El Paso, Texas

Since the days of silent cinema, audiences in El Paso, Texas, were able to see the latest movies produced across the Rio Grande. One of the most publicized was *Santa*. The film caused great stir in 1919, when it played on the screens of several local theaters: the Alcázar, Eureka, Rex and Iris. For only six cents admission, people witnessed the disgrace of Santa, the young heroine of the film interpreted by Elena Sánchez Valenzuela. The tale described the fall of an innocent peasant woman, who is seduced by a soldier and thus degraded by her family. Sad as it was, the story moved through three chapters: "Purity, Vice, and Martyrdom," coming to an end with Santa's pitiful death. Its commercial success in El Paso gave the editors of a local newspaper an opportunity to express: "El espectáculo novedoso que ha venido a darnos vida; porque *Santa* estrujando nuestros nervios, sacude la monotonía de la vida de El Paso y nos transporta a las regiones de nuestro México" (The newest spectacle that has brought us life; because *Santa*, crushing our nerves, shakes the monotonous living of El Paso and takes us to the depths of our México).[1]

In addition to the gloomy dramas in the style of *Santa*, a more cheerful depiction of life permeated earlier Mexican films. The promotion of these pictures through the pages of two Spanish-language newspapers of El Paso, *La República* and *La Patria*, was advanced by typically exalting the public's patriotism. When the Teatro Alcázar played *Por la patria*, a short feature filmed in El Paso, the advertisement called for every true Mexican to: "Forget the rancor! Forget the political parties! Let there be peace for all Mexicans! Viva México!" At a time when the country was still recovering from the trauma of the Revolution, these words seemed to find an echo in the minds of hundreds of immigrants and exiles. The theater impresario Juan de la Cruz Alarcón, who was general manager of the Compañía Internacional de Diversiones, had produced *Por la patria* with the aim of showcasing the local festivities celebrating Mexican Independence Day. After it opened in this city, the movie was programmed to tour several theaters in México.[2]

A handful of movie houses catering to Mexicans in El Paso were advertised in the local Spanish-language newspapers in 1919. They were the Alcázar, Eureka, Paris, Rex, and Hidalgo Theaters, all of them belonging to the Compañía Internacional de Diversiones. Three prominent businessmen in the El Paso-Ciudad Juárez area headed this vigorous circuit: Rafael Calderón, José U. Calderón and Juan Salas Porras. Across the border and throughout the state of Chihuahua, many entertainment venues were connected to this circuit, also known as the International Amusement Company.

The Teatro Colón in the 1920s and 1930s

Located in downtown El Paso, the Gran Teatro Colón was originally a theater for stage plays and operetta. Its current manager, Silvio Lacoma, announced in December of 1919 a season of zarzuela (light opera), presenting two of the most admired Mexican actresses: Mimí Derba and María Caballé. The following year, the Colón began to show films, competing with the Estrella and Cristal Theaters. Moving pictures could also be seen at the Alameda Theater, on Alameda Avenue and San Marcial Street, and at the Teatro Iris, operated by J. C. Ontiveros. These were two popular sub-run houses for the Mexican working classes. Across the international border, in Ciudad Juárez, some of the places programming Mexican films were the Anáhuac and Edén Theaters.

In 1921, the Teatro Colón featured several important films. One of them was the serial *La banda del automóvil*, which like another picture of similar title was based on real-life events. Everyone reading the news from abroad had learned of the atrocities of a México City band of thieves, who disguised as army officers and rode on a luxurious gray automobile. *La banda del automóvil* was a success upon its release in El Paso. Other films shown at the Colón this year were *El escándalo, Alas abiertas, México pintoresco* and *Tepeyac*. A sophisticated drama, *El escándalo* "demonstrated that our social life also has the refinement and culture of the most advanced nations of Europe." *Tepeyac* was a patriotic movie with religious overtones that focused on the miraculous apparition of the Virgin of Guadalupe to an Indian; it was double-billed for the occasion with the Hollywood serial *El fantasma del enemigo*. The Colón was one of the more expensive venues, charging twenty cents admission for adults and ten cents for children. Sometimes the attraction consisted of a live show, as when the Justiniani brothers made their debut here. Wearing Far East garments, José and Daniel Justiniani performed a number of mystery tricks and several "acts of mind transmission" that left audiences perplexed.[3]

El Paso's Alcazar Theater targeted its Mexican audience with the locally produced 1919 film *Por la Patria* (Agrasánchez Film Archive).

The impresario Silvio Lacoma had a second amusement center, the Teatro Estrella, which in September of 1924 showed the film *De pura raza* while announcing the debut of Celia Montalván, a frivolous vaudeville actress from México. A cheaper theater, the Estrella attracted mostly people from the lower classes. Lured by its vaudeville program, a reporter working for the local *La Patria* newspaper joined the crowd attending the Estrella. His opinion of the young but inexperienced Montalván was quite negative, as *La Patria*'s article made plain. Yet his remarks about the run-down condition of the theater were even more pointed.

> Miss Montalván is now being applauded at the Estrella. She was presented with great fanfare, but she hasn't really attracted the attention of the public... Besides, the Teatro Estrella leaves much to be desired regarding hygiene. The moment you walk in, a strong odor of uric acid is perceived throughout the place; there is no ventilation and the air gets stalled. In one corner, you could watch an incessant opening and closing of doors, as if it were a public restroom: it appears that women like to come to the theatre not for diversion but to do their necessities. However, since the tickets are cheap the people go the Estrella in spite of all the discomfort.[4]

As expected, the management of the Estrella did not take long to complain to the editor of the newspaper. This protest, by all means, was very effective. Although the following day the *La Patria* reporter continued attacking the awful singing of Celia Montalván, the only thing he added about his previous commentary on the filthiness of the theater was the cryptic and old-fashioned phrase: "Ni le meneallo" (Don't even mention it).

When theaters in El Paso were converted to the new system of sound pictures in the late twenties, the transition was anything but smooth. Immediately after the first experience, patrons and management began complaining about bad acoustics, defective sound equipment, and especially the poor manners of people in the audience. Rafael Calderón, who by 1929 had acquired the Teatro Colón and other movie houses, warned of the chaotic consequences of the introduction of "talkies."

> Because our audiences are very little disciplined... and they do not stop in their customary gibberish, affecting seriously the optimum exhibition of talkies. People coming in; people coming out, children that cry or yell, plus whistling and all sorts of things. This state of affairs regarding our viewers will cause a lot of nuisance and worries [to exhibitors]. I know this from my own experience.[5]

One of the first Mexican "talkies" exhibited at the Teatro Colón was *El águila y el nopal*. The Colón advertised it as "The first picture spoken, sung, and danced that has been produced in México." This folkloric film about a rancher who accidentally discovers oil on his property played in El Paso, in May of 1931. Other exhibitors, cashing in on the fever of sound movies and wanting to lure the Mexican population to their business, also began to show Spanish-dialogue pictures. The powerful Publix Theatres, Inc., announced the conversion of the Teatro Palace to this policy. *Un caballero de frac*, a Paramount Pictures production starring Roberto Rey and Gloria Guzmán, played at the Palace this year and was billed as a "Noisy and energetic film like a champagne glass." Many of the local theaters engaged in a competitive race to win the favors of Mexican audiences, who showed great enthusiasm for these "noisy" pictures. The Teatro Rex, located on 413 South El Paso Street, reopened under new management in December "to exhibit silent and spoken movies in Spanish." Among other things, the Rex boasted a "magnificent heating system for the comfort of the public."[6]

The newspaper publicity for the Teatro Colón emphasized the cleanliness of the spectacle offered, recommending it as suitable for the whole family and speaking for its "moral flavor." Smart ads referred to the Colón as the place "where art, joy and the respect to the public can be felt." Community-oriented functions often took place here. For example, as a reaction to the devastating effects of the economic depression this theater promoted special matinees for the benefit of "Los sin trabajo," the unemployed. Charging "the extremely low price of 25 cents," the theater followed the current admission policies of major Hollywood theater chains in response to the financial crisis. Another charity effort of the management helped raise funds for the Mexican poor, or "indigentes repatriados," that voluntarily returned to their homeland during the Depression.[7]

Throughout the 1930s, the Teatro Colón alternated the exhibition of Mexican and Hollywood films. A double bill, for instance, presented the Mexican melodrama *Tierra, amor y dolor*, supplemented by an American movie subtitled in Spanish starring Lionel Barrymore. Artists from across the border came regularly to perform at the Colón, as when Adriana Lamar and Ramón Pereda, interpreters of *La Llorona*, appeared on stage to demonstrate "how the love scenes and fights were done in the movies." Adriana Lamar also presented her latest picture, *Chucho el Roto*, which was hailed by the press in Mexico City as "the most expensive production filmed in the country." Theaters catering to English-language audiences sometimes advertised a Mexican picture. The Alameda, for instance, played *Madre querida*, a picture exalting the love of a son for his missing mother. Likewise, the Palace showed *El primo Basilio*, a story about a "deceitful wife who, in the absence of her husband, revives an old passion for her cousin." This ambivalent view of Mexican womanhood reached a climax in 1936 when the Colón Theater advertised a series of films starting with the exemplary melodramas *Madres del mundo, Mater nostra* and *El calvario de una esposa*. To demonstrate that women can also be the objects of damnation, the Colón showed *Malditas sean las mujeres*, subsequently re-releasing two hits: *El primo Basilio* and *Madre querida*.[8]

By 1937, theaters in El Paso were well supplied with Spanish-language movies. Azteca Films, the pioneer distributor of Mexican motion pictures based in this Texan city, provided the exhibitors throughout the region with most of their programs. For this distributor, the Teatro Colón became the main outlet for Mexican films, presenting the public with the most recent productions. This year it released several features such as *Cielito lindo, ¡Ora Ponciano!, Juan Pistolas* and *Jalisco nunca pierde*, all of them taking enormous profits at the box office. The pictures appealed to the majority of moviegoers because of their popular musical content, and their depiction of typical regional customs from across the border. The exhibition of *¡Ora Ponciano!* at the end of July was a milestone in the history of this theater, as the doors of the Colón remained opened from twelve noon until midnight. Thus allowing the crowds a chance to laugh at the occurrences of comedians *Chato* Ortín and Carlos López *Chaflán*. Most features typically played one or two days, but this film was held for a full week at the Teatro Colón, returning again the following month. The extreme heat of that summer prompted the management of the Colón to advertise this house as "The freshest theater along the border."

During the 1940s, several movie houses opened in Texas as a result of the bonanza in the exhibition business. Until the opening of San Antonio's Alameda Theater in 1949, the Teatro Colón remained as the most important house for Mexican movies in this large state. Located on 507 South El Paso Street, the Colón had a capacity for 1,078 seats (728 on the main floor and 350 on the balcony). Rafael Calderón, founder of Azteca Films distributors, also owned this theater and was the head of the International Amusement Company. Needless to say, Don Rafael always strove to bring to the Colón the best features, having to compete locally against the Alameda, Alcázar, Mission, and several English-language houses: the Plaza, Ellanay, Texas Grand, Palace and Wigwam (these five belonged to the Interstate Circuit, Inc.).

A 1936 melodrama shown at the Teatro Colón: *Malditas sean las mujeres*. Original one-sheet poster (Agrasánchez Film Archive).

Besides the existing competition in El Paso, a theater like the Colón had to contend with the entertainment centers across the international divide. Ciudad Juárez offered a good variety of places for viewing movies, and at cheaper prices. This meant that, in order to be successful, the Colón had to be innovative in all its business practices. Pictures released here were selected carefully and promoted wisely. The returns of this theater during the 1940s attest to the importance given to selective programming and good advertising. As a general rule, the most popular subjects included well-known stars. For example, some of the Colón's biggest receipts at this time were obtained from films starring Jorge Negrete. This star attracted large crowds during the weeklong engagements of *El rebelde* ($4,895), *Tierra de pasiones* ($4,958), *El peñon de las ánimas* ($6,009). Compared to a regular film like *Al son de la marimba*, which made $2,480 in one week, Negrete's color feature, *Así se quiere en Jalisco*, ripped $6,432 from ticket sales alone. These pictures played for a full week between 1943 and 1945. Yet, *Un día con el Diablo*, a comedy with Mario Moreno *Cantinflas*, was able to gross at the Colón $7,298 during its seven-day exhibition in 1946.[9]

Pedro Infante, Screen Idol

Without a question, the absolute attraction for the fans of Mexican movies was Pedro Infante. Having his name spelled out on the marquee ensured the theaters of excellent box office results. In 1945, at the start of Infante's career, two of his pictures made top receipts at the Teatro Colón: *Mexicanos al grito de guerra* ($3,837) and *¡Viva mi desgracia!* ($4,068), both of which played for one week in this first-run theater. Other subsequent hits of the Mexican idol were *Los tres García*, *Nosotros los pobres*, *Angelitos negros*, and *Los tres Huastecos*. The Colón exhibited these subjects with more frequency than any of Pedro Infante's pictures distributed by Clasa-Mohme. This company handled thirty films starring Infante, while its competitor, Azteca Films, had in stock about twenty movies of the star's total of 59.

Pedro Infante's movies were heavily in demand by theaters everywhere. This popularity increased over time, especially after his untimely death in 1957, when the thirty-nine-year-old actor was at the top of his cinematic career. His many recorded songs (344) and a string of unbeatable films cemented his

Pedro Infante's movies made top receipts at all theaters. He starred in a total of 59 films, winning an award for *La vida no vale nada* (1954) (Agrasánchez Film Aarchive).

reputation as one of the icons of Mexican popular culture. Since Infante's debut in the early forties, the charismatic star became a gold mine for the music and film industries. At a time when radio and the cinema were at a high point, his melodious voice and his exploits in films guaranteed the success of any show. Whether the movie was a new release or a re-release, it always grasped the attention of the crowds. For that reason, when an exhibitor deemed a program weak, he usually requested a Pedro Infante movie as supporting feature. This assured the theater of obtaining good returns. As one distributor pointed out: "A powerful filler has a good deal to do with the success of any picture, regardless of the [importance] of the head of the program." Thus, the management of the Teatro Colón frequently tested the effectiveness of a Pedro Infante film to back up the main attraction. Time and again, it was said, "An Infante filler definitely improves receipts."[10]

For the release of *Guitarras de media noche*, a film starring Lola Beltrán and José Alfredo Jiménez, the Colón added a popular tearjerker with Pedro Infante made in 1948, *Angelitos negros*. This powerful combination resulted in cash receipts of $3,586 for the weeklong engagement in the summer of 1958. Benefiting from a period of school vacation, this double bill was made even more successful because "in Texas the summer business is better than the winter, for air-conditioned or air-cooled theatres attract a good deal of patronage so that people can escape the heat for a short time." Even during the exhibition of big pictures like *La Cucaracha*, the Colón Theater programmed a Pedro Infante film as a companion to the main feature. For that occasion, the management of the Colón requested *Pablo y Carolina* as a filler. On its first day, *La Cucaracha* grossed $1,394 at the ticket booth. Admission prices for adults were 70 cents downstairs or 50 cents in the balcony, while those for children were 25 and 20 cents.[11]

When the Ascárate Drive-In opened in January of 1957, its inaugural Eastman color picture starring Luis Aguilar, *El Siete Leguas*, made $810 at the box office in three days. A similar amount was harvested by *Los gavilanes*, a Pedro Infante picture that had been released previously in El Paso and was finally playing at this drive-in. After Infante's death in April, the Ascárate registered an increase in ticket sales for the deceased idol's movies. In July of that year, it exhibited *A toda máquina*, obtaining $1,029 on a three-day weekend. The same month, Infante's *El inocente* made almost $1,500 in four days. An assortment of films performed by the late star was brought to the Ascárate Drive-In within a year of Infante's deadly plane crash. The distributor Clasa-Mohme booked nine pictures to this theater in that interval, including the hits *Los tres García*, *Dos tipos de cuidado*, and *Pablo y Carolina*. This last movie played under lots of rain and snow during its four-day engagement in January of 1958. Still, the receipts of the drive-in amounted to $1,174, when most of the other Mexican releases exhibited under normal conditions that winter hardly exceeded the $600 mark.[12]

There was almost no week without a Pedro Infante film showing in the theaters of El Paso. Throughout the 1950s, the Colón and the Mission Theaters, as well as the Azcárate, the Trail and the Bronco Drive-Ins were supplied with this actor's movies on a regular basis. Pedro Infante belonged to the screen of every theater catering to Hispanic audiences. The significance of this idol of Mexican cinema is only hinted at by his movies' performance at the box-office. It is true that a lot of money was involved whenever his pictures were booked by theaters. But beyond the realm of quantifications, the impact of Infante's personality on audiences had a deeper meaning in those days (and probably it still has). A

Opposite: After Pedro Infante's death in 1957, his popularity grew even more. He acted alongside his brother Ángel Infante in *Por ellas aunque mal paguen* (1952) (Agrasánchez Film Archive).

¡ESTA SI ES UNA VACIADA!
¡UN DERROCHE DE "PUNTADAS" Y DE BUEN HUMOR!

FERNANDO SOLER y PEDRO INFANTE

apadrinando el debut estelar de

ANGEL INFANTE en

POR ELLAS, AUNQUE MAL PAGUEN

UNA COMEDIA REBOSANTE DE AGUDEZA Y PICARDIA,
CON BELLISIMAS CANCIONES
QUE MEXICO ENTERO CANTARA

GROVAS, S.A.

contemporary author, the novelist Denise Chávez, has been able to capture in prose the essence of the cult to this famed artist. At the same time, Chávez has characterized in one of her novels the intimate atmosphere of the Teatro Colón of El Paso.

> In the darkness of El Colón movie theater, larger than life and superimposed on a giant screen, Pedro Infante, the Mexican movie star, stares straight at me with his dark, smoldering eyes. It is here in the sensuous shadows that I forget all about my life... It is here that I prefer to dream. It's dinnertime on a hot July night. I should be at home, and yet I find myself lost in the timeless transparency of El Colón watching Pedro Infante in the movie *La vida no vale nada*. The temperature inside El Colón is ninety degrees. The main floor and the balcony are packed with people of all ages, families hovering close to each other, young lovers, older couples resting like torpid flies near the water cooler. Outside, it's hotter. The married men wander down to the concession stand to get a Coke and stare hard at the young girls... Voices call out incessantly to the actors on the screen, without any hesitation or embarrassment, as if the audience knows them... We're all children in the darkness. In here no one watches us and tells us what to feel. Each of us yearns for Pedro, for the world he creates: a world of beauty, physical perfection, song.[13]

This interpretation of what it meant for movie fans to sit through one of their preferred movies in a place like the Colón Theater, touches upon a typical stance of the Latin American theatergoing public. For them, the spectacle was a good pretext to bring forth their emotions, amidst a concealed surrounding. While the attentive individual became absorbed in the filmic narrative –in this case the misfortunes of Pedro Infante in *La vida no vale nada*— the same viewer participated in a broader, collective ritual: the act of dressing up for the movies, entering a theater, and relaxing prior to the opening of the curtains. Above all, going to the movies has always been a social activity, and part of the appeal of the spectacle has been the mingling of attendees under the unique atmosphere of the theater. As author I. C. Jarvie noted: "There was an element of meeting people in the foyer before, in the interval, and afterwards (especially in small towns), an element therefore of showing off, and there was something to talk about subsequently at home."[14]

Pleasing All Audiences

The tastes of the public that attended the Colón varied a great deal. But Mexican audiences in the 1950s typically patronized heavy dramas, in the style of *La vida no vale nada* or any film depicting circumstances of intense personal conflict. In this Pedro Infante story, for example, the hero goes through life as a melancholic, lonely man, unable to stick to one job or woman. The acting is superb and the action builds up to a potent finale. Infante won an Ariel award for Best performance in this film. Another drama of this star with excellent box-office appeal was *La tercera palabra*, playing at the Colón a full week during its release in November of 1956.

The Teatro Colón also engaged all kinds of comedies and action pictures. Its management knew that variety was the best antidote to boredom. The supplier of films, Clasa-Mohme, considered that there were two classes of public that went to the Colón. One was "El público grueso," the majority of people who liked straight action pictures and comedies with lots of thrills and laughter. The other half of the public consisted of a more selective audience; those that wanted sophisticated films with "real-life" content. The question of how well a particular film performed at the box office depended on many factors. But this dual partition of audiences helped explain the appeal or repeal of numerous movies. When the action western *Estampida* was released in January of 1960, the Clasa-Mohme

The Teatro Colón of El Paso offered entertainment since the days of silent movies. Photograph taken in the 1980s (Library of Congress. HABS, TEX, 71-ELPA, 4-118).

distributor compared this film to two dramas, advancing an opinion of its reception at the Colón Theater:

> I don't know how to interpret the returns from the Colón, in El Paso, with respect to the movie *Estampida*. The four-day gross amounted to $1,446. That is better than average, but less than *Cada hijo una cruz* and *La edad de la tentación*. The taste of the people who attend the Colón is rather an educated one and they like strong dramatic stories, as they do in Mexico City.[15]

According to the box office records of the Colón Theater for the year 1960, certain action/adventure films were not as successful as the "strong dramatic stories." Two adventure pictures; *Socios para la aventura* ($1,178) and *Ochocientas leguas por el Amazonas* ($1,276) grossed less than the dramas *Ama a tu prójimo* ($1,466) and *El derecho a la vida* ($1,542). Another tearjerker that was already eight years old when shown, *El derecho de nacer*, produced more money than any other picture on a four-day engagement. This all-time favorite was effectively double-billed with *Los que no deben nacer*, a typical drama, making it possible for the Teatro Colón to collect an exceptional $1,742 in ticket sales.[16]

A few movies, on the other hand, turned out to be complete flops. Between 1955 and 1960, the Colón Theater registered some of the lowest grosses with films such as *Se solicitan modelos* ($744), *Al compás del rock'n roll* ($706), *Secreto profesional* ($682), *Pepito y el monstruo* ($640), *Kid Tabaco* ($548), and *Sublime melodía* ($370). Perhaps the most exiguous taking was $203 made by *Pepito as del volante*, backed up by *Azahares para tu boda*. These pictures, however, usually played three or four days, from Tuesday to Saturday, without the advantage of a Sunday showing. Also accounting for bad receipts was when the exhibitor mismatched the films in a program. For example, *Las señoritas Vivanco*, starring

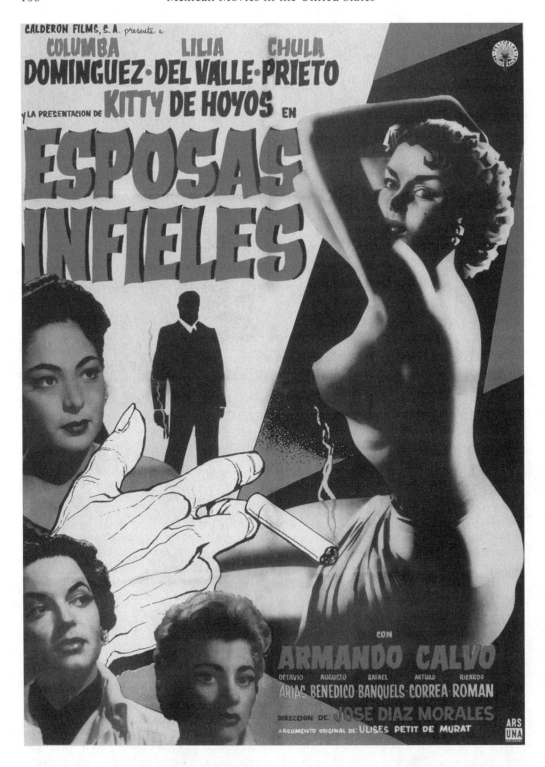

Poster advertising was a key element for the commercial success of a film. *Esposas infieles* (1955) (Agrasánchez Film Archive).

Sara García and Prudencia Griffel, and *La pasión desnuda*, with María Félix, were paired in an unusual combination of a comedy for all the family and a film that seemed to suggest adult content. Perhaps for this reason the returns of this double bill on a Sunday were only $662, when in comparison a good movie usually made two or three hundred dollars above this figure.[17]

In a more informal atmosphere at the drive-in theaters, however, some of these movies fared better. *Pepito as del volante* and *Pepito y el monstruo* were two children's comedies that had excellent results when exhibited at the Azcárate Drive-In. In an effort to please the adult audiences who were fans of Zully Moreno and Sarita Montiel, these comedies were complemented by the melodramas *Calle del pecado* and *Yo no creo en los hombres*, starring Moreno and Montiel respectively. By this logic, odd combinations such as *Camino del mal/El sultan descalzo* and *La tercera palabra/Piernas de oro* gave the patrons of the Azcárate a convenient mix of tears and laughter. Tin Tan's frolics in *Campeón ciclista*, matched with the naughty wives' behavior in *Esposas infieles*, made for an attractive double bill aimed at two distinct age groups, the youngsters and the grown-ups.

Toward the end of the fifties, theaters in the United States showing American and Mexican movies were generally having a hard time trying to keep afloat. Their record low receipts were due principally to the proliferation of televised programming. To make matters worse, Spanish-language films suffered from a lack of big names: the deaths of Jorge Negrete, Pedro Infante, Miroslava, and other stars left a void that was hard to fill. A shift in audience's preferences was added to this. The icons of American popular culture that the cinematic world of Hollywood promoted fascinated the younger generation of Hispanics.

Notwithstanding, the era that saw the expansion of Spanish-language movie entertainment left an indelible mark upon its generation. Definitely, this mixture of Mexican and Hollywood films, with their differing styles, traditions, and languages, offered the Hispanics in the United States a rich variety that is in essence exceptional. For the assiduous moviegoer, the experience of growing up in the midst of two cultures was enhanced by the images that the cinema created.

6

San Antonio, Texas

San Antonio, Texas, with its two hundred thousand inhabitants in 1924 and a growing economy, earned the name of the Metropolis of the Southwest. Of the total population in the city, around 70,000 were of Mexican origin. Far from being homogeneous, this Spanish speaking community was made up of three main groups. At the top came the elite immigrant families, most of them arriving in the country as political refugees. Next, there were the Texas Mexicans or "Tejanos" that had populated the region since the nineteenth century. Finally, the largest group comprised the "casual laborers," a varied mix of immigrants in search for jobs in the fields and factories. The majority of the Mexican immigrants made their quarters on the west side of San Antonio, in a *barrio* with a thriving commercial activity provided mostly by Mexican businesses. This West Side constituted "a city all to itself, existing side by side with the gringo city across San Pedro Creek."[1]

The segregated Mexican quarter of San Antonio mirrored in many ways the lifestyle of the homeland: with its streets named typically after several towns and states of México; its plazas, cantinas, and movie houses serving as social and cultural centers that complemented the daily routine of working people. While the upper middle class preferred entertainment in the form of dramatic plays, opera, or perhaps an American movie, the working classes dutifully gathered in the plazas, where vernacular music could be heard alongside a row of Mexican food stands. And for those willing to pay the admission ticket, there were several neighborhood theater houses that offered vaudeville and moving pictures.[2]

There was a flourishing theater business targeting Mexican-Americans and immigrants from Spanish-speaking countries. An Italian-born shoemaker, Sam Lucchese, initiated a chain of theaters dedicated to the Hispanic public. The Lucchese family would later become famous for its boot manufacturing enterprise, but starting in the 1920s it actively promoted theater entertainment among the people of San Antonio's West Side. As patronage increased, so did the number of stages and screens operated by this family. During the next four decades, the names of the Zaragoza, Nacional, Guadalupe, and Alameda Theaters became synonymous with Mexican live shows and filmed entertainment.

Gaetano Lucchese's Nacional and Zaragoza

One of the first theaters for Spanish-speaking audiences in San Antonio was the Teatro Zaragoza. In 1910 Sam Lucchese, who had been prospering with his shoe-making business, bought the property of an old "shooting gallery" (the Red Wing Theater) with the purpose of expanding his downtown boot factory. This purchase also included the theater's aged but still functional equipment. The projector, screen, curtains, and 250 chairs were put to good use and moved to a new location on Commerce and Laredo Streets, on the West side of town. At the beginning, the Zaragoza had a limited capacity of only 250 seats. Sam Lucchese took his son, young Gaetano, out of the shoe business where he had been working "and made him the house manager of his newly acquired theater." Very soon the patronage of the Zaragoza grew substantially, making it imperative for the Lucchese family to consider expanding the size of the business.[3]

The Zaragoza, located in the heart of the Mexican barrio, increased its capacity to one thousand seats in 1921. Gaetano Lucchese invested a total of $35,000 in its complete renovation. The new facilities incorporated ventilation improvements as well as modern safety devises that made the interior a more comfortable place.[4] The theater, with its "red grand drape," was the stage for a wide array of performers, including singers, dancers, acrobats, magicians, trained animals, vaudeville actors and comedians. Its program consisted generally of "cine y variedad," a live show of various acts complemented by the exhibition of moving pictures. These silent pictures first came with English titles, and afterwards with added Spanish titles. But always they were enhanced by a piano or small orchestra musical accompaniment. On a typical night, one could see a stage show featuring the troupe of "Los Pirríns." This versatile comedy group, directed by Casimiro Torres Pirrín, became a favorite of the local Mexican audiences and visited San Antonio regularly to perform at the Zaragoza. To round up the program, an American movie like Pola Negri's *Barbed Wire* or Rodolfo Valentino's *The Arab* played on the screen.

Catering to the working class, this establishment only charged twenty to thirty cents admission. Almost anybody could afford a "tanda de variedades" and a moving picture. On weekends, the theater attracted a bundle of people eager to spend a few hours mesmerized by the glitter of the spectacle. According to scholar Nicolás Kanellos, a contemporary satiric newspaper put forth a fanciful story lampooning the Zaragoza and its audience: "A father is content to let his daughters go daily to the Zaragoza since he cannot afford the first-rate theatres. The two daughters are joined by their boyfriends, who snuggle and smooch with them during the movies and whose eyes pop out at La Carcachas (María Luisa García), Sara Villegas, and Chelo Tiesta in their song-and-dance routines." The article also made fun of "the ignorance of the common folk and the pretensions of the elite while also satirizing the artlessness of the actors and the physical conditions (dirty stage) of the Zaragoza as a second-class theatre."[5]

Although motion picture production in Mexico was very sporadic at this time, the few stories made for the screen were eagerly sought by the Lucchese's West Side theaters. *Confesión trágica*, a drama that was filmed at the renowned colonial monastery of Tepozotlán; and *María*, a love story based on the widely read novel by Jorge Isaacs, played on the screen of the Zaragoza in February of 1921. Also exhibited this month was a film called *Fiestas del Centenario de 1910*, a documentary of the centennial festivities commemorating Mexico's Independence. According to one ad, the *Fiestas* were "presided by General Don Porfirio Díaz," who appeared frequently in the film. Finally, in November the Zaragoza Theater showed *El caporal*, starring Miguel Contreras Torres and featuring several aspects of Mexican ranch life, including festivals, bullfights and rodeos.[6]

Another center for live entertainment and moving pictures was the Teatro Nacional, located on the corner of Commerce Street and Santa Rosa Avenue, next door to the Zaragoza. This coliseum occupied a two-story structure and had its exterior walls covered

San Antonio's Teatro Zaragoza (in the background) as seen from the nearby Nacional Theater. Photograph taken in the 1940s (San Antonio Conservation Society).

by large posters and advertising signs. Sam Lucchese, who owned the Nacional, turned it into San Antonio's most prestigious place for Spanish-language stage shows. Having a capacity for 1,000 people, the Teatro Nacional opened its doors to the public in 1917. Sam and his son Gaetano took the lease of the building from Alexander Joske, finally acquiring it in 1926. They paid $112,000 for the property.[7]

The Nacional was a nicer and better-equipped theater than the Zaragoza. It quickly became a successful business, "offering operatic and dramatic entertainment or movies and vaudeville." Over the years, many important stage artists from México performed at this theater, including the celebrated Virginia Fábregas, María Caballé, María Conesa, and others. Renowned theatrical authors Pablo Prida Santacilia, Carlos Ortega, and composer Manuel Castro Padilla arrived in San Antonio to stage their folkloric and nationalistic pieces here. Before debuting at the Nacional, this company made an appearance at the Strand Theater of Laredo, Texas, which was currently operated by Sam Lucchese. Likewise, the "Compañía de Revistas" stage show, headed by *Guz Águila*, performed at the Nacional. Antonio Guzmán Aguilera, better known as *Guz Águila*, was a popular vaudeville author that specialized in political satire; he also wrote screenplays for several important movies, like the 1936 hit *Allá en el Rancho Grande*.

In July of 1920, the Teatro Nacional sponsored the showing of Mexican movies for the first time. Three silent films were proudly announced: *La soñadora*, *En defensa propia*, and *La Tigresa*, which were co-produced by filmmaker Enrique Rosas and stage actress/writer

Mimí Derba. Each film played for two consecutive nights, drawing an impatient multitude ready to see the exploits of stars Mimí Derba, Sara Uthoff, and María Caballé. Before the end of the year, two more south-of-the-border films were shown at the Nacional Theater: *Cuauhtémoc,* a poetic story centered on the last Aztec emperor, and the popular action serial *El automóvil gris.* Based on a true story of a band of gangsters that had recently besieged México City, this last movie incorporated scenes of the actual execution of the band's members by a death squad. The theater management divided the serial into three installments, each playing in the Nacional for a full day. Taking advantage of the popularity of the subject, a new movie with a similar title, *La banda del automóvil* was brought to the Nacional the following January 1921. The enormous success of these two serials made it compelling for the Teatro Zaragoza to offer *El automóvil gris* a year later. To maximize profits two daily episodes were screened to the public, keeping audiences coming back to the theater throughout the week until the serial reached its dramatic end.[8]

In April, *El Escándalo* was billed as "a superb society drama, awash with luxury and art." The management of the Nacional promoted it as "the first Mexican movie that has been praised by the metropolitan newspapers" of México City. The publicity also recommended the scenes taken at a number of historical places in that city and in Guadalajara, thus targeting the audience's nostalgic remembrance of the homeland. To commemorate the day of Mexican Independence on September 16, the Teatro Nacional entertained its public with a documentary of the patriotic festivities of 1910. The movie showed "the brilliant entourage of foreign dignitaries, and the notable self-assurance of General Porfirio Díaz, who was noisily applauded every time he appeared on the screen."[9] Many Mexicans

El automóvil gris was very popular among audiences and inspired another serial called *La banda del automóvil* (both made in 1919) (Agrasánchez Film Archive).

still regarded General Díaz as a national hero, even though he was driven from office and into exile in 1911.

The program of the Teatro Nacional usually combined live and filmed entertainment, as when it advertised side by side a performance by Mexican tenor José Merino and a screening of the MGM feature with Spanish titles *Thy Name Is Woman*, starring Ramón Novarro and Barbara La Marr. The MGM movie had been released a year earlier at the Palace Theater of San Antonio in its English-titled version. Always keeping an eye on popular subjects, the Nacional offered double-bill programs that included a Mexican and a Hollywood attraction. One of them announced a bullfight event that took place in México City: the last performance of famous matador Rodolfo Gaona before retiring. Complementing this feature was the American picture *Revelation*, with Monte Blue and Viola Dana. During Holy Week, the management brought films of religious significance, of which two French dramas "in color" with Spanish titles, *La pasión de Cristo* and *Vida, pasíon y muerte de Nuestro Señor Jesucristo*, were the most popular.

A Mexican feature that recounted the miracles of the Virgin of Guadalupe, *Tepeyac*, played at the Teatro Unión in 1921. This theater, operated by the Empresa Garza, was located at the intersection of Matamoros and Pecos Streets, in the Mexican barrio. It offered a different program every night, composed of "cine y variedades." *Tepeyac* ran on Saturday and Sunday, enhanced by the live performance of two popular comics, "la simpática pareja Sarita Villegas y Paco Escalera." The Unión also showed *Recuerdo*, "the first film from Spain exhibited in the United States."[10]

Special events often took place at the Nacional for the benefit of charity organizations. To help collect funds for the construction of schools in Guanajuato, México, a live spectacle was advertised in 1921. These efforts extended as well to favor the children of San Antonio's low-income families. The management of the theater and the newspaper *La Prensa* sponsored a "Fiesta de Navidad" every year, giving free tickets to one thousand children. This Christmas celebration consisted of a raffle and the exhibition of comedy films. Prizes to the winers of the drawing ranged from toys, trousers, blankets, books and miniature sewing machines, to "gallinas, cabritos, sodas y chocolates." Attendance in 1924 increased to 1,200 children under age twelve. Looking at the newspaper photos of this event, one could gain an idea of the theater's spacious interior: one picture shows 1,000 children enjoying the movie comfortably seated in the auditorium, while 200 more are looking down from their seats in the balcony.[11]

Mexican artists looked to the Nacional as the ideal place to promote their movies. Such was the case of pioneer director Guillermo *Indio* Calles, who started as an actor in several Hollywood films featuring William Duncan. Calles visited San Antonio in 1929 for a personal appearance and presentation of his picture *Sol de gloria*. Along with the movie he also brought its leading actress, Carmen La Roux. It became customary to invite to these special screenings the representatives of the consulate of México and other important guests, including the editors of San Antonio's Spanish-language newspaper *La Prensa*. After this successful screening, the artists engaged their film for a subsequent showing in Houston. The same year, another silent Mexican melodrama was announced at the Nacional: *El Cristo de oro*. Directed by Manuel R. Ojeda, it was hailed as "La bellísima película basada en la leyenda colonial de las angustias del México viejo" (The most beautiful picture based on the legend of colonial times depicting the suffering of Old Mexico). *El Cristo de oro* featured a cast that included young Fanny Schiller, "the favorite actress of the people of San Antonio."[12]

Sam Lucchese's death in 1929 left his son, Gaetano, in full control of the operation of both the Zaragoza and Nacional Theaters. Besides these principal houses, he also managed other minor entertainment centers that flourished in the twenties: the Azteca, on El Paso Street, and the Hidalgo, on Laredo Street. Each of these theaters had about 500 seats and offered live and filmed programs. Enterprising and hard working, Tano –as his friends and family called him– gradually improved the conditions of these houses, making them conform to the demand of their patrons. According to a member of the Lucchese family, "the business expanded so fast [...] and they were all making money, every one of them; they kept growing and they kept growing."[13]

"Películas habladas en español"

In June of 1930, Gaetano Lucchese finally succeeded in furnishing the Nacional with a sound-on-film projection equipment. The Hollywood production *Sombras de gloria* was the first Spanish-language "talkie" shown at the Nacional. This Spanish-language version of *Blaze of Glory*, starring José Bohr and Mona Rico, had been exhibited a month earlier at the local State Theater. The Nacional pompously displayed signs at the door that read: "Mire y oiga películas en su propio idioma" (See and hear movies in your own language). Starting this year, Tano's principal movie house began competing with San Antonio's English-language theaters (State, Majestic, Aztec, and Texas) for the showing of Hollywood's Spanish "talkies."

The Majestic announced in the Summer of 1930 the Hollywood picture *Charros, Gauchos y Manolas*, an early effort at providing filmed vaudeville mixing the folklore and music of México, Argentina, and Spain. The following month, the same theater played *El precio de un beso*, which was the Spanish-language version of *One Mad Kiss*. This version, produced by Fox Film Corporation, featured the Mexican opera singer and actor José Mojica, Mona Maris and Antonio Moreno. At the beginning, these "talkies" were enjoyed by viewers. The pictures represented a novelty and were expected to lure Latin American audiences.

By the mid-thirties, however, the Spanish-language films crafted in the Hollywood studios began to falter. For example, the musical romance *La buenaventura*, which was based on the operatic tale *The Fortune Teller* and had been lavishly produced by Warner Brothers, collapsed during its 1934 release at the Empire Theater of San Antonio. After the first day of showing, unluckily, this downtown deluxe house decided to withdraw the film. The management conceded that the people were indifferent to this Spanish-language picture, even though it featured familiar names like Enrico Caruso Jr. and Anita Campillo. One of the reasons for the failure of the movie, according to an observer, was that it did not portray true-to-life characters with which Latin Americans could identify. Further, "We figure that the pictures in Spanish made by Americans, although they have luxury and good presentation, can never have the niceties of our culture, which always have the Mexican productions; these are greeted with enthusiasm by the Spanish speaking public."[14]

After more than two years of playing Hollywood's Spanish-language "talkies," the first Mexican film with optical sound was released. Interpreted by Lupita Tovar, Carlos Orellana and Mimí Derba, *Santa* had been a major south-of-the-border success before coming to the United States. The prestigious Aztec Theater premiered the movie in San Antonio during a special midnight show, on May 14, 1932 (a week before its opening in Los Angeles, California). As expected, the picture captivated the attention of a large crowd that filled the theater to its 2,455 capacity. A few days later, *Santa* played at the Teatro Nacional during regular hours and at lower admission prices. Because the movie continued to arouse the public's interest it was held over for a full week, an unusually long engagement. *Santa* proved to be more successful here than in México, according to its promoters. The theater's manager enthusiastically asserted: "The Mexican public of the United States is more satisfied and shows more pride of the triumph obtained by *Santa*, than the public that live in our country."[15]

A year later, another large coliseum, the Texas Theater, announced the exhibition of *Almas encontradas*. United Artists Corporation distributed this feature, which played for one night at the Texas, in July of 1933. The Texas premiere preceded the México City debut of the film for six months. Oftentimes Mexican movies were sent to the United States for their world premiere. For instance, director Fernando de Fuentes, who had lived in San Antonio for some time, chose this Texan city for the release of his picture *La Calandria*. An adaptation from a novel, the film told the story of a young woman in the bucolic town of Orizaba, who is seduced and abandoned before tragically taking her own life. Also shown first in San Antonio was De Fuentes's revolutionary drama *¡Vámonos con Pancho Villa!*, considered by many as one of the masterpieces of Mexican cinema. Just a month before its release in México, the movie premiered at the Teatro Nacional in a simultaneous engagement that included several cities in the United States.[16]

While the Spanish-language productions made in Hollywood in the early thirties were shown in all the local theaters, Gaetano Lucchese's Nacional and Zaragoza began to take the lead in the exhibition of imported films from across the border. These were obtained through the Latin American Film Exchange, a local business headed by José J. Jiménez. Azteca Films distributors of El Paso, Texas, in turn supplied this exchange. With a few exceptions, all of the box-office hits of the thirties presented in San Antonio were released by these companies and exhibited in the theaters owned by the Lucchese family.

One of the earliest sound movies shown at the Nacional was *Sobre las olas*. This picture dramatized the life of Mexico's most famous composer in the 19th-Century, Juventino Rosas, who died at an early age and whose celebrated waltz gave name to this movie. Its advertising campaign made known the compliments to the film from distinguished intellectuals like Federico Gamboa, the novelist of *Santa*. With much fanfare, *Sobre las olas* played in July 1933. Other pictures of merit like *Los de abajo*, *Juárez y Maximiliano*, *La noche de los Mayas*, *¡Vámonos con Pancho Villa!*, and *La Zandunga* conveyed a sense of national pride among audiences. The films portrayed historical events interwoven with legend, providing a narrative filled with action, romance and folklore. Also, these pictures were produced during a period of unprecedented national fervor, which coincided with the mandate of Lázaro Cárdenas, a president much revered by Mexicans. In such context, the Teatro Nacional became the center for the promotion of south-of-the-border nationalist cinema, as well as a radiating medium of popular culture.

An era of Mexican hits began in June 1935, when the State Theater presented the tear-jerker *Madre querida*. The crowds were larger than expected making this engagement to stretch for four days, with screenings starting at 12 p.m. and ending at midnight. *Madre querida* had another run at the Strand Theater for an extra four days. The success of this melodrama encouraged the management of these two houses to show other imported Mexican product, opening a competition for the best Spanish-language pictures in the market.

Among them was *Allá en el Rancho Grande*, which turned into a mythical film since its release in 1936. The movie initiated a popular genre that later came to be known as "comedia ranchera." Its principal stars were Tito Guízar, Esther Fernández, René Cardona

Los de abajo (1939), a movie about the Mexican Revolution, was adapted form a famous novel of the same name (Agrasánchez Film Archive).

and Carlos López *Chaflán*. The last-named was an excellent comedian much praised by the public for its characterization of the happy-go-lucky of the countryside. When *Chaflán* died in an accident in 1942, everyone who had seen his films remembered him with emotion. That year, San Antonio's newspaper *La Prensa* paid tribute to this artist of stage and screen in a series of articles depicting his life and cinematic career.

Already, several theaters in San Antonio competed against each other to secure the exhibition of *Allá en el Rancho Grande*, which premiered at the Texas Theater on June 5, 1937. After a few days, the film went to the Prince Theater for a one-week run, and subsequently to the Plaza for a four-day engagement. This theater brought back the movie as a reprise the following month. All in all, over 15,000 people attended these screenings, according to the film's distributors. *Allá en el Rancho Grande* was exhibited over and over by theaters in every city. During the forties and fifties, the mythic aura of *Allá en el Rancho Grande* continued to attract Hispanic audiences. Aware of its worth, the distributors of the film made new prints and advertising accessories for its ongoing exploitation in the United States.[17]

The appeal of the "comedia ranchera" had its roots in the populace's need for a well-rounded form of entertainment that could combine songs, folklore, dances, drama and comedy, as in the popular stage performances of the "teatro de revista." The scenery of the countryside, the lively musical numbers, the life-like characters and brisk dialogue, together with an resourceful dramatic plot; all resulted in a formula that gave birth to a unique Mexican genre. An outpouring of nostalgic sentiment was central to these stories, as can be exemplified by another picture: *Nobleza ranchera*. When the film played in San Antonio in 1939, the newspaper ads remarked:

> *Nobleza ranchera*, a Mexican film of local customs...will be released tomorrow at the Teatro Nacional. This production reflects small-town life, with its afflictions, its pleasures, love affairs and other meeting points (sic) that are common in every village of our country. The plot is very interesting, with plenty of drama; and it will make any viewer homesick remembering the place where he came from before migrating to the United States.[18]

The popularity of the genre was evident in the programming of several hits in San Antonio. For example, in March 1938 *Allá en el Rancho Grande* and *Bajo el cielo de México* played at the Nacional, competing with two other money-makers being exhibited at the Zaragoza: *¡Ora Ponciano!* and *Jalisco nunca pierde*. These examples became the first blockbusters of the era and were re-released many times afterwards. During the showing of one of these films, the publicity slogan asked: "When will *Bajo el cielo de México* end its exhibition? Only after the 82,000 Mexicans in San Antonio have admired it."[19]

In August 1939, the Teatro Nacional closed temporarily for renovations. The management selected for a last screening *¡Ora Ponciano!*, which had been a favorite of the locals. The film blended together a good amount of romance, humor, and songs in a comedy of ranch life. One of the tunes with spicy lyrics, "Tú ya no soplas," fueled the public in an uproar every time they heard it.

A comedy that stirred the hearts of the public: *¡Ora Ponciano!* (1936). Left to right: Carlos López *Chaflán*, Jesús Solórzano and *Chato* Ortín (Agrasánchez Film Archive).

Nuevo Nacional and Guadalupe Theaters

After four months of intensive restoration work, in December 1939 the Nuevo Teatro Nacional proudly opened its doors to the clientele. The Zaragoza Amusement Co., presided by Gaetano Lucchese and his brother Sam, was said to have invested nearly $100,000 in expanding and renovating the old theater. A top-notch architect, N. Straus Nayfach, designed the new look of the building, and general contractor Victor Prassel took care of the construction work. The inauguration of the Nuevo Teatro Nacional attracted a lot of attention. Among the people invited were the Mexican consul general in San Antonio, the City's Mayor, the County Judge and other local leaders. Movie director Gabriel Soria, producer Jesús Grovas, and several guests of honor representing the Mexican motion picture industry made the trip to San Antonio to attend the ceremony. Film star Rafael Falcón and his wife, the "cupletista" Maruja Gómez, came also to perform during the opening of the Nacional.

On the screen played *La reina del río*, starring Rafael Falcón, Gloria Morel, and Pedro Armendáriz. Patrons of this theater had been asked a month before to cast a vote on their favorite Mexican movie, which would be programmed for the inauguration. A large majority selected *La reina del río*, a comedy produced and provided with music by two of the most popular Mexican artists of the thirties, Lorenzo Barcelata and Ernesto Cortázar. Nearly every successful movie of the period contained songs by the duo Barcelata-Cortázar; their music was an essential part of the Mexican *ranchera* genre.

As expected, the opening of the Nuevo Teatro Nacional drew more than enough people, forcing a large crowd to remain outside. But the theater manager had shrewdly placed extra speakers in the street, so that those who were unable to get tickets could at least hear the movie and get a glimpse of the pompous inaugural ceremony. Apart from its beautiful look, the theater boasted some of the most advanced comforts of the era. A new heating and cooling system unit, "the largest in Texas," was capable of blowing 27,000 cubic feet per minute to provide "pure and healthy air all the time." The newspaper *La Prensa* gave a detailed description of its architecture:

> The enlargement of the Teatro Nacional has concluded; its transformation is complete. The architecture of a new theatre of classic Mexican style now rises up; bestowed of the ambience of the nationals of México, and of the structural beauty that they are capable of molding. There is a profusion of tile, fountains, large windows and lattice in the decoration, and a bold combination of the colors that are preferred by Mexicans. In the exterior, the façade reminds us of the severity of our plateresque churches, in amalgamation with the simplicity and strength of the frontal parameters of the haciendas. And the top resembles old colonial style.[20]

Three colors dominated the interior decoration of the Nacional: orange, blue and white. The cushioned leather seats were tinted blue, with a bright orange in the back. The curtains in the proscenium were of different shades of red and orange. It all added to a very Texas-Mexican flavor. Gaetano Lucchese expressed his satisfaction in being able to give to the community a theater where everybody "could really feel at home." He restated that the renovation of the building was planned with one thing in mind: to provide all the comforts for the moviegoers. "It is now their chance," said Lucchese, "to take care of the theater and perpetuate it with their daily attendance."

An unpleasant incident occurred the night of the inauguration of the new Teatro Nacional. Following the screening and reception, movie director Gabriel Soria and the local film distributor José J. Jiménez drove off in a car. It was 2 a.m. and the streets were empty

The Teatro Nacional was a focal point for stage acts and the exhibition of Mexican movies. Photograph taken in the 1940s (Ignacio Torres Collection, San Antonio Conservation Society).

when another car collided with the vehicle occupied by Soria and Jiménez. Director Soria was the only one injured; he received treatment for broken ribs at a hospital.

Two weeks later, the Nacional became the scene of a passionate crime. After watching a movie –directed by Gabriel Soria, incidentally — , a man by the name of Leopoldo González and his lover, María G. Aguayo, walked out of the theater mixing with the rest of the public. Across the street waited Elías Aguayo, husband of the unfaithful woman. Aguayo approached the couple, firing his gun on González's forehead. The following day, the newspaper *La Prensa* ran a front-page account of the murder. This sensational news gave free publicity to the theater as well as to the current movie attraction.

> Mexican Attacked Last Night When He Was Leaving The Teatro Nacional. He was shot in the forehead, and remained agonizing... A bloody and true drama was witnessed involuntarily by the many who attended the last show in El Teatro Nacional, after they had watched on the screen, ironically, the sensational drama *La bestia negra*. A man fell to the ground, the agonizing victim of a sure shot from a gun that another man in jealousy fired. Without speaking a word, he took out his pistol and made three shots, one of them mortally wounded Mr. González. Another bullet sunk in the walls of the theatre lobby, while the third one got lost.[21]

Gaetano Lucchese, owner of the Zaragoza and Nacional theaters, opened a brand-new house for pictures in 1942. The Teatro Guadalupe, on the corner of Guadalupe and South Brazos Streets, was strategically located in the heart of a west side Mexican neighborhood. The construction of the Guadalupe ran into several problems, as the scarcity of building

Presiding the inauguration of the Nuevo Teatro Nacional in 1939, left to right: Rafael Falcón, Maruja Gómez, Lula V. Lucchese and Gaetano Lucchese (Ignacio Torres Collection, San Antonio Conservation Society).

materials in the war years slowed down its completion. A shortage of hand labor and other limitations imposed by the government during World War II hindered the conclusion of this enterprise. The architect of the project was N. Straus Nayfach, designer of the new Teatro Nacional and planner of several other important buildings in the city. General contractor D.G. Janssen took care of construction.

When it opened, the Guadalupe had 862 seats and was promoted as "El cine de barrio más elegante de la colonia mexicana," the most elegant neighborhood theater of the Mexican colony. It boasted "air conditioning for the hot months and steam heating for the winter." The exterior façade of the theater combined the style of the old missions in San Antonio with a modern look. Beautiful tile work decorated the interior walls and a couple of stone fountains adorned the foyer and the entrance hall. People attending the opening night were dazzled by the neon lights and the dream-like glitter reflected off the walls, as well as by the recently polished floor.

For the inauguration of the Guadalupe, on July 3, 1942, several local officials were invited: the city's Mayor, the consul of México, the county Judge, a representative of the U.S. armed forces, and various important businessmen. The program included the U.S. premiere of the Mexican film *Águila roja*, followed by a short feature with *Cantinflas* and the Mexican cartoon in color, *Chema y Juana en el tesoro*. Ticket prices were very affordable: adults 17 cents, children 5 cents. On Tuesdays and Thursdays, the Guadalupe had special admission prices of "two for one."[22]

Teatro Guadalupe, in the heart of Mexican *barrio*. It opened in 1942 (Agrasánchez Film Archive).

The Progreso and Other "stomp and whistle" Theaters

Besides the Guadalupe, Nacional, and Zaragoza, there were other popular entertainment spots in San Antonio for Hispanics: the Obrero Theater, located at 416 W. Houston Street, and the Teatro Progreso, on 1306 Guadalupe Street. The brothers Juan and Paul Garza owned these venues. The Obrero had a capacity of 400 seats, and as its name indicated it was frequented by the *obreros*, the working classes. The slightly larger Progreso, with 550 seats, had been in business since 1931 and was flamboyantly advertised as "El Templo del Arte." But after 1942 it had to compete with Tano's new Guadalupe Theater, which stood just across the street from the Progreso. The Garza's theaters catered mainly to the low-income families. Their program included fifth or sixth-run American movies "that thrilled the public many years ago." Every once in a while, there was a Spanish-language picture on the screen. The informal atmosphere encouraged audiences to "stomp and whistle" during the film's climatic moments, but more often when the projector or sound system failed.

Admission tickets to the Progreso were ten cents adults and five cents children. For those with tight budgets, a "función popular" during day hours cost no more than two pennies. On Saturdays, the theater entertained its patrons with a midnight show and gave away several prizes in a raffle. The night of December 23, 1939, for example, the audience watched the film *The Hounds of Baskerville*. At the end of the movie, a drawing took place and the lucky ones were able to take home some of the "15 cabritos y un elegante colchón" (15 goats and a fancy mattress). The Progreso Theater often organized charity functions giving its proceeds to the unemployed. One such benefit took place at the end of 1938 with the billing of *Corazón bandolero* complemented by a vaudeville attraction.[23]

Competition among theater operators led to the promotion of live performances that enhanced the screening of a film. For example, the program of the Teatro Progreso in its sixth anniversary of June 24, 1937, consisted of two Hollywood color movies: the two-reel short *La Cucaracha* and the R.K.O. feature *Dancing Pirate*. As an added attraction, it announced the appearance of popular singer Lydia Mendoza. The Teatro Zaragoza, meanwhile, contracted local comedians like the group of the "Compañía Alegrías," who took the stage on Saturdays to entertain noisy crowds. Very aptly, these special engagements were advertised as "función de medianoche de borlote" (riotous midnight shows).

Without a doubt, the Progreso's chief rivals were the theaters of the Lucchese family: the Zaragoza and the Nacional, and most recently the Guadalupe. The Lucchese houses monopolized the Spanish-language movies that the local Azteca Films and Clasa-Mohme companies distributed. In 1947, the Progreso's Paul Garza made an official petition for product to Clasa-Mohme, underlining the legal right of this exhibitor to "request a first suburban run on Spanish speaking features, following their first run in the Nacional Theatre." However, this distributor decided at the time not to serve any films to the Progreso Theater, thus eliminating any potential competitor to the Lucchese businesses.[24]

Gaetano Lucchese also ran the Teatro Maya, on 5045 W. Commerce. In 1946 the Maya

For those with tight budgets, the Teatro Progreso offered a "función popular" for only two cents. Photograph taken in 1938 (Institute of Texan Cultures at San Antonio).

was advertised as an open-air theater with a Mexican picture program on Thursday-Friday-Saturday. Admission prices were 25 cents for adults and 9 cents for children. Every so often, due to bad weather the show had to be cancelled or "rained out." Perhaps because of its distant location and lack of roof, the Maya failed to attract a large clientele. Movies like Pedro Infante's *Nosotros los pobres* and *Vuelven los García* barely made receipts for the theater to break even. Other times, as when *Los hijos de don Venancio* played, the electricity went off and the crowd demanded a full refund. After some ups and downs, people quit going to the Maya, and the management decided to close its doors permanently in August 1950.[25]

Another small venue, the Rio Theater operated as an open-air movie house supplied by Clasa-Mohme distributors. It opened in May 1948, remaining in business for only a short period. The category of the Rio was behind that of any other theater. It probably functioned on the west side of town, where the Maya and Guadalupe Theaters were located.

Paul Garza, co-owner of the Teatro Obrero and Teatro Progreso, opened a new house for Mexican movies in 1948: the Follies Theater. Again, it was a short-lived enterprise that only played subsequent-run movies. The Follies rented films from Clasa-Mohme distributors for a period of eight months, the first of these being *¡Ay Jalisco no te rajes!* which grossed an estimable $286 on a three-day show. But very quickly box-office receipts began to drop. At the beginning of 1949, the theater fell behind in its remittances of film rentals and the distributor stopped providing any more movies. Mr. Garza delayed paying Clasa-Mohme a bill for $75 as well as another note for $36, with the result that it took more than two years to obtain a partial liquidation of this debt.[26]

Most shows offered a double bill, sometimes combining a Spanish-language movie and a Hollywood production. For example, during March 1949 the Nacional exhibited *Ángel o demonio*, a Mexican movie featuring the backbreaking Cuban dancer María Antonieta Pons who was billed as "la mujer que en su alma trae un volcán y en la cintura un terremoto" ("the woman that carries a volcano in her soul and an earthquake around her waist). The program's second feature was Hollywood's *Romance of the High Seas*, a musical filmed in Technicolor. Similarly, the Guadalupe advertised *Rayando el sol*, with Pedro Armendáriz, complemented by the American picture *Riding Down the Rail*. Finally, the Zaragoza offered the Warner Brothers drama *To the Victor*, together with a live show that included Las hermanitas López, Don Goyo, and Jean Valjean.

The theaters were usually packed on Sundays, when the entire family went to see the double feature program and the occasional vaudeville performances. These attractions usually lasted several hours. Besides the normal overcrowding of most theaters, a typical complaint concerned the noisy atmosphere during the shows. For sure, having four or five hundred people and lots of restive children in an enclosed space made it hard to keep it tidy all the time. Anything could happen while the film was running, including a sudden quarrel or the unexpected birth of a child.

> For the manager of the Teatro Nacional it's just one thing after another. A few days ago, a señora gave birth in the theatre. After that, another woman almost died from a heart attack. And yesterday two gentlemen gave themselves a good exchange of blows. Let me add that the police arrived just like a rainbow, after the storm. Talking about policemen... they should bring to order scores of people talking so loud that the rest of us are unable to enjoy the movie being shown on the screen. Also, they should discipline hordes of children running like foals along the aisles, stepping on someone's calloused feet and knocking down other patrons.[27]

One of the outstanding box-office hits of Mexican cinema in the forties was *Juan Charrasqueado*, a rural drama with Pedro Armendáriz and the lovely Miroslava Stern. Based

Overcrowding on Sundays: anything could happen during the showing of a film. Teatro Nacional in the mid-forties (Ignacio Torres Collection, San Antonio Conservation Society).

on the popular ballad *El corrido de Juan Charrasqueado*, the movie promised to tell "la triste historia de un ranchero enamorado, que fue borracho, parrandero y jugador" (the sad story of a love-struck rancher, who was a drunken reveler and a gambler). *Juan Charrasqueado* became the first Mexican movie to be exhibited in three local theaters simultaneously. It opened at the Nacional, Zaragoza, and Guadalupe, during a "sumptuous avant premiére" on February 27, 1948. The movie broke all the records for a Mexican or even an American production, attracting literally thousands of people. On that day, all three theaters opened their doors to the public starting at 9 a.m., "in order to avoid a dangerous overcrowding." Still, the lengthy lines stretched beyond the block of each theater.

The Alameda: "A magnificent show place"

The exhibition of Spanish-language movies in San Antonio entered a new phase with the construction of the Teatro Alameda. On March 9, 1949, after three years of planning and hard work, Gaetano Lucchese was finally ready to give to the community its most opulent movie house. With a capacity of 2,500 seats, the Alameda became the largest theater for Mexican films and live entertainment built in the United States. The vast structure, on 510 W. Houston Street, was part of a complex that included the International Building or "Casa de México." It housed the studios of KIWW "La voz de las Américas," a radio station

The imposing Teatro Alameda, on 510 W. Houston Street, an icon of San Antonio's Hispanic heritage. Photographer: Jim Keller (San Antonio Conservation Society).

broadcasting in Spanish and English. A photography business that specialized in children's portraits, a jewelry outlet, and a real estate broker were some of the commercial offices occupying this building.

The architect of the Teatro Alameda was N. Straus Nayfach, who had also designed the two other movie houses of the Zaragoza Amusement Company: the Nacional and the Guadalupe. His project for the Alameda had been in the making since December of 1946, when the cornerstone of the "Casa de México" was officially laid. Mr. Nayfach, unfortunately, did not live long enough to see the completion of the Alameda. The interior decoration of the foyer was the work of Pedro Terán and Frank Lackner. Two impressive murals on each side of the auditorium depicted the histories of Texas and México. A symbol of the coming together of two cultures, the Alameda was regarded as an example of the advancement of filmmaking in México: "The cathedral of Art, where the culture of two nations can converge. It will be the most powerful spiritual linkage, and will allow everybody in South Texas to admire the highest degree which Mexican cinema art has reached."[28]

All of the comforts and innovations of a modern theater were incorporated into the design of the Alameda: air conditioning, acoustic materials, projector and sound equipment, special lighting, and a baby-sitter room. The construction of the theater and business annex cost its owner one million and a half dollars. The editors of two trade publications, *Exhibitor* and *Theatre Catalog*, made the Alameda the recipient of the 1949 Merit Award. Also, it was awarded the "International Oscar that honors the year's Best among the World's new theatres."

For the inauguration of the Alameda, several prominent people were invited: local and state authorities, banking and business executives, film exhibitors and distributors, national and foreign press representatives, in addition to performing artists. The ceremony started with the intonation of the national anthems of the United States and México, followed by the singing of "The Eyes of Texas." Chaplain Ora J. Cohen, of the Association of Christians and Jews, made the benediction of the theater. There was also an invocation by San Fernando Cathedral's Reverend Esteban Emaldía.

Among the local newspaper reporters was *La Prensa*'s César Serrato, author of an entertaining and informative column about daily happenings in San Antonio. Serrato said of the opening of this new theater that

> There was an enormous line of people; it almost made it around the block. At the door of the theatre, a group of strikers holding their banners went around and around. Across the street we saw several police vehicles, ready to go into action. Because it was rumored that there would be a fuss, but there was nothing. Some mothers brought their kids to the theatre and they were a pain. Other people showed their good manners by talking when the speakers gave their address.[29]

Various Mexican actors and actresses attended the Alameda's inauguration, including Carmen Montejo, Hilda Sour, Lilia Michel and Rafael Baledón. Mrs. Lula V. Lucchese, wife of Gaetano Lucchese, announced the appearance of the singing cowboy Gene Autry, a surprise guest who took the stage to sing a popular ballad in Spanish. For its opening gala, the Alameda exhibited a brand-new Mexican film, *Revancha*, starring Ninón Sevilla, Agustín Lara, Toña la Negra and Pedro Vargas. All in all, the audience that night was delighted with the show and positively impressed by the gorgeous atmosphere of the new theater. The branch manager of Clasa-Mohme distributors, Gordon B. Dunlap, said of the Alameda: "It truly is a magnificent show place."

Not surprisingly, several movie theaters in Texas were named after the Alameda of San Antonio. The prestige of this movie house reached all corners, naturally inspiring many

Prominent people from México and the U.S. attended the opening of the Alameda in 1949, while the film *Revancha* played on the screen (San Antonio Conservation Society).

exhibitors. Cities such as Falfurrias, Edinburg, Elsa, Sebastian, Crystal City, Olton, and Lamesa, each one had its own Alameda. The name became synonymous with the best entertainment for *Mexicanos* and Mexican-Americans. Ignacio Torres, manager of San Antonio's Alameda Theater, instituted many of the policies that made this a favorite place for Spanish-language movies. His expertise and commercial instinct made him a valuable asset for the Alameda.[30]

At the same time that the Alameda opened in 1949, modern mercury lighting was installed and parking meters were posted along Houston Street, where the new theater stood. In the nearby Broadway Avenue, new traffic lights for pedestrians could be operated conveniently to cross the street. Already with a population of 400,000 inhabitants, San Antonio had 15 major movie places; eight of them exhibited films in Spanish.

The decade of the forties brought a significant expansion in the distribution and exhibition of Mexican films in the United States. Azteca Films, Inc., had been the most important distributor until the establishment of Clasa-Mohme, Inc., in 1942. Both Spanish-language film companies competed during the forties and fifties for the distribution of their product. The San Antonio branch of Clasa-Mohme, for example, kept a busy schedule servicing 150 theater accounts in 1946; most of which were in Texas and some as far away as Kansas, Colorado, and Florida. As a proof of its success, the company reported this year profits from movie rentals in the sum of $400,000. In some instances, the monthly revenue of this exchange surpassed that of the main office in Los Angeles, California. These were

San Antonio's Clasa-Mohme personnel. Gordon B. Dunlap (second from left) was the head of this film exchange from 1944 to 1961 (Agrasánchez Film Archive).

optimistic times, as the 1947 projected sales of Clasa-Mohme for the territory of Texas were calculated at $540,000.[31]

Exhibitors Lured by Mexican Pictures

The 1950's brought about the consolidation of Mexican films in the international market. Many movie theaters in the United States, which had previously shown only Hollywood pictures, were readily accommodating Spanish-language features. In San Antonio, for example, the Empire Theater decided to shift to Mexican movies starting in September of 1957. The Empire, which had an exclusive contract with Azteca Films distributors, calculated the importance of the Hispanic public in this city. The first picture to be shown was the "all-color super-production" with Pedro Infante and María Félix, *Amor indio* (aka *Tizoc*). This drama attracted a tremendous crowd, not only because of the untimely death of Infante earlier this year, but because the theater had the privilege of showing the film almost two months in advance of its premiere in México City. The Empire made approximately $12,000 on the week of the release of *Amor indio*.[32]

Another picture with the idol of the masses, Pedro Infante, played at the Empire in November of 1957. The comedy *Escuela de rateros* was Infante's last movie before he was killed in an airplane accident. It opened in San Antonio almost six months before its release in the capital of México. Likewise, *Cantinflas*'s first color film, *El bolero de Raquel*, played simultaneously at the Alameda, Nacional and Guadalupe Theaters in September of that year, a month before its opening in México City.

The Empire, which started out as the old Orpheum in the twenties, had the advantage of being centrally located on the corner of Houston and St. Mary's Streets. Its manager, Bob Otwell, was very optimistic with the change of policy to Mexican pictures. Otwell's confidence in the new business relied to a great extent on the exceptional location of the Empire.

> The theatre is almost next door to one of San Antonio's leading Catholic churches, St. Mary's Catholic Church, which is attended by thousands and it is about half-way between the Majestic and the Aztec Theatres, and close to the Texas and Prince Theatres. Practically every bus in San Antonio passes within a block of this theatre, with many passing directly in front of it.[33]

The manager of the Empire Theater made a good effort in publicizing his business. He believed in the method of direct-mail advertising, announcing the films and stage shows "to a select list of 8,000 names of people in the Latin American Colony." He also used posters and promotional material profusely for the decoration of the theater lobby. When programming special shows, more costly radio and newspaper campaigns were launched. As usual, the local film distributor Clasa-Mohme was keeping an eye on the performance of the Empire.

> There is one thing to be said about Otwell, he does more in exploitation than anyone I know, having an almost uncanny ability along these lines. He will always gamble a lot of money on advertising. Right now it is his belief that if he can make this theatre show a profit, he will stay with it from now on out. I think he has a fairly good chance, even though the Alameda Theatre is doing terrific business with *Sube y baja*. On top of that, five English-language drive-in theatres start *Around the World in 80 Days* tonight. Of course, Otwell is going up against rough competition.[34]

The Empire did in fact have a difficult time trying to lure its clientele. After a year experimenting with Mexican films, it went back to playing American movies. In order to draw more people, the theater was showing three Hollywood pictures on a program. Then the Empire closed for a few months and reopened for the exhibition of English-language sexy pictures. But in May 1959, its manager wisely reversed the policy sticking to Mexican movies once again.

Interstate Circuit's State Theater of San Antonio also shifted to Spanish-language movies at the end of 1959. It was re-painted and re-decorated in order to welcome a different kind of audience. The distributing company Clasa-Mohme played a pivotal role in the conversion of the State to a policy of Spanish-language pictures. The president of Clasa-Mohme in Los Angeles, California, had been exploring the possibility for an alternate first-run theater in San Antonio for Mexican product, because the Alameda was able to book only half or less of the pictures offered by this exchange. For Clasa-Mohme's executives, "the State Theater in San Antonio would be ideal for the release of our films." Since the State had been doing poorly with American pictures during that year, the directors of this distributing company privately concluded: "They need us as badly as we do them."[35]

For its premier, the house showed a Luis Aguilar western movie, *Estampida*, together with the melodrama *El caso de una adolescente* as filler. Both productions had been photographed in Eastmancolor, but *Estampida* had an extra box office value because it was an action movie, and also because it contained several popular songs. People spoke with enthusiasm about the excellent business of the first day.

The State Theatre opened yesterday to what I would call a big success with receipts of $1,016. The downstairs was full; the mezzanine floor was filled and at 4:30 p.m., there were many people in the huge balcony. It is the first time that the balcony has been used in almost anyone's memory. Perhaps they used it during the first week of the Spanish version of *The Ten Commandments*. By the first hour yesterday they had sold 200 adult tickets. They sold a total of 1,550 adult tickets at 60 cents, 319 children's tickets and 20 'movie discount' tickets at 35 cents. Mr. Moss [the manager] was a very happy man. He told me that the Interstate people would have been very well pleased had they done only $750 on the day, so they must be extremely happy with such a turn-out... They had gotten customers they hadn't ever seen before. Many complimentary things were said about the theatre and the new policy.[36]

The State had a good start at seducing moviegoers. In order to add a little glamour to the show, the management brought to the theater popular Mexican stars. For example, Fernando Casanova, a handsome leading actor featured in the movie *Cuando se quiere se quiere*, made a special appearance at the State for a full week in March 1960. The City of San Antonio even honored Casanova with the official designation of "Alcalde Honorario de San Antonio." Other popular movie stars, like the comic duo *Viruta y Capulina*, were scheduled to perform at this theater, but the competing Alameda fought over to get the comedians' contract.

By now, the State Theater had already developed a steady and loyal clientele. A local newspaper reported that a "little girl had bought tickets for her parents, sister and self with 230 pennies." This kind of publicity, cemented on a true story, worked wonders for a theater that had just started to exhibit Mexican films. Besides, the management of the State recognized the importance of a steady promotional campaign for the films it was showing. Adding to the regular advertising columns in the popular *San Antonio Light*, two radio stations, KCOR and KUBO, announced upcoming attractions every week.

However, all these efforts were not enough. For observers like Clasa-Mohme's Gordon B. Dunlap, the State needed a more aggressive campaign that could get the attention of people out in the streets. What the business required was true "showmanship of the exploitation variety." Dunlap wrote: "The theater needs a little more circus atmosphere. I wish they would do something to give this theatre a warmer and friendlier appearance. They are missing the boat when they do not use a lot of circus type advertising... Not that their lobby doesn't already look attractive; it is just that the theatre needs more oomph, as the saying goes."[37]

Diligently, the manager of the State provided the theater's lobby with nice publicity displays and red-colored frames for the posters. But Dunlap also suggested that this exhibitor should spread around in commercial establishments some photographs of the films to be shown. "There are a lot of stores and markets on the West side that are mostly patronized by Spanish speaking people," said the Clasa-Mohme executive, and added: "The Alameda and the Nacional used to do this very successfully, they were able to display advance advertising on the pictures," in exchange for free passes to the owners of the stores.[38]

In an effort to lure more theater owners into the business of Spanish-language movies, the Clasa-Mohme distributors placed a five-word ad in the pages of a trade magazine, tersely asking: "Why not try Mexican pictures?" Perhaps influenced by this ad, an exhibitor in Amherst, Texas, took "the big step of changing his drive-in theater from a policy of mostly Hollywood pictures to 100% Spanish-language films." By doing so, he was "gambling everything on the success of Mexican pictures, which will be shown four days per week." The Clasa-Mohme distributors felt their duty to stimulate the new business, as it played to "everyone's advantage to make the theater a successful venture."[39]

From Big Business to Decline

One of the biggest grossing pictures of Mexican cinema in the fifties was *El derecho de nacer*, a movie starring Gloria Marín, Jorge Mistral and Martha Roth. During its release in México City in June of 1952, the picture broke all the records at the downtown Cine Orfeón, which engaged the film for seven straight weeks. This adaptation of the famous novel written by Félix B. Caignet was billed as "the greatest motion picture ever made in Latin America." *El derecho de nacer* effectively used publicity phrases such as: "Following the highest moral standards of the Catholic Church," and also advancing: "The story concerns a Cuban doctor that is visited by a young girl who wishes to renounce her unborn child. He refuses to comply with her request and [then proceeds] to impress her with the sacredness of motherhood."[40] The movie's immense popularity was due, to a large extent, to a radio serial of the same title that had seduced listeners for many months in preparation of the film's release.

In San Antonio, *El derecho de nacer* premiered at the Alameda on August 11, 1952. It played for a full week generating receipts of $18,063, a record-breaking figure by all means. With admission prices at fifty cents adults, fifteen cents children and eight cents special passes, a total of 41,734 tickets were sold. The following month, the feature had a second run in the same theater, drawing an extra $5,650 with attendance of 14,613 people in one

Everybody went to see the record-breaking movie *El derecho de nacer* (1951). Martha Roth and Gloria Marín confer in a climatic scene (Agrasánchez Film Archive).

week. Soon, the movie was playing at the Nacional and Guadalupe Theaters. The Alameda showed it again three years later with the first-run Argentine movie *Deshonra*, to receipts of $6,926, also a record figure for a re-release. During a five-year period, *El derecho de nacer* had a total of 22 runs in San Antonio's Spanish-language theaters; making it the number one grosser in Clasa-Mohme's catalog.[41]

But the era of fervor for Spanish-language cinema was obscured by an impending thundercloud. While the Alameda, Nacional and Guadalupe successfully fought the irruption of television and drive-in theaters, the old Teatro Zaragoza gave up the fight and succumbed in 1952. After more than forty years in operation, it finally closed its doors. Audiences were lured instead to the drive-in theaters, some of which exhibited Mexican features. Because of their low admission prices, informal atmosphere and other conveniences, the Fiesta and the El Capitán Drive-Ins appealed very much to the masses.

The Teatro Nacional also suffered with the new competition from drive-in theaters. Its management designed all sorts of strategies to keep ahead. Besides double-feature programs that combined Mexican and American pictures, the Nacional promoted live shows that included singers, magicians, dwarfs, telepaths and so on. Every Thursday night, the house gave away one hundred dollars in a contest that was known as "Péguele al gordo" ("Hit the fat one"). By mid–1954, this theater changed its policy and started exhibiting only American movies. The management announced the installation of the new Cinemascope and Stereophonic system in the theater. Sixteen speakers gave the audience "the impression of

San Antonio offices of Clasa-Mohme distributors, on 501 Soledad Street. Photograph taken in 1944 (Agrasánchez Film Archive).

being inside the happenings." *The Robe*, a religious film featuring Victor Mature, played in May of that year followed by the 3-D movie *Creature from the Black Lagoon*. Customers received free glasses to watch the innovative films. Thus, the Nacional was turned into "el coliseo mexicano más moderno de San Antonio."

Mexican movies exhibited at the Alameda Theater continued to show a profit in the mid-fifties. Productions with recognizable stars were sure to grab the public's attention, like the comedy *Caballero a la medida*, starring Mario Moreno *Cantinflas*. It played the Alameda for two consecutive weeks in 1956. A color film with a catchy title was ¿*Con quién andan nuestras hijas?* This modern urban melodrama recounted the problems and afflictions of several teenage girls, who wind up in the company of unscrupulous and corrupted men. Even before its exhibition in 1957, the film's distributor in San Antonio predicted that it would be "a big money maker for the company." "I can't say how well it will be received by those audiences," the distributor said, adding that "many of them will be highly impressed, and no one with an education above that of a moron could fail to be deeply stirred by the treatment of the serious social problems that are involved in the various stories, which are interwoven in the picture."[42]

An advance preview of ¿*Con quién andan nuestras hijas?* at the Alameda Theater on a Friday resulted in a total gross of $2,574, with admission prices of 75 cents for adults and 25 for children. This was an outstanding box-office figure. The enormous profit from ¿*Con quién andan nuestras hijas?* was even more surprising because, as the distributor of the film pointed out: "Everyone knows that the Mexican theaters do their top business on Sundays, so it is really something when a picture can be shown on a Friday and have receipts which far exceed the Sunday business with another good picture."[43]

The state of affairs of Azteca Films and Clasa-Mohme was complicated by the arrival of Columbia Pictures as a major distributor of Mexican product. In 1958, Columbia had a stock of only 25 Spanish-language features for release, among which there were two Disney cartoon re-issues (dubbed), three *Cantinflas* pictures (one of them a new release), plus one film from Spain. Several of these features were guaranteed hits, like *Sube y baja* with *Cantinflas*, *Cuatro copas* with Libertad Lamarque and Miguel Aceves Mejía, and *Maratón de baile* with Luis Aguilar and Ninón Sevilla. Columbia Pictures would eventually increase its catalog of foreign films, adding principally 28 titles that featured the popular Mario Moreno *Cantinflas*.

Although Clasa-Mohme's inventory for 1958 totaled 103 pictures, of which 23 were all-color productions, the head of the Los Angeles office did not feel too confident in the face of the existing competition. He urged San Antonio's branch manager to secure the renewal of contract with the Alameda Theater in order to book as many films in this theater as possible for the year 1959, "before it is done by Azteca or Columbia."[44]

Revenue from the Teatro Alameda had always been of vital importance to film distributors in San Antonio. Both Azteca Films and Clasa-Mohme supplied the Alameda with their best pictures throughout the year. But competition turned very stiff for the latter in 1958. A comparison of the grosses from this theater during the months of February to October revealed that Clasa-Mohme's product was making only $42,784, when Azteca Films made it possible for the Alameda to reap $80,350 in the same period. The highest gross for a single Clasa-Mohme picture had been $5,790, with the western *El Rayo de Sinaloa* (aka *La venganza de Heraclio Bernal*). This figure was doubled by Azteca's tearjerker *Tu hijo debe nacer*, which scooped $10,705 in just one week.[45]

Further proof of the importance of the Alameda for the local distributors can be seen in the correspondence of Clasa-Mohme's Gordon B. Dunlap. In one letter, the executive

CARTEL DE LA SEMANA

NACIONAL
—EXTRA—

Lunes 9 a Domingo 15

Motivo de Verdadero Orgullo es para la Empresa, la presentación de esta bellísima película!

Dolores DEL RIO
y PEDRO
ARMENDARIZ

La pareja ideal del Cinema Nacional, conquistadores del Primer Premio en el Concurso de Cannes, Francia en

'BUGAMBILIA'

La Historia de un Amor Arrebatador
...Impetuoso... y Sublime a la Vez!

ELLA era una mujer irresistible . . . voluptuosa, de una coquetería encantadora . . . Por ello era el blanco de la envidia de las mujeres y de la codicia de los hombres! Se llamaba AMALIA! Era la hija predilecta de un acaudalado.

EL amaba la vida - su predilección era la música y sus aliados inseparables eran la audacia y el valor - la temeridad y el arrojo. No tenía miedo a la muerte y la desafiaba en cada lance!

DIRIGIDA POR EL INDIO FERNANDEZ!

EL era rudo, arrogante y fiero . . . de una voluntad recia y de indómito espíritu! . . . Para él la justicia y el deber eran sus primordiales normas de vida . . . Se llamaba RICARDO - Era el jefe de mineros!

PERO el destino contra el cual nadie puede, hizo que se conocieran . . . se comprendieran y se fundieran en el AMOR más fuerte que la muerte! . . . Un amor que desafió todo: Prejuicios de casta, orgullo, calumnia e iras!

FOTOGRAFIA DE GABRIEL FIGUEROA!

ELLA rechazaba el amor que le brindaban los de su aristocrática casta . . . porque había nacido para amar a un HOMBRE VERDADERO — incapaz de ser vencido por ssu hechizos!

BUGAMBILIA le conmoverá hondamente, pues en argumento y emotividad supera a FLOR SILVESTRE, MARIA CANDELARIA y LAS ABANDONADAS! . . . Sus portentosos protagonistas le harán vivir momentos de inefable romanticismo!

ARGUMENTO PROFUNDAMENTE HUMANO!
NO DEJE USTED DE VERLA: LE GUSTARA MUCHO!

FILMS MUNDIALES, S.A.

DOLORES del RIO
y Pedro ARMENDARIZ
en BUGAMBILIA

UNA SUPERPRODUCCION MEXICANA

Con
JULIO VILLARREAL
STELA INDA
ALBERTO GALAN
PACO FUENTES

Dirección de
EMILIO FERNANDEZ

CLASA-MOHME, Inc.

PROXIMA SEMANA—UN FORMIDABLE CARTEL DOBLE — EL ESTRENO

LIBERTAD LAMARQUE en "YO CONOCI A ESA MUJER"
y a petición general
RICARDO MONTALBAN en la bella cinta "NOSOTROS"

Flier advertising for *Bugambilia*, a 1944 film starring Dolores del Río (Agrasánchez Film Archive).

expressed his worries because the picture *Música de siempre* was "doing very badly" at the Alameda Theater. "This often happens after a week of stage shows, as the people are either 'broke' or not in the mood for moving picture entertainment," he explained. Weather conditions also affected the business and lots of rain meant poor attendance to theaters. In short, Dunlap granted, "little revenue from downtown San Antonio hurts exceedingly, for the largest single billings that we ever have in this territory come from the Alameda Theatre."[46]

Flier advertising for *Caballero a la medida*, playing in 1956 (Agrasánchez Film Archive).

Even distant events had a bearing on the business performance of theaters. For example, during the screening of *Los salvajes*, in October 1958, the news of the death of Pope Pius XII had a tangible impact on the Alameda's box office results. The management of the theater "did not attribute the rather low receipts of $4,327 to any weakness in the picture, but to the shock of the people in this area over the passing of such a great man."[47]

Difficult Times for the Movie Industry

The size of San Antonio grew constantly during the fifties. In 1955, the population was calculated at approximately 510,000. Of this total, 150,000 people were Hispanics. The number of movie houses operating in 1957 increased to 33, including 18 drive-in theaters. Spanish-dialogue pictures were shown primarily at the Alameda, Guadalupe, and Nacional, in addition to the Fiesta and El Capitán Drive-Ins.

This was a difficult period for the motion picture industry. *The Wall Street Journal* reported at the end of 1957: "Movie receipts at the box office have fallen sharply in recent months. Attendance is now at a post-war low ... and some 1,200 theaters across the nation have closed since the start of the year."[48] Part of the reason for this decline in theater attendance was that more people owned television sets, a less expensive form of mass entertainment. Another factor, ironically, was the large number of movie places operating within the same city. All this kept exhibitors very busy competing against each other.

A decade after it opened, the Alameda Theater of San Antonio began to show signs of mismanagement. Gaetano Lucchese, head of the Zaragoza Amusement Company that owned this and other theaters, had died from a heart attack in August of 1957. His son, Robert, took over the business. But within a

Press sheet advertising for *Tizoc*, aka *Amor indio* (1956) (Agrasánchez Film Archive).

year the Alameda was losing money. Even before the death of Gaetano Lucchese, the financial burden of this company had become considerable, as "they owed money right and left."
S. G. Heath, the company's treasurer, did his best to keep it out of bankruptcy. Then, in
1958, Lula V. Lucchese, the widow of Gaetano, replaced her stepson Robert as head of the
Zaragoza Amusement Co. Immediately, she put herself to the task of "cutting out a great
deal of dead wood in the operation of this theatre."

> The Alameda Theatre has been having a hard time and Mrs. Lucchese has resorted to every
> possible economy, having eliminated the two-for-one policy on Wednesday, the special
> passes which were given to people who would get one free admission after having bought
> tickets for three weeks, passes to merchants for advertising space in windows, and all per-
> sonal passes, including all employees of the three Spanish-language distributors located in
> this city. She has also cut down on overhead and I understand was successful in getting the
> Union, which controls air conditioning and heating, to reduce the number of men perma-
> nently on the job from two to one, having told the Union that she could not stand the
> expense and it was 'that or else.' [49]

According to Clasa-Mohme, the theater had already declined in popularity by 1959.
It so happened that "the young people and kids have almost quit going to the theater as
nothing is being done to interest them in following Mexican pictures, their stars and featured players," informed the distributor. Newspaper advertising for this theater had also
been neglected. Even though the manager of the Alameda, Ignacio Torres, maintained a
reputation for being a dynamic publicity agent, the inadequate business practices of Mrs.
Lucchese and her excessive control on expenditures affected adversely the standing of the

Alameda. Torres became alarmed because of Mrs. Lucchese's "niggardly and stingy tactics." From the point of view of Clasa-Mohme, she was "so penny-pinching that she will not even pay the cost of the big [advertising] fronts that the Alameda used to have on the sidewalks and on the building. She won't pay for window cards or simply anything."[50]

To make matters worse, people began complaining of the poor treatment they were given at this theater. For example, when the *Cantinflas* comedy *Sube y baja* was exhibited, a man with two daughters under the age of eleven went to the Alameda to buy tickets only to find out from the cashier that the girls would be charged the adult fare. Obviously displeased, he swore that he would never again attend this theater. "People no longer consider it fun to go to the Alameda," Gordon B. Dunlap sentenced. This distributor also observed that

> Mrs. Lucchese hasn't the slightest conception of showmanship or how to treat the public... It looks as though she is so determined to save money that she is running her customers away from the theatre. I don't like to exaggerate, but it looks to me like this theatre is going downhill very rapidly. There is no such thing as a big gross business any longer. A picture that used to do $8,000 is now lucky to do $6,000.[51]

Clasa-Mohme was definitely feeling the pinch at the end of the decade. Although its inventory of pictures was still significant, it released only a handful of movies that could be considered top-notch. This was the case of the extremely successful revolutionary drama with María Félix and Dolores del Río, *La Cucaracha*, which opened in México in November of 1959. The film's release in Texas was strategically withheld until the summer of 1960, for maximum returns at the box office. As soon as they learned of the excellent performance of this film, many theaters in the U.S. jumped to get the first booking of the picture. San Antonio's Clasa-Mohme placed an order of five prints, ten trailers, and one thousand window cards (posters) of *La Cucaracha*, to take care of its playing dates in Texas. This distributor regarded the María Félix film as "probably the greatest attraction this office has had in prospect since the 1952 release of *El derecho de nacer*."[52]

But theater attendance continued to drop as a general rule. Television entertainment was the biggest challenge to the theater's business. Although few Spanish-language pictures were being shown on T.V. at this time, the ones that did get aired raised the concern of some film distributors. For instance, when the local KENS presented *A la sombra del Puente*, a Mexican film made in the forties, Clasa-Mohme's Dunlap expressed: "I am sure that it was entertaining to the people who sat at home to see it on their T.V. sets. That may be one reason why the Alameda Theatre receipts were quite low Sunday night; and if we are going to face the competition of halfway decent Mexican pictures through the medium of T.V., it is likely to get a little tough for our company."[53]

The first three months of 1960 had been very inauspicious for outdoor entertainment in San Antonio. Film distributors complained frequently about poor weather, as "it conspired to keep people away from the theatres and has been terribly detrimental to everyone's business." Not just Spanish-language movie houses were affected by adverse weather conditions, but the rest of the theaters in the area suffered as well. A heavy flu epidemic cut down theater attendance in January. Also, the long strike of five industrial labor unions, which involved plumbing, electrical, common labor, air conditioning and hoist engineers, had its toll on the overall economic situation.[54]

One last factor that had considerable influence on the general business of many theaters in downtown San Antonio was the increasing "suburban exodus." Clasa-Mohme's Dunlap pointed out that "fewer and fewer people are coming downtown to do their shopping due to the tremendous growth of Community Centers that are located, in many cases,

La Cucaracha was a prestigious film for its distributor, Clasa-Mohme, when it played in the U.S. in 1960 (Agrasánchez Film Archive).

miles from the business district that, in the past, represented most of the retail trade of this area."[55]

The lack of money seemed to be the main issue of the day: it was just not flowing to the theaters and film exchanges as it used to. "Most weekends have been partial or total failures," said Dunlap referring to the movie business in 1960 and adding: "I don't see how some theatres are hanging on and I don't believe that many of them could have resisted except that the owners have other sources of income." He explained that there were a few exhibitors who could maintain their business afloat in bad times by pitching in from alternative cash reserves. A wealthy man that had an extensive lumber business besides being a road and general contractor, for example, owned the Towne Twin Drive-In. This exhibitor, who had been showing Mexican films on one of the Twin Drive-In screens, could do "the heaviest newspaper advertising of any independent or circuit drive-in theatre."[56]

But other people in the business did not have the same economic solvency. The owner of the Fiesta Drive-In was "having a tough time getting the money in." Not knowing how to improve attendance to his theater, he contemplated putting up the drive-in for sale. This situation extended to several other people outside of San Antonio, like the owner of the Rio Theater in Alice, Texas. He was forced to shut down this venue, as his debt to film distributors had increased substantially. Clasa-Mohme requested this theater the liquidation of overdue movie rentals. After many letters, the distribution company received a check for $876, which represented the full amount due. "This was almost a miracle," Dunlap wrote, "and I can hardly get over the shock of it yet. It took the sale of a farm to accomplish it."[57]

Finally, in 1962 the Alameda Theater, one of the most important houses for Spanish-language films in the United States, changed ownership. Mrs. Lula V. Lucchese, president of the Zaragoza Amusement Company, sold the Alameda and its annex building "Casa de México," together with the Guadalupe and Nacional Theaters, to the New York-based Jack Cane Corporation. Henry Rosenberg and Maurice Braha, the company's president and vice president respectively, kept a long-time employee of the Zaragoza Amusement Co., Ignacio Torres, as administrator of the Alameda. A large staff of 30 people was put in charge of running the facilities, as the theater continued its traditional policy of exhibiting first-run Spanish-language films and staging live performances.[58]

The Alameda changed hands again in 1976, when associates Al Zarzana of Houston and Gary Hartstein of the Dallas-based Texas National Theaters, bought this San Antonio venue from Maurice Braha. The new owners paid $600,000 for the Alameda and the adjacent International Building, continuing its operation as a Spanish-language movie house. With its decline in the mid-eighties, the Alameda became endangered by the city's growth as well as by ambitious developers. A group of private investors proposed the demolition of the theater in order to make room for a 12-story medical building. People like María Berriozabal, representing the City Council, opposed this plan saying: "The Alameda is a treasure for downtown, and I will fight anyone who wants to tear it down."[59] Fortunately, the theater survived and was converted to a triple screen theater, without destroying its original design and decor. However, in 1990 the machine projectors of this 40-year-old entertainment center stopped running for good, as the supply of films that had been the life and blood of the Alameda was cut off. That year, the Azteca Films distributor closed its offices in San Antonio. All in all, competition from videocassette movies, together with the decline of the Mexican motion picture industry, accounted for the demise of Spanish-language theaters in this city and throughout the United States.[60]

Today, the remnants of an era of movie going in San Antonio are being rescued by a new generation that looks back to its cultural roots. Thanks to the many people promoting the city's Hispanic heritage, the Teatro Alameda and the annex building "Casa de México" have been restored and designated as the central part of a "cultural zone" project. As the new century begins, this committed generation has demonstrated an authentic appreciation of a by-gone era and its preeminent symbols. Scholar Tomás Ybarra-Frausto exemplified this attitude when he stated, "the Alameda may be the most significant building in the nation relating to Mexican-American culture and history."[61]

In the same manner, another theater built by Gaetano Lucchese, the Teatro Guadalupe, survived the passing of time and was restored through the efforts of the artistic community of Mexican-Americans in San Antonio. The theater, which was originally opened in 1942, is now under the administration of the Guadalupe Cultural Arts Center. Thankfully, both entertainment landmarks, the Alameda and the Guadalupe, have been preserved and are now cultural icons of the city's Hispanic heritage. They also serve today as reminders of the vibrant cinema of México that once stirred the local populace.

7

The Rio Grande Valley

The area in South Texas known as the Rio Grande Valley extends some one hundred miles along the river that serves as an international border with México. From the busy entry port of Brownsville, near the Gulf coast, to the urban communities of McAllen and Mission, a succession of 20 small and medium-sized cities dot this semi-tropical region. Agriculture has played a central role in the economy of the Valley, with citrus, cotton, vegetables and canning as the main cash products. Cotton became the "king of crops" in the region from the 1940s to the 1960s. Throughout this time, its production required the concourse of thousands of laborers who came mostly from México, both as legal braceros and as "wetbacks."

Like in many parts of the country, the development of business in the Valley can be linked directly to the influx of Mexican migrant workers before, during and after World War II. Agricultural production in the Rio Grande Valley was heavily dependent on the importation of a large labor force. In 1954, for example, approximately 250,000 contract workers from Mexico entered the United States. Many of them were hired as cotton pickers in the Valley and elsewhere. Illegal immigration, on the other hand, by far exceeded these numbers. While the majority of "wetbacks" arriving that year found jobs in the country, an estimated 300,000 of them were deported by authorities.[1]

Migratory workers definitely had an impact on the economy of this region. In fact, their presence stimulated the activity of many businesses, including the establishments offering entertainment to the public. A distributor of Mexican films in San Antonio, Texas, appraised the cotton economy of the Valley as of great importance to the well being of the theater industry. Estimating at 65,000 the number of braceros that came to work in the fields in the summer of 1959, this motion picture concern projected that "everybody is going to have a huge amount of extra business" in the area.

> Spanish speaking people by the thousand start migrating from Texas for other states, but some of these are replaced by Braceros from Mexico and the ones that remain in Texas have better work opportunities, which means an increase in money in circulation... In Texas the summer is always better than the winter. It is true that until about July, our business from the Rio Grande Valley is likely to decrease, due to the heavy exodus from that region, but this doesn't last too long because, with the start of the cotton picking about the first ten days of July, things really hum down there and the tempo is kept up throughout the State as this great crop matures in different temperature zones.[2]

Entertainment for Hispanics started to flourish in the 1930's when radio programs, live shows, records and moving pictures in the Spanish language became a regular fare.

Although Hollywood film production dominated the screens of the Rio Grande Valley, Spanish-speaking people just as easily could select from an assortment of Mexican movies playing locally. Approximately twenty theaters in the Valley specialized in Spanish-language motion pictures in the early forties. By 1953, this number increased to thirty-two. As drive-in theaters began to be built, the exhibition outlets for imported movies equally expanded.

When the top-notch picture *La Cucaracha* was released in July of 1960, already 38 screens in the area were open to the trade. This all-color all-star feature played in fourteen of those theaters. Every movie business in the Valley had to compete with the rest for a share of the Spanish-language population, a constituency that represented a good deal of money for exhibitors. In the exceptional case of *La Cucaracha*, box-office proceeds from fourteen theaters amounted to a good $15,515 collected during its first run in the Valley. As with all films, this picture was re-released many times after its initial showing, promising a continuous flow of cash that benefited both the distributor of the film and the local exhibitors.[3]

Besides their regular attendance to Hollywood entertainment, Hispanics also indulged in a varied and steady supply of films in Spanish. The assortment of Mexican movies that a person could draw on in one week was staggering. For example, in the last eight days of 1949 the Valley's movie theaters offered some 27 Spanish features and an equal number of short subjects. A movie fan could decide on a wide range of pictures representing any genre, stars, or category. Thus, he or she may choose from the action-packed westerns like *Cielito lindo, El gallero,* or *Espuelas de oro,* to the strong dramas portrayed in *Nosotros los pobres, Dios se lo pague,* and *La casa colorada.* If he was in a light mood, there were plenty of comedies: *Los tres Huastecos, A volar joven, Pito Pérez se va de bracero,* or *El ropavejero.* Finally, a variety of sentimental melodramas invaded the screens of almost every theater: *Amor de una vida, Corazones de México, No me quieras tanto,* and *Chachita la de Triana.* Featuring the most popular singers, actors and actresses, these films drew enthusiastic crowds at a time of peak activity in the business of Spanish-language pictures.[4]

Early Exhibition of Mexican Films

Very few entertainment spots in the Rio Grande Valley catered specifically to Hispanics in the twenties. In Harlingen, for example, the Park Theater sometimes offered "interesting and varied pictures" for Mexican families. In May of 1929, it played the seven-part serial *Historia de la Revolución Mexicana,* a documentary about military and political events occurring in Mexico in the recent past. As these movies were silent, they often had musical accompaniment provided by the theater. The Teatro Anahuac, in McAllen, offered movies with popular Latin stars of Hollywood. *El Pagano,* a silent film with Spanish titles featuring Ramón Novarro, played here in March 1930. Another theater catering to Hispanics at this time was the Teatro Chapultepec of Donna. One of its programs advertised the serial *The Big Diamond Robbery,* starring Tom Mix: "A cowboy full of life and strength who is not afraid of anything or anybody."[5] A new movie house opened in Edinburg in 1930. The Grande Theater, owned by Mrs. Montague, was located on Harriman Street, the main artery of the Mexican neighborhood. Mrs. Montague had planned this theater with the explicit intention of showing films to the "many people that lack the most indispensable knowledge of English."[6]

The area's show business gained momentum during the thirties. People gathered inside *carpas*, or tent theaters, to view the latest attraction. Some establishments, like the Teatro Carpa Jalisco, in the town of San Juan, enjoyed unrivaled popularity. Its main fare were Spanish-dialogue pictures, offering every once in a while a "variedad" or live show. At the beginning of 1938, the public attending this tent watched the Mexican films: *Chucho el roto, Mater nostra, Payasadas de la vida, Luponini, Madres del mundo, Corazón bandolero,* and many more. In adition, Carpa Jalisco entertained its patrons with religious pictures like *Vida, pasión y muerte de Nuestro Señor,* a French film dubbed in Spanish. The town of Pharr also had its own tent theater that spread under an Ebony tree, from where it took the name of Carpa Ébano.[7]

In Mission, a city known as "the Valley's greatest citrus development" and "the home of the grapefruit," locals could attend La Lomita Theater. In the fall of 1937, for instance, La Lomita exhibited many films, among them *Cielito lindo, Rosario, Tras la reja, Todo un hombre, Los desheredados,* and *¡Ora Ponciano!* Besides these pictures in Spanish, the theater offered movies in English, such as *Tex Ritter in Arizona Days,* and also *Thin Ice,* with Sonja Henie and Tyrone Power.[8]

The Benítez Circuit

As film production soared in México during the thirties, several Valley theaters began to have a regular program that included Spanish-language pictures. Enterprising residents carried out the construction of buildings for the sole purpose of showing movies. The impresario Miguel Benítez of Weslaco, who had been running a theater called the Iris, opened the Teatro Nacional in the same city. The weekend of June 22, 1935, it showed the Mexican film *El compadre Mendoza.* This 300-seat theater underwent major reforms and was re-inaugurated in March of 1938. The manager of the Nacional proudly announced that a "modern and expensive equipment for the reproduction of sound has just arrived from New York and it is now installed." For its premiere, it exhibited *La madrina del Diablo,* an adventure film featuring Jorge Negrete in his cinematic debut. The Nacional was privileged to show this movie for the first time in Texas, bypassing theaters in other cities that were much larger. To advertise the picture, Mr. Benítez had a pamphlet of *La madrina del Diablo* distributed to people, so that they could become acquainted with the story before watching the movie. An announcement in San Antonio's *La Prensa* informed: "Now, more than 600 spectators can be seated comfortably. Hereafter, the manager intends to keep an eye over strict order and morality, preventing the disagreeable spectacle that certain people give, without any respect for the fair sex, when they smoke in their own seats and stay with their sombreros pulled on."[9]

A year later, Mr. Benítez opened a new theater in the town of Edcouch, a few miles north of Weslaco. The Teatro Texas was built under the direction of Primitivo Chapa, a skilful carpenter and contractor. An attractive front in the Spanish colonial style decorated the building, which measured 36 feet wide and 90 feet long. The Texas was the only theater in Edcouch; it exhibited Mexican pictures continuously for a period of over two decades.[10]

The enthusiasm of Miguel Benítez for Spanish-language entertainment developed into a serious and profitable family business. By 1961 Mr. Benítez, his wife Lupita, and his four sons (Miguel Jr., Héctor, René, and Reynaldo) controlled 12 outlets for Mexican pictures in the Rio Grande Valley. This was the largest theater circuit in the area catering to Hispanics. Besides the Iris and Nacional of Weslaco, and the Texas of Edcouch, the Benítez

The Teatro Nacional of Weslaco showed films since the 1930s (Carlos Hinojosa private collection).

Circuit operated the following theaters: Palacio, in Donna; Rio, in Santa Rosa; El Capitán, in Pharr; Alameda and Roxy, in Edinburg; Alameda, Tropic and Sky-Vue Drive-In, in Elsa; Benítez Drive-In, in Weslaco. The circuit later expanded to other Valley towns, like Harlingen (Grande Theater) and Brownsville (Benítez Twin Theaters). In the 1970s, the family's business surpassed the Valley area to include other movie places in Houston, Austin, Laredo and Corpus Christi. All of these entertainment centers opened eight days a week and consumed loads of pictures annually. Alone, the Sky-Vue Drive-In of Elsa required four Mexican pictures per week; this meant almost 200 a year.[11]

According to a family member, their interest in motion pictures began in the 1920s when Mrs. Lupita Benítez "became fascinated by movies and ordered a small hand projector camera, she came up with the idea to show films in their backyard by using blankets and making them into a makeshift tent, and charged the neighborhood kids 5 cents to come over and watch films." As attendance to these functions increased, the Benítez family decided to bestow the show with a more formal atmosphere.

> In 1924 they built their first movie theater called the Iris, and adjacent the Iris came the Nacional. They began screening American silent films and converting over to talkies when they came into market. In the 1930's, the Benítez theaters found their audience by catering to the Spanish-language films. On Fridays and Saturdays, the movies began showing at 11 a.m. to midnight, admission now at 25 cents. Mrs. Benítez found herself making 250 candied apples for an evening's sale, in addition to making hamburgers, malts and popcorn. A talent show was offered before screening of films to entertain the audience. The show was called 'Los Aficionados.' Kids or adults from the audience would go on a stage that was built under the screen and sing and dance or tell a joke for prizes. The contestant who received the loudest clapping from the crowd won.[12]

The Teatro Nacional brought to Weslaco the most successful Spanish-language movies. In June 1937, it exhibited *Allá en el Rancho Grande*, a lively picture starring singer Tito Guízar that had broken all records. The Nacional was the first theater in the Valley presenting the picture, which played for three days attracting a very large crowd. *Allá en el Rancho Grande* became a classic folkloric movie and was re-released in the forties with nearly the same success. During a function in 1945 at the Nacional, the film produced an enviable gross of $1,092 in only three days.[13] Another big movie that came to the Nacional in 1937 was *¡Ora Ponciano!* It depicted daily life in a ranch, with its bullfights, fiestas, romances, and mariachi songs. Exhibitors found this to be a favorite subject among the public.

Still, the job of theater operators was anything but easy, as it also carried its risks. Exhibitors, no doubt, had many things to worry about. Among them, the most dreaded were theater disasters, as when the Teatro Rio of Donna caught fire in 1940. No one could ascertain the origin of the flare that caused the fiery destruction of this business. A year before, the Teatro Alamo, in the city of the same name, had suffered an equal fate. Then, in March of 1946, Miguel Benítez's Roxy Theater in the town of Elsa burned to the ground. Two small cafes and two small homes were also destroyed in a blaze that originated in the Roxy's projection room. Although no one was injured, "a sizeable crowd hurriedly left the building when the alarm was sounded... The theater roof collapsed soon after the fire started. Three fire departments battled the flames for nearly three hours," a newspaper reported. Mr. Benítez estimated the losses at $8,000, which included projectors, screen, seats and other furniture. Unrelenting, its owner rebuilt the Roxy the following year and put it back in business. Another movie house owned by Benítez, the Rex of Santa Rosa, burned down in 1948, after it exhibited the *Cantinflas* comedy *A volar joven*.[14]

By force of habit, Miguel Benítez and sons developed a keen instinct for good programming. They were very selective and often quarreled with film suppliers regarding the sort of movies that drew more public. Their decisions were fundamentally audience-oriented, with a marked tendency to please the largest group of patrons, who were Mexican farm workers. By these standards, the distribution companies acknowledged: "The Benítez circuit always tries to make long-range plans for the right kind of pictures. And no one can blame the exhibitors, for they have had countless years of experience that show that unless they can offer either action pictures or comedies, they can't make the kind of grosses that the presence of many uneducated laborers demand." Thus, the film distributing company Clasa-Mohme described the preferences of exhibitors and their regular customers:

> The independents in the Rio Grande Valley are only impressed by big pictures or those which have lots of popular appeal for their public; namely, films in which such stars as Antonio Aguilar, Piporro, Tin Tan, Luis Aguilar, and Miguel Aceves Mejía appear. Very few pictures appeal to the average Spanish speaking resident of the Valley. These people have uncultured tastes and would rather see a picture like *Los santos reyes* and *Tres desgraciados con suerte* than the finest picture made.[15]

Frequently, a bargaining battle took place between a film supplier and the Benítez over the worth of certain pictures. In a typical tug-of-war situation, the distribution company set the price for pictures, while the exhibitors insisted in paying a lower fee for their rental. This habitual business was accepted by Gordon B. Dunlap, the Texas representative of Clasa-Mohme, when he confided: "All distributors have to work out their own salvation if they want to get the Benítez revenue, which is very important, and we have to put up with a lot of things. If we didn't have the pictures that we do, I would really feel sorry for ourselves because they certainly know how to be rough, but in the long run they need us as badly as we do them."[16]

Edinburg's Teatro Juárez attracted large crowds when *El derecho de nacer* played here in 1952 (Agrasánchez Film Archive).

In fact, Clasa-Mohme's Dunlap had "to put up with a lot of things" from the Benítez. In the summer of 1952, a hot-tempered Miguel Benítez, Jr., telephoned Dunlap to complain about the company's refusal to serve his Roxy Theater in Edinburg. The San Antonio-based distributor reminded Benítez that, because he did not allow a theater checker to go into the Roxy to verify the box-office receipts, his theater would be cut out of film service immediately. Upon hearing this, Benítez yelled through the phone "words uttered in an angry, menacing, extremely serious and threatening tone, which start with: I'm going to sue the shit out of you. And ending with..." Dunlap was aghast and took note of the discussion. For a few weeks, a tense situation persisted between Benítez and the Clasa-Mohme distributor. Under the pressure of his family, however, Miguel Jr. finally apologized to the head of the San Antonio exchange and made a commitment to "continue an ever ending friendship by which both of us may gain."[17]

When the color super-production *La Cucaracha* was announced for release in the Valley in the summer of 1960, every exhibitor rushed to get the first booking of the picture. Before making any deal with the Benítez, Clasa-Mohme offered it to the Interstate Circuit, which handled three Spanish-language theaters in the Valley, and also to Dave Young's México Theater of Brownsville. This move guaranteed certain lead to *La Cucaracha*'s distributor, who clearly wanted to obtain a better percentage from the rental of the picture to the Benítez Theaters. To the distributor's satisfaction, a fifty percent arrangement was reached. This drama of the Mexican Revolution featuring an explosive duo composed of María Félix and Dolores del Río, was expected to break all previous records for an imported movie. Towards the end of July, Benítez and sons exhibited *La Cucaracha* in the towns of Edinburg, Pharr, Weslaco, and Elsa. In six days, the four theaters harvested more than $3,000 from ticket sales. Just their 500-seat Alameda Theater in Edinburg made a fantastic $1,198 at the box office, doubling its highest gross of $503 obtained that year.[18]

Apart from the outstanding ticket turn out, the Benítez were also happy with the substantial profits from the concessions sale. Invariably, theater records did not reveal extra income from items such as popcorn, sodas and candies. But in this instance the earnings can be inferred from the testimony of some observers. Carlos Hinojosa, a loyal customer of the Valley's theaters showing Mexican films, remembered the crowds that attended these screenings. The extent of business at the Benítez's El Capitán Theater in Pharr, came to his attention more than once. Specifically, Mr. Hinojosa recalled that the sale of popcorn at this 250-seat theater usually amounted to between five and six hundred dollars on a busy day, not counting sodas and other items. This extra income certainly helped make ends meet for the theaters.[19]

The Show Business of the Ruenes Family

Another important name in the history of motion picture entertainment in the Rio Grande Valley is the Ruenes family. Don Ramón Ruenes, a Spanish immigrant who came to the United States in 1902, established his home in San Benito, Texas. He built one of the first movie houses in town, the Teatro Juárez, a wooden structure with 200 seats located at the northeast corner of Hidalgo and Landrum Streets. This entertainment center served as a stage for many plays and vaudeville acts. Mr. Ruenes also showed silent films with a projector run by hand. The theater made the transition to sound movies in the thirties; at approximately the same time it started exhibiting Mexican pictures. As the business developed through the years, the Ruenes family opened other movie houses.

> After the death of Ramón Ruenes, his wife, Ester Ramírez Ruenes continued to run the business. She had the Ruenes Theater built on Díaz and Robertson Streets, in [1944] which wasn't easy for a widow to do, especially during time of war when building materials were rationed. Her four children, Ramón, Ester Yzaguirre, Paquita Cañas, and Cristina Brady eventually went on to operate the business they knew best, the theatre.[20]

The powerful drama starring María Félix, *Doña Bárbara*, played at San Benito's Juárez Theater before closing in October of 1944. The new Ruenes Theater, with its 416 seats and a better location, opened the following month with one of Dolores del Río's finest pictures, *Flor Silvestre*. As customary, there were several special guests in the audience the night of the inauguration. Among them, Enrique Ballesteros, Mexican Consul in Brownsville and Manuel I. Ugalde, Consul General of Costa Rica. The Ruenes business had to compete with the Palace Theater in the same city, which also played Mexican movies and was run by the Interstate Circuit of Dallas. Another competitor, the Rivoli, exhibited English-language films; it was located on the American side of town, just across the railroad tracks that divided the city.

While Ester R. Ruenes operated the new theater in San Benito, her oldest daughter Ester R. Yzaguirre managed the Rex. This 800-seat movie house was located in Mission, about 40 miles from San Benito. Also, in 1946, Paquita R. Cañas took the lease of Harlingen's

The Ruenes Theater opened in 1944 with Dolores del Río's *Flor Silvestre* (Agrasánchez Film Archive).

Teatro Azteca for the exhibition of Spanish-language pictures. The same year, Ramón Ruenes, Jr. together with his associate Ed Brady built the Victoria, Brownsville's most modern theater. Three years later, Mrs. Ruenes and her daughter Ester R. Yzaguirre completely remodeled the old Azteca of McAllen, and inaugurated it as the México Theater. For its grand opening, in October 1949, the Ruenes family brought a special attraction. Pedro Infante, the most revered figure of Mexican film and radio, took the stage that night accompanied by the Trío Los Arrieros. Also, a double feature program composed of *El amor de mi bohío* and *Jesusita en Chihuahua* played on the screen. The local newspaper published dramatic photographs of the crowds waiting outside of the theater, as well as of Infante's stage performance. Witnessing the enthusiasm of the public during the opening night, the paper reported: "Movie fans jam traffic. Hundreds of McAllen's Latin American citizens turned out Monday night and jammed 17th Street traffic during the opening of the new Teatro México and the appearance of Pedro Infante.[21]

The entertainment interests of the Ruenes family did not stop here. In the 1950s, Paquita R. Cañas began operation of the Rex Theater in Rio Hondo, as well as the Roxy in Port Isabel. Also, in the larger city of Brownsville, Ramón Jr. opened the Ruenes Drive-In, and in Raymondville he became a business partner with the manager of the local El Rey Theater. Further, Eddie Yzaguirre, son of Ester R. Yzaguirre, operated two other drive-ins in Mission: the Valley Drive-In and the Buckhorn Drive-In. Infused by the success of the drive-in business, Mrs. Ruenes and her daughter Paquita built the Juárez Drive-In Theater in 1962, located on Highway 83, between San Benito and Harlingen. Over the years, the number of movie places controlled by the family extended far beyond the Valley. In San Antonio, for example, Ramón Jr. managed two drive-in cinemas; while in Corpus Christi, Ester R. Yzaguirre owned and operated the Gulf Drive-In.

   An advantage of the extended businesses of the Ruenes family was that it allowed them to offer lucrative contracts to personalities of the Mexican screen and radio. These artists came to tour the Valley's circuit, and the crowds they attracted at each town were significant. In this way, the Spanish-speaking people of the area had the opportunity to interact with stars like Pedro Infante, Tito Guízar, Matilde Sánchez *La Torcacita*, Fernando Soto *Mantequilla*, Virginia Fábregas, Jorge *Che* Reyes, Leopoldo *Chato* Ortín, Rafael Baledón and other artists coming from across the border in the 1950s. Many times the stars alternated with local Texas talents.

   The smooth operation of nearly all of the Ruenes' movie houses was made possible, principally, because the family relied on the good services of selected people. The projectionist Santos Aranda, for instance, was perhaps the oldest and most loyal of their employees. He started working for the Ruenes circuit at age 14, and remained a trustworthy element for fifty years until his death in 1984. Aranda's last day was spent working at the Juárez Drive-In. It was there that "he started feeling chest pains but refused to go home until the movie was over and the last car was out and he had secured the building for the night." Personnel like Santos Aranda were a "vital ingredient" of the success of any business.[22] But a good staff was not always available for every theater operated by the Ruenes family, as was the case of the Rex Theater in Mission.

   In the mid-fifties, the Rex Theater lost favor with the suppliers of films. The deplorable conditions of this house were manifest when the exhibitor decided not to allow the representative of Clasa-Mohme distributors to check the sale of tickets. A regular practice of Clasa-Mohme in monitoring the performance of exhibitors was to send an occasional "checker" to theaters. But the operator of the Rex consistently refused to allow such an intrusion. This resulted in a confrontation between the exhibitor and the distributor. For 18 months, the Rex did not play any picture distributed by Clasa-Mohme. Then, it resumed business again but the film distributor required that all pictures sent to this theater would only be delivered against a C.O.D. payment. An infamous report by the "checker" Mrs. Esperanza Whiteley, who worked for Clasa-Mohme, stated:

> The last time I checked the Rex Theater was in the fall of 1955. I checked the Rio Theater too. There is a big difference between how the Rex is run and the Rio is run. The Rio is owned by Mr. Flores, who is always there and takes very good care of the theater and treats the public very nice. He never lets the 'pachuco' element run in and out of the theater like they do at the Rex. Mr. Ruenes of the Rex is only in the theater on weekends and the theater runs itself the rest of the time. Mr. Ruenes at the Rex encourages the tough young Mexicans to run in and out of the theater dating up girls, and doesn't care what noise or commotion they make. Almost no families go to the Rex. It is only mostly Braceros and the tough 'pachuco' element and the bad girls. At the Rio it is completely different. Mr. Flores will not allow any commotion in the theater and all the decent people in town prefer to go to the Rio.[23]

   While many operators accurately reported on the theater's box office receipts, some others quietly meddled with the statements. Frequently, the latter opposed the visit of "checkers" to their businesses giving various excuses for this refusal. Almost any reasoning was valid in order to distance from the theater the observing eyes of the distributor. Meanwhile, the film exchanges tried to do their best to monitor the exploitation of their product. Clasa-Mohme regularly dispatched to the theaters one of its most trusted agents. "It has been our experience that Mrs. Whiteley is a very *lucky* checker," this distributor said with irony, "because many times wherever she goes the business just 'happens' to be a great deal better on the day she is present than it is at any other time."[24]

Besides the Benítez and the Ruenes, a few other Valley exhibitors operated more than one theater simultaneously. A. R. Peña, for instance, managed two movie places: the Teatro Alamo, in the city of Alamo, and the Teatro Murillo, in San Juan. These venues were showing Mexican films since the mid–1930s. Peña's theater in Alamo was partially destroyed by a fire in 1939, but he reconstructed it soon afterwards. This impresario consistently advertised his business in the pages of *The Brownsville Herald*. Beyond these two movie houses, the *Texas Theatre Guide* of 1956 lists a Murillo Theater in Dilley, Texas, owned by A. R. Peña. This 250-seat theater, however, was not in the Rio Grande Valley. Another important exhibitor, David J. Young of Brownsville, operated the México Theater together with the Teatro Iris. An account of Young's entertainment business follows.

Brownsville, a Good Market for Films

The exhibition of Spanish-language pictures in Brownsville, Texas, can be traced back to the 1930's. A few downtown American movie theaters occasionally included in their program some of the earliest sound films made south of the border. In 1934, for example, the Dittmann Theater advertised *La mujer del puerto*, a story of "a woman thrown by destiny into an abyss of suffering." The film had been acclaimed in México, and its debutant actress, Andrea Palma, was thereafter catapulted to fame. The following year, the Queen Theater announced another drama with Andrea Palma, *El primo Basilio*, which was shown for two days. At the beginning of 1936, the Queen brought to the screen one of the first Mexican westerns: *Juan Pistolas*, featuring Raúl de Anda in the title role. A Hollywood movie, *Check Your Sombrero*, and a cartoon complemented this feature. The imported films in Spanish were usually exhibited on Sundays and Mondays.[25]

David J. Young, a Brownsville entrepreneur, owned a moving picture gallery that had been operating in the late thirties as El Tiro Theater. It accomodated 590 seats and developed soon into a successful business catering specifically to Mexicans. Mr. Young's son, his wife and daughter-in-law aided the impresario in running the business efficiently. In 1937, El Tiro exhibited one of the biggest attractions that came from the Mexican studios: *¡Ora Ponciano!* This musical comedy of ranch life and bullfighting was released simultaneously in San Antonio, Laredo, Houston, and Corpus Christi.

Shortly before 1940 the name of El Tiro Theater was changed to the more popular designation of Teatro México. From then on, the Young's movie house became a focal point of entertainment for the Spanish-speaking people of this border city. The theater showed hundreds of Mexican-made films during its five decades in operation. Admission prices in the early forties were 20 cents for adults, 15 cents for balcony seats, and 5 cents for children. The program sometimes offered a combination of vaudeville act and a picture, as when it advertised the performance of Toño el Negro followed by the Mexican movie *La india bonita*. On weekends, tickets cost a little more (25, 15, and 10 cents). The movie *El superloco*, with Chato Ortín and Carlos Villarías, played in June 1940, during a special Friday function. This program was advertised as "Noche del centavo," meaning that patrons purchasing a ticket at regular price could get an extra admission for only one cent. An illustrated ad for the pictures shown at the Teatro México appeared regularly in the pages of *The Brownsville Herald*, which contained a Spanish-language section since 1940.

On time, all of the biggest attractions came to the México Theater. The classic movie *¡Ay Jalisco no te rajes!* played in December of 1942, drawing hundreds of people. It grossed

In Brownsville, the Teatro México was renovated in 1945 (Agrasánchez Film Archive).

$1,240 at the box office in five days, setting a record for other Spanish-language theaters in the Rio Grande Valley. Only the Azteca of McAllen came close to this figure with earnings of $872 for a similar run.[27] The songs included in *¡Ay Jalisco no te rajes!* undoubtedly had an impact on the masses, more so because Jorge Negrete, México's most virile actor, performed in the movie. The popular tune that gave name to this film remains a trademark of Negrete's superior singing to this day.

There were many films during the forties that achieved great financial success at the Teatro México. One of them, *Soy puro mexicano*, was an amusing adventure set during World War II in which three wicked spies from Nazi Germany, Italy, and Japan are fought and defeated by a noble Mexican bandit played by Pedro Armendáriz. The México engaged this film in April of 1943, grossing $1,356 in six days. Another popular feature, *¡Qué lindo es Michoacán!* attracted a large crowd that bought tickets for a total of $1,218 during its release. At the beginning of 1944, a film with Dolores del Río and Pedro Armendáriz, *Flor silvestre*, garnished $1,439 during a six-day showing. A year later, the Pedro Infante picture *¡Viva mi desgracia!* was able to top this with $1,500 in theater receipts.[28]

In 1945, the owner of the México Theater completely renovated the building to make it conform to the modern standards of the day. Before the opening night, the local newspaper gave a detailed description of the new facilities, offering also a historical account of this theater.

The picture *¡Ay Jalisco no te rajes!* (1941) delighted theater patrons (Agrasánchez Film Archive).

> Brownsville will have the finest all–Mexican moving picture in the United States' South-
> west when Teatro Mexico, Eleventh and Washington Streets, downtown, open its doors
> Tuesday night at 8:30. The structure is air-conditioned throughout, even to the cashier's
> box... The Mexico Theatre is a family operated partnership, and is wholly owned in
> Brownsville. D. J. Young Sr., dean of Valley moving picture theatre operators, with more
> than thirty-five years in the business, is the senior partner and managing head of the
> enterprise... 'We have long seen the opportunity in Brownsville for voice pictures in the
> Spanish language, featuring well-known Mexican and other Latin American actors', Mr.
> Young declared. 'So, when Mexico's moving picture production moved up into real quan-
> tity, we laid our plans accordingly. The Mexican and other Latin American actors are
> highly popular with the Spanish speaking section of our population. They want to see and
> hear the Mexican actors, and we are giving them the opportunity.[29]

On Tuesday April 24, 1945, the remodeled Teatro México opened its doors to the public. For the inauguration, a gem of the Mexican screen was chosen: *María Candelaria*.
Directed by Emilio *Indio* Fernández and featuring Dolores del Río and Pedro Armendáriz,
this film later won the main prize at the Cannes Film Festival. In Brownsville, it grossed
$1,022 during its four-day run. An average movie at the México usually harvested about
seven hundred dollars for a mid-week run. Bigger receipts were made on weekends, as
when *La leyenda del bandido* played the following month bringing in $1,609 for a Saturday-
Tuesday run. A Jorge Negrete picture, *El rebelde*, harvested $1,843 during a similar run in
July, the highest ticket sale for a movie in this theater.[30]

Without a doubt, the most popular pictures among Mexicans and Mexican-Americans of the area featured male stars with singing abilities, like Jorge Negrete, Pedro Infante, and Luis Aguilar. A four-day exhibition of Luis Aguilar's *Guadalajara pues* brought one thousand dollars to the box office of the México Theater. *Yo maté a Rosita Alvírez*, another Aguilar film, made $1,244 in just three days. *Los tres García*, starring Pedro Infante, produced $1,311 on a Tuesday-Wednesday-Thursday run. A tearjerker drama of race prejudice featuring Infante, *Angelitos negros*, made $1,297. Besides movies with singing charros, the comedies starring Mario Moreno *Cantinflas* were big moneymakers. One of his funniest films, *Soy un prófugo*, was exhibited during the city's annual festivities of "Charro Days," earning at the booth $1,181. With no exception, the pictures of this popular comedian meant good business for the exhibitor. This was confirmed by the showing of *A volar joven*, a film that made $1,556 in only two days. All of these movies were exhibited at the Teatro México during the late forties, guaranteeing every time a full house. In May of 1950, another *Cantinflas* picture made the top receipts: *Puerta joven* earned an incredible $2,652 during its five-day show. These examples help illustrate the appeal of Mexican cinema for Spanish-speaking audiences in Brownsville, at a time when theater going offered the best entertainment for the family.[31]

One of the most successful pictures that played at the Teatro México in 1952 was the melodrama *El derecho de nacer*. Over and above all expectations, it attracted thousands of people during the week of August 16–23. The movie made an incredible $4,748 at the box office, the highest gross in the history of this theater. Nearly nine thousand adults and 2,458 children attended the México Theater, with admission tickets at fifty and twenty-one cents respectively. As an indication of the pull of movies, twenty-five Spanish-language theaters in the Rio Grande Valley exhibited *El derecho de nacer* to full capacity that year. The film's earnings in the Valley totaled $26,430, which came from ticket sales alone. Seven years later, the *Cantinflas* comedy *Sube y baja* was able to beat *El derecho de nacer* at the Teatro México, reaping $6,924 during its eleven-day run. A newspaper reported that the crowds were so enthusiastic to get in the theater that they almost tore down the ticket booth.[32]

Once again, the cash receipts demonstrated that the México Theater could be held as one of the most important movie houses in Texas. In fact, the film distribution company Clasa-Mohme decided in 1959 that this Brownsville venue "may now be established as our release theatre in the Rio Grande Valley as we cannot depend on San Antonio under present conditions." These remarks implied that a city like Brownsville could become a good substitute market for first-run films, if the Alameda Theater of San Antonio did not comply with Clasa-Mohme's business deals.[33]

David J. Young, owner of the México Theater, opened a new house for Mexican films in 1946: the Teatro Iris. Young's amusement centers were located a few steps from each other, on the busy downtown Washington Street. A smaller-size house, the Iris could accommodate 454 people. Its inauguration took place on August 18th with the exhibition of the drama *Entre hermanos*, a film set during the Mexican Revolution and starring Pedro Armendáriz and Carmen Montejo. The Young's theaters were now competing for a share of the local Spanish-speaking audience. While the better-equipped Teatro México announced this year a personal appearance of the Trío Tamesi, providing music accompaniment for the singers Leonor and Gudelia La Oaxaqueña; the screen of the Iris presented an entertaining Mexican gangster film, *Virgen de medianoche*, followed by *Cantinflas'* comedy *Águila o sol*.

Three months after the Iris opened, a competitor theater entered the business. Ed Brady and Ramón Ruenes, Jr., joined efforts to build the Teatro Victoria, located at Fourteenth and Harrison Streets in Brownsville. The construction of this house–undertaken around the end of WWII — was finally completed "despite the limitations placed upon us

Another Mexican movie house opened in Brownsville in 1946: the Teatro Victoria. Photograph taken in 1990 (Agrasánchez Film Archive).

by the various restrictions in building materials, labor, fixtures, etc.," the owners informed. The Victoria boasted several unique features, among them "the most modern projection and sound equipment in the Valley, like in the theaters of great cities." Its construction, furthermore, had been made under strict fireproof standards. It was also provided with a special glass-encased room "for the comfort of the mothers who want to see and hear the movie even when the baby cries." These technological advantages, Brady and Ruenes advertised, "signified a step ahead for Brownsville and a heavy investment for our enterprise."[34]

The Teatro Victoria had 1,000 cushioned seats for the comfort of its patrons. It likewise featured a concession stand connected to the lobby, an advantage that kept customers from "having to go out of the building." For the opening night, on November 25, 1946, several city representatives were invited, including the Mayor of Brownsville and the Mexican Consul. The atmosphere was filled with music played by a marimba orchestra, while the picture *¡Ay Jalisco no te rajes!* made the delight of the patrons. The new theater stood several blocks from the main downtown businesses, in a semi-developed neighborhood for low-income families. Notwithstanding its location, the management advertised the facilities as "Clean, spacious and comfortable; where you and yours may enjoy to the very fullest measure the latest and cleanest films released."[35]

Stage shows were brought frequently to the Victoria Theater. A personal appearance of Pedro Infante, the idol of the masses, was scheduled for November 7, 1948. However, to the disappointment of management and public, the Mexican star did not arrive. Instead, a musical show was announced for the following week, billing Amanda del Llano as the "Notable Mexican actress that has appeared in films with Jorge Negrete, Luis Aguilar and Pedro Infante." The attraction also included Crox Alvarado, "Young actor and ideal type of any girl's dreams"; and the Trío Tamaulipeco, a well-known musical group that provided one hour of good entertainment. Topping all this, two movies were offered: *Lo que va de ayer a hoy* and the *Cantinflas* short *Jengibre contra Dinamita*. Only after a year did Pedro Infante show up on the stage of the Teatro Victoria, competing with the screening of the film *La Malagueña*.

Brownsville had ten major movie theaters in 1956. American pictures played at the following: Majestic, Capitol, Grande, Queen, and the two drive-ins, El Charro and the Star. Mexican films were exhibited at the México, Iris, Victoria, and Fiesta Drive-In Theaters. David J. Young, owner of the Iris and México Theaters, inaugurated the Fiesta Drive-In in May of 1954. One of the first Mexican movies shown here was the comedy *Baile mi rey*, featuring the speedy dancer and comedian Adalberto Martínez *Resortes*. It played for three days grossing $445, an exceptional figure for an open-air theater. The Fiesta aggressively fought competition by promoting popular "Bargain nights," charging only forty cents per carload. In January 1965, the Fiesta closed, only to re-open as the Ruenes Drive-in the following month. This venue exhibited a mix of Spanish and English-language movies until it was shut down in the late 1980s.

Brief mention should be made of the Grande Theater in Brownsville, owned by the Leon Circuit of Dallas and which exhibited Spanish-language movies around 1952–1953. This 550-seat theater offered double-feature programs, typically consisting of a Mexican and an American picture. One such combination, for example, paired *Si Adelita se fuera con otro* and *Bullets Ablazing*. Likewise, Pedro Infante's *Vuelven los García* played side by side with the Hollywood production *Treasure of Lost Canyon*. A film that made good money for this business was the patriotic, war-related *Escuadrón 201*, exhibited in the same program with *Forbidden Jungle*. *Escuadrón 201* was a story about the volunteer Mexican Air Force pilots who served in the Pacific with U.S. forces during World War II. The Teatro Grande played only a handful of Mexican pictures, as competition from the other established Spanish-language houses made it impractical to maintain this film policy.[36]

Interstate Theater Circuit

The powerful Interstate Circuit of Dallas, Texas, controlled several movie houses in the Rio Grande Valley, including five Spanish-language theaters. These were the Teatro Palace, in San Benito; the Teatro Rio, in Mercedes; the Teatro Grande, in Harlingen; the El Rey Theater, in McAllen and the Cactus Drive-In in Pharr. Starting in 1935, Interstate Circuit had acquired the lease of the old Teatro Mercedes, situated in the Mexican section of the city of the same name. Reopened as Teatro Rio, this 325-seat house was equipped with a modern projection system that incorporated sound. A large crowd gathered for its inauguration, on March 31, to watch the film *La sombra de Pancho Villa*.

A few miles away, in the city of Harlingen, few theaters catered to Hispanic audiences prior to 1942. Interstate Circuit had three houses in this town showing Hollywood films: Arcadia, Rialto and Strand, with the latter also offering Spanish-language pictures on Saturdays. That year, the Rialto Theater offered to the Hispanic community an exceptional program on the night of November 8. Mexican film star Pedro Armendáriz appeared in person for a 'Función de Media Noche', a midnight show that included live music by the Trío Los Dorados de Villa and a run of the movie *Padre mercader*. The need for an establishment that specialized in Spanish-language pictures in this town led to the opening of a new theater.

At last, a large movie house with a capacity for 700 people was inaugurated in Harlingen. Interstate Circuit's Grande Theater began operation in 1942, when Spanish-language films were picking up in popularity. An example of this is *La leyenda del bandido*, an action western starring Raúl de Anda, the celebrated "Charro Negro" of the Mexican screen. On the last day of 1944, this film made $328 during a midnight show at the Teatro Grande, beating the American picture playing a few blocks down. The Arcadia Theater offered a New Year's Eve midnight show announcing *Something for the Boys*, with Carmen Miranda and the cherry blonde Vivian Blaine. One of the biggest grosses for the Grande was made in 1943, during a four-day exhibition of *¡Qué lindo es Michoacán!*, which harvested $1,100. Some of the most successful films shown at this theater belonged to the "comedia ranchera" genre. For example, the public applauded *¡Viva mi desgracia!*, *Adiós Mariquita linda*, and *Amanecer ranchero*.[37]

An abundance of features from México came to the Grande Theater, which very soon began to compete with another Spanish-language house. In 1946, the Teatro Azteca opened for business in Harlingen. Located on "F" Street, in the heart of the Mexican neighborhood, it was run by the Ruenes family. With this, the exhibition of Spanish-language films reached a wider audience. However, some people complained about what they considered bad movies. A resident of Harlingen, José Guadalupe Treviño, was not fully satisfied with the theaters' choice of product. In a letter written in 1951, he called upon the Mexican film distributors to supply this town with better films.

> There are no words to describe the bitter aftertaste produced by a number of trashy films given to us recently, pictures lacking interest and with nothing artistic. In the past, there have been some films that are worth praising. People liked very much: *Angelitos negros*, *Nosotros los pobres*, *Salón México*, and above all *Pueblerina*. But ever since this year everything has been of

Interstate Circuit's Teatro Grande of Harlingen opened in 1942. The building still stands today as a memory of a bygone era (Interstate Collection, Harry Ransom Humanities Research Center, University of Texas at Austin).

the worst kind, with the exception of *La loca de la casa*, which is pretty good. Let me tell you, gentlemen. We have here movie houses with all the modern comfort, but we do not pay for that. Rather we pay for the spectacle. We do not want any more tacky things, so make a good selection and send us the best. Show all these 'pochos' who prefer Yankee cinema that México still has a punch.[38]

Treviño stressed the fact that "Mexican enthusiasts of the Seventh Art," like himself, knew how to appreciate fine movies. Finally, he requested the distributors to send to Harlingen three specific titles: *Inmaculada, En la palma de tu mano*, and *Paraíso robado*. A year later, the Teatro Grande showed these films, prompting Treviño to write a thank-you note and express his admiration for *Inmaculada*. This melodrama was the work of Julio Bracho, one of the most talented Mexican directors. The film recounts the story of Consuelo (Rosario Granados), a young and decent woman that is forced to wed an immoral and cruel man (Carlos López Moctezuma). Although later falling in love with another man, she remains faithful to her husband who is by now paraplegic and confined to a wheel chair. Movie fan Treviño said of this film:

> We have been given *Inmaculada*, which is a great movie, praiseworthy all around: its adaptation, direction, acting and an excellent screenplay. It is free of vulgar things and scenes of bad taste. It is a serious work that gets inside and convinces even the most refined and exigent public. Whether the movie has any defects or not, is beside the point; we know that it did not get Ariel awards, but it doesn't need them. The opinion and the applause of film fans is worth much more than what the scholars of cinema might think.[39]

The Teatro El Rey, in downtown McAllen, was another Interstate Circuit theater. Promoted as one of the most modern and beautiful movie houses in the Valley, it opened in May of 1947. As with all theaters controlled by Interstate, El Rey got much publicity through the pages of the local newspaper. Live shows added to the popularity of this new house, making an extra income of six to eight hundred dollars during a two-day engagement complemented by a picture. That year El Rey offered several of these "variedades." Beginning with the appearance of magician Wu Li Chang, the theater staged the shows of Miguel Inclán, Juanito Fedol, Dueto Atotonilco, and the musical group Sensación Mexicana, among other attractions. Famous Texas singer Lydia Mendoza also performed here in combination with the screening of the movie *Sol y sombra*. Receipts for the Sunday-Monday shows of Mendoza amounted to $1,065, the second biggest earnings of the year for a single attraction. The top receipts were obtained with the movie *A volar joven*, a comedy starring *Cantinflas* that established a record $1,500 on its three-day show.[40]

Over the years, people with a preference for Spanish-language entertainment became assiduous customers of the Teatro El Rey. The management emphasized this preference when it advertised the theater as "El mejor cine mexicano en el Valle." On the occasion of its ninth anniversary, El Rey's manager, Bill Rast, sought to treat patrons with a special souvenir. Clasa-Mohme, a film supplier of the theater, gladly cooperated with him.

> I am going to have an assortment of [photos] shipped to you with our compliments for the principal artists who appear in certain Clasa-Mohme pictures that you will be showing for the balance of the month. For example, María Antonieta Pons, who is in *Necesita un marido*, Chachita, who is in *Padre nuestro*, Rosa Carmina, who is the star in *Bajo la influencia del miedo*, and Charito Granados, who starred in *Secreto profesional*. You can give some of these stills to your customers, which I hope they will appreciate and perhaps treasure in their homes. This would tie in with your plan to thank the Mexican people for their loyal patronage during the time which your theatre has been in operation, for they have been very loyal, partly through gratitude for such a beautiful theatre, although mostly because they are very rabid fans.[41]

People enjoyed films like *Inmaculada*, a slick melodrama made in 1950. Original one-sheet poster designed by renowned artist Josep Renau (Agrasánchez Film Archive).

The Teatro Grande of Harlingen equally followed this policy of Interstate Circuit with respect to patronage development. In some instances, it offered the public free "cancioneros," which were attractive little song books advertising movies such as *Alma de acero, Camino de Guanajuato,* and *Guitarras de media noche.* The distributor of these films strongly recommended their use because "they have the words of all the songs that appear in these western

Cine El Rey, a favorite theater for McAllen's residents, is now listed as a site of historic importance. Photograph taken in 1950 (Interstate Collection, Harry Ransom Humanities Research Center, University of Texas at Austin).

pictures, and they also carry some illustrations." These booklets were sold to the theater at one cent a piece. For the movie *Alma de acero*, starring the popular Luis Aguilar, the manager of the Grande Theater ordered 5,000 copies from Clasa-Mohme. This company made one more point in favor of the handy leaflets: "This is the type of advertising that no one throws away. On the contrary, the Spanish speaking people, great lovers of music, will keep the booklets until they are worn to shreds."[42]

In order to draw in more people, the Grande Theater promoted personal appearances of artists as well as amateur shows. Its only competitor of Spanish-language pictures in the neighborhood, the Teatro Azteca, likewise announced a live show every once in a while. In December of 1949, for example, the Azteca proudly presented Pedro Infante in person. While the Grande was considered a higher-class theater showing first-runs or "estrenos," the Azteca specialized in second-run pictures at lower admission prices. Estela S. de la Fuente, a local resident, retained an impression of the atmosphere at these two houses.

> When we were about seven or eight years old, my brother and I went to the Grande in the company of our parents. It was usually on Sunday afternoons in the summertime, when it was too hot to be outdoors. That's when we were introduced to Pedro Infante, Jorge Negrete, La Abuelita (Sara García), Libertad Lamarque, María Antonieta Pons, and so many others. The Grande was also well known for its "aficionados" (talent shows) during the week, usually on Thursday nights. The "estrenos" or new features would start on Friday... My parents did not like the Azteca Theater, which showed the second-run movies,

so the only times I went there was with my cousins. I remember not liking to go there because they had vendors who would walk up and down the aisles during the movie, calling out what they were selling. I remember that's where I first heard a vendor call popcorn "palomitas." The vendors also called popcorn something that sounded like "pacón."[43]

The business of movie entertainment suffered deeply as a consequence of the arrival of television. Already, in the mid-fifties, picture shows and broadcast programs were competing in earnest for the attention of audiences. Weslaco's T.V. station KRGV promoted a "Fiesta Latina" that was broadcast three times a week in 1954. The program invited the public to take part of a talent contest designed specifically "to discover the greatest shining stars for the future of television."[44]

With the construction of drive-in theaters throughout the Valley, the foundations of the traditional hard top houses began to shake. People saw many advantages in driving their own vehicle to one of these amusement centers. Among the blessings counted was the experience of more privacy while watching the show. According to some customers, drive-ins were a draw because one could hear better the movie, as "there are no women making noises with chewing gum or talking about what is going to happen in the picture."[45] This and other advantages made the drive-ins a popular alternative. In 1956, there were twelve open-air theaters in the Rio Grande Valley. Those that showed Mexican pictures were the Fiesta, Sky-Vue, Cactus, Corral, Depot, and El Patio Drive-Ins.

What else could a household enjoy more on a Sunday evening than watching a movie at a drive-in theater? After all, it was very convenient for the whole family to be able to go to the nearest drive-in and pay only one dollar per carload. On Wednesdays and Thursdays, Edinburg's El Patio charged no more than fifty cents for each automobile. Walk-ins were welcomed, too. The Benitez Drive-In Theater in Weslaco opened in December of 1956, and it attracted a large audience with Tin Tan's movie *No me defiendas compadre,* which

In the fifties, drive-ins became popular throughout the U.S. Many of them also exhibited Spanish-language movies (Agrasánchez Film Archive).

made over two hundred dollars on a Sunday-Monday run. The following year, on account of Pedro Infante's death, the Benitez Drive-In programmed some of the idol's pictures making top receipts at all times. For a film like *Pepe el Toro*, one hundred and seventy-five vehicles showed up on a Sunday, with an average occupancy of five people per car. Concession sales, obviously, were the major income for this business.

Interstate Circuit operated the Cactus Drive-In Theater since the late forties. It programmed Hollywood movies almost exclusively, with some Mexican films shown sporadically. Located on a highway east of Pharr, the drive-in had a capacity for 450 automobiles. By the late 1950s, the Cactus had updated its projection equipment and was able to offer motion pictures in Cinemascope. If it was unusual for this theater to show a Mexican movie, rarer still was the exhibition of two Spanish-language Cinemascope films: *La doncella de piedra*, starring Elsa Aguirre, and *Primavera en el corazón*, with Irasema Dilián. The distributor Clasa-Mohme suggested both pictures on the grounds that "they ought to show up very nicely on the wide screen of the Cactus Drive-In Theater." Billed as "the extraordinary Indian legend of a beautiful girl who leads her people from slavery into freedom," the Cactus played *La doncella de piedra* in January of 1960.[46]

The 1980s brought an abrupt end to the drive-in and hardtop theater business in Spanish, as the new media of cable television and video-home entertainment became prevalent. Today, all that remains are the memories of the people that regularly attended these shows. Some individuals working for the theaters have fascinating anecdotes to tell. Alton Moore, for instance, remembered when he was hired at the Cactus Drive-In as the flashlight boy that directed traffic to open spots. "It was also my job to go around with the flit gun, and offer to spray for mosquitoes. I also had to walk around to every damned last speaker on the lot and turn the volume down at the first intermission, and after the last feature," said Moore.[47] While the places once occupied by these theaters have been converted into strip malls and flea markets, the fond recollections of moviegoers prevail, making up for an invaluable testimony of the history of local filmed entertainment.

Of the more than thirty Spanish-language theaters in the Rio Grande Valley, only a few of their buildings survive today: the Teatro El Rey, in McAllen; the Rio in Mission; the Grande in Harlingen; and the Victoria in Brownsville. As part of an important revitalization effort of downtown McAllen, a group of concerned movie fans led by Luis Muñoz restored to its former glory the Cine El Rey. Since 2003, it shows specialty films and is open to performing arts events as well. The Rio Theater is still standing and physically in good shape, but there are no plans to put it to use. Also waiting its turn for restoration are the Teatro Grande and the Victoria. Both of them closed in the 1980s and have since been vacant.

Epilogue:
An Era of Mexican
Film Entertainment

Theatrical exhibition of Mexican motion pictures in the United States followed an upward trend since the 1920s; a phenomenon that ran parallel to the rising number of Hispanics in this country that demanded a popular entertainment in their own language. Although Hollywood experimented for a while with Spanish-language films when sound movies were introduced, the successful production and exploitation of pictures for the Hispanic market belonged from the beginning to México, Argentina, and Spain. During the thirties, Mexican cinema developed in such a way that it surpassed its competitors and was able to furnish U.S. theaters with approximately ninety percent of their booking needs in the Spanish language.

For many years, the suppliers of Mexican movie entertainment in the United States were Azteca Films and Clasa-Mohme. Both companies obtained the rights to distribute films from the producers in México and other Spanish-speaking countries. Azteca operated practically without competition from 1932 until 1942, at which point Clasa-Mohme entered the arena tapping into a very lucrative business. A healthy match between these two film distributors resulted in the opening up of more theaters for the product they carried. Also affecting positively the development of Mexican cinema was the advent of World War II. Because of the wartime alliance with the United States, film producers south of the border benefited significantly. They likewise took advantage of the fact that European and Argentinean film production diminished considerably during the war, making the demand for Mexican films soar. Under these circumstances, México became the world leader of Spanish-language motion pictures, supplying product to Latin America, Spain, and the United States in a steady fashion.[1]

Theaters sprung up wherever there was an audience for these pictures. In the United States, scores of movie houses were converted to Spanish-language shows, while new buildings were erected for the sole purpose of exhibiting Mexican films. The owners of these houses represented a varied mix of business enthusiasts. From the large theater chains to the small-town exhibitors, including clubs and non-profit institutions, the number of screens catering to Hispanics grew to nearly seven hundred in the early fifties. For the most part, the swelling of this line of business was due to the influx of Latin American immigrants.

161

Throughout the forties and fifties, legal and illegal workers crossing north of the international border significantly added to the regular crowds that attended Spanish-language movie theaters. Because racial discrimination existed in many parts of the country, an extra effort by film distributors was needed in order to convince theater owners of the advantage to show films to the Hispanic public.

Spanish-language film distributors and exhibitors found an extremely loyal audience among Hispanics. As the majority of this public craved for simple, genuine film entertainment, they turned to the local theater for a respite from daily work and routine. People were also drawn to Mexican movie houses because these places provided ethnic minorities with a sense of identity and cultural pride, amidst an often-hostile environment dominated by the Anglo-American way of life. Presumably, the Mexican attractions were greeted with even more enthusiasm than it was due to them in their native soil. The opening of a theater or the presentation of a patriotic film provided a reason for the local Hispanic communities to celebrate with pomposity. Typically, special functions and inaugurations were presided by a consul or another representative of the Mexican government. Also attending these events were prominent local businessmen and city servants, who on the occasion were entertained by the appearance of a popular star from México. Many theaters complemented their film program with live shows, either presenting professional artists or local aficionados. In essence, the community turned theater entertainment into one of the most important assets of cultural life.

The preference of Mexican films by a large majority of Hispanics resulted from cultural inclinations as well as from the cinema industry's own commercial strategies. It is the contention of some scholars that powerful business interests alone created the environment for the predominance of Mexican movies, to the exclusion of the cinema of other Spanish-speaking countries. One such view, espoused by Amy B. Beer, concludes that the popularity of films from México did not originate "from cultural similarities among Latinos or from audiences' preferences, but rather from industrial and political relations in local, national and international spheres."[2] While this assertion may shed some light on the pragmatic basis for the successful exploitation of movies, it tends to obscure the vital question of the cultural appeal of movies. For one thing, if any cinema has enough sway over the public, it is principally because of its spontaneity and inherent values. As another film scholar has explained, the cinema "is not just a product of a particular culture, but rather a projection of its most fundamental needs, desires, and beliefs."[3] For that same reason, non–Mexican Spanish-speaking audiences in the United States and Latin America recognized the representations of classic Mexican film narrative as their own, making the connection through a common denominator of language and customs. Thus, the imagery of an urban melodrama like *Pepe el Toro* or *El derecho de nacer* reverberated in truth in the collective mind of spectators from San Antonio, Texas, to Lima, Perú.

Going to the movies entailed not only witnessing the details of a story, but also enjoying the music included in the film. One of the most important elements of Mexican cinema was the selection of songs that accompanied a movie. People invariably reacted to musical themes in vogue, and movie producers knew from experience that attractive tunes meant more to the crowds than the specifics of a film's story. At their disposal was an assortment of rhythms made popular by the record and radio industries. Next to the Mexican mariachi tunes –*rancheras* and *corridos* — was the music from other Latin American countries: *bolero*, *mambo*, *rumba*, *danzón*, *tango*, etc. In all of Latin American music ran a medullar substance

Opposite: Azteca Films distributed hundreds of films in the U.S. since 1932 (Agrasánchez Film Archive).

EN 1957

Con Orgullo Presenta

UNA SELECCION
SOBRESALIENTE
DE LAS
MEJORES PELICULAS
HECHAS EN MEXICO

Con Las Estrellas Más Famosas - Los Mejores Directores
La Música Más Encantadora - Soberbia Fotografía
Los Productores Más Eminentes

**Vea Próximamente Estas
Extraordinarias Películas
En Su Teatro
Favorito**

Pepe el Toro was released in the U.S. in 1954. Ad from the movie catalog of Clasa-Mohme (Agrasánchez Film Archive).

that captivated the public instantly. The romantic songs and ballads not only provided an excellent pretext to tell a story in film, but also gave movies their catchy titles. Naturally, the populace took pleasure in seeing an idealized version of their sentimentality projected onto the silver screen and endowed with flavorsome tunes. Many movies owed their success to the magic invoked in their absorbing music and rapturous rhythms.[4]

Folkloric themes and bucolic settings bestowed Mexican cinema with extraordinary acceptance from the public. Movies with *charro* interpreters and *ranchera* songs were the staple of many small-town theaters in the Southwest, where patrons came mainly from rural areas. Urban and psychological dramas, on the other hand, became more popular among Hispanics residing in metropolitan districts. But it was the big names on the marquee that usually attracted the populace. Idols like *Cantinflas*, Sara García, Jorge Negrete, María Félix, Libertad Lamarque, or Pedro Infante had their throng of faithful admirers in every city, large or small. Films also benefited from the inclusion of well-known musicians in their casts. For example, *Toña la negra*, Pedro Vargas, Agustín Lara, or even a trio like *Los Panchos*, or *Los Calaveras* were indispensable for the success of a movie. The cinema's popular appeal depended not just on the type of story or its physical setting, but perhaps more importantly on the star values and choice of musical interpreters.

Significant changes took place in the Mexican film industry toward

Singer Luis Aguilar starred in *Guadalajara pues* (1945), a folkloric picture with many typical "ranchera" songs (Agrasánchez Film Archive).

the end of the fifties, when television entertainment began to chip away the rewards of theatrical business. Traditional movie going experienced a shift after 1960, as audiences began to favor attendance at popular drive-in theaters. Faced with an overwhelming presence of Hollywood and European movies, along with a shrinking world market for their own films, the majority of Mexican producers resorted to financing low budget movies with the aim of making a quick profit. Hasty economic decisions and a lack of long-term investment policies only made matters worse. Audiences, in the meantime, succumbed to the polish and glitter of the cinema of Hollywood. As expected, the younger generation of moviegoers was automatically assimilated to mainstream American popular culture. Still, the exhibition of Mexican motion pictures in the U.S. continued to be profitable for theater owners, whose earnings were complemented by personal appearances of artists and, more frequently, by the sales from the concession stand.

The emergence of video-home entertainment in the 1980s finally brought to a halt the

The spacious Alameda Theater of San Antonio: red drapes, 1940s decor and a capacity for 2,500 spectators (San Antonio Conservation Society).

theatrical exhibition of Mexican movies. Before the end of the decade, the leading U.S. distributor, Azteca Films, went out of business. Very few pictures were released in theaters after 1991, a year that saw the collapse of the government-backed Mexican Producers Cooperative and its distribution arm, CIMEX. While electronic media (television, videos, and DVDs) carried on the task of popularizing Mexican cinema, the original setting of theaters where large crowds once celebrated these movies almost completely faded. Happily, in some regions of the United States, Hispanic communities and steadfast cultural institutions have engaged in restoring the remaining movie houses as homage to our forebears' favorite pastime.

Understandably, the preservation of movie theaters is only one aspect of today's enthusiasm for the history of mass entertainment. The rise of scholarly research has also increased our awareness of the importance of Spanish-language live and filmed spectacle. In this respect, the recovery of Clasa-Mohme's business documents comes at a suitable moment, throwing new light on the consumption of Mexican movies. The files of this film distributing company are indeed a rich legacy; the information they contain let us envisage an essential facet of Latin American culture in the U.S.

The reconstruction of an era also takes place in the oral history programs devised by dedicated scholars and lay people, who are now paying attention to their communities' past. A systematic compilation of testimonies regarding the exhibition of Spanish-language films in the United States is certainly worthwhile. Beyond the chapters contained in the present book, this panorama should grow to include other localities like Chicago, San Francisco, Laredo, Houston, etc. Every town, large or small, deserves a detailed account of the leisure-time activities of its people. In an age when the study of cinema and its public is beginning to yield illuminating narratives, a glance at the movie going habits of Hispanics may prove still more rewarding.

Appendix: U.S. Theaters That Exhibited Mexican Movies, 1920–1960

Alabama

City	Theater*	Address	Owner	Seats	Showing Mexican Films Since
Tuscaloosa	ALBERTA		Gerald Little		1953

Arizona

City	Theater	Address	Owner	Seats	Showing Mexican Films Since†
Ajo	OASIS		R.E. Griffith	400	1943
Benson	BENSON	234 E. 4th	R.E. Griffith	150	1943
Bisbee	LYRIC	10 Naco Road	Lyric Amusement Co.	1,050	1943
Casa Grande	CHIEF		Griffith Long		1943
Casa Grande	PARAMOUNT	420 M. Florence	R.E. Griffith	750	1943
Chandler	ROWENA	W. Boston	Joe Woods	400	1943
Clarkdale	GRAND		Verdi Valley Theatres	350	1943
Clifton	MARTIN	Coronado Rd.	F.C. Martin	500	1943
Coolidge	COOLIDGE		Louie Long Circuit		1943
Cottonwood	RIALTO		Nace & Becchetti	300	1943
Douglas	GRAND	12th & G St.	Lyric Amusement Co.	1,454	1943
Eloy	DUST BOWL		R.E. Griffith	450	1943
Flagstaff	LIBERTY		Nace & Olmstead	400	1943
Flagstaff	ORPHEUM	15 W. Aspen Ave.	Ray Olmstead, Northern Arizona Thea.		1943
Florence	ISIS		R.E. Griffith	500	1943
Gilbert	FALCON	Main St.	Harry L. Nace		1943
Glendale	GLENDALE		Wade Loudermilk	300	1943
Glendale	PLAZA	36 N. First Ave.	Ray Olmstead		1944
Hayden	REX		R.E. Griffith	350	1943

Original name of theaters in parentheses.
  †Earliest recorded showing; according to the Clasa-Mohme records in most cases; with a date prior to 1943, information was taken from other sources.

City	Theater	Address	Owner	Seats	Showing Mexican Films Since
Jerome	RITZ	1st & Hull St.	Ritz Theatres Inc.	480	1943
Mesa	RITZ	52 W. Main St.	Harry L. Nace	500	1943
Miami	GRAND	603 Sullivan	Nenes & Souris	800	1943
Morenci	ROYAL		F.C. Martin	350	1943
Nogales	LYRIC			450	1943
Nogales	NOGALES	741 Morely Ave.	Lyric Amusement Co.	800	1943
Oatmen	OATMEN		W.H. Ridenow	225	1943
Phoenix	RAMONA	Washington St.	Harry L. Nace	800	1943
Phoenix	REX		W. T. Gregg	400	1943
Ray	IRIS		R. E. Griffith	350	1943
Safford	RAMONA		Louie Long	700	1943
Safford	SAFFORD		R. E. Griffith	675	1943
Seligman	SELIGMAN	Chino & Main St.	Wade Loudermilk	240	1943
Sonora	JUAREZ		R. E. Griffith	400	1943
Somerton	SOMERTON		Silvercrest Thea.	350	1943
Superior	UPTOWN		R.E. Griffith	600	1943
Tiger	TIGER		Louie Long		1943
Tombstone	CRYSTAL	412 Allen St.	Lyric Amusement Co.	250	1943
Tucson	PLAZA	132 W. Congress	Nick Diamos Amusement Co.	700	1943
Williams	SULTANA		Harry L. Nace	400	1943
Winslow	RIALTO	Kinsley St.	Harry L. Nace	640	1943
Winslow	CHIEF	E. 2nd St.	H. L. Nace, Silvercrest Theatres	270	1943

Arkansas

City	Theater	Address	Owner	Showing Mexican Films Since
Lake City	LAKE		Ned Fraser, Jr.	1957
Osceola	TENT			1953

California*

City	Theater	Address	Owner	Seats	Showing Mexican Films Since
Albany	ALBANY	Kains and Solano	W. I. Garren	500	1943
Alvarado	ALVARADO	March Rd.	E. Naharro	150	1943
Anaheim	GRAND	304 E. Center	Mr. Trott.	500	1943
Azusa	JUÁREZ		Santiago Ruff		1930
Bakersfield	VIRGINIA	1224 19th St.	Pete Simous.	300	1943
Bakersfield	RIALTO	960 Baker St.	Fred Conley.	425	1943
Blythe	LIBERTY		Robert Donagan	600	1943
Brawley	MÉXICO		Benjamín Aranda, Sr.		1928
Brawley	AZTECA		Rafael Corella	400	1931
Brawley	EUREKA	925 Main St.	Benjamín Aranda Jr.	350	1943
Brentwood	DELTA	Main St.	Petersen Theatre Cir.	300	1943
Calexico	AZTEC	114 Hefferman St.	Frank Ullman	600	1943
Calexico	FOX CAPITOL	321 Second St.	West Coast Theatres	1,000	1934
Calistoga	RITZ	348 Lincoln St.	G. W. Page	250	1943
Carlsbad	IRIS		Vicent Ullman Araiza	750	1943
Chino	WOODS	328 Sixth St.	Ashley L. Woods	350	1934
Chula Vista	SEVILLE	3rd Avenue	John F. Keorg	500	1943
Claremont	VILLAGE	3rd and Harvard	Richard Barre	498	1943
Coachella	PARAMOUNT	1st St. South	L.A. Pawley	400	1943

*Sources: El Cine Grafico, Anuario: 1943–194, México, D.F.; La Opinión, Los Angeles, Calif.; El Espectador, Pomona, Calif.; Semanario Imparcial, San Francisco, Calif.; Cinema Reporter, México, D.F.

City	Theater	Address	Owner	Seats	Showing Mexican Films Since
Colton	HUB CITY	N. 8th St.	Dietrich & Feldstein	592	1943
Corcoran	CORCORAN	1215 Whitney Ave.	Arthur Fukuda	400	1943
Corona	CHAPULTEPEC	407 Main St.	José Cruz & Sons	250	1928
Corona	CIRCLE	407 Main St.	Benjamín Aranda Jr.	350	1943
Cucamonga	MÉXICO	547 24th St.	L.C. Rodríguez	250	1937
Delano	STAR				1928
Delano	WEST	1008 Freemont St.	Frank Panero	300	1943
Dinuba	DINUBA		Edward Levy		1943
Dinuba	STATE	Fresno & L St.	Redwood Midland Theatres	1,222	1943
El Centro	BROADWAY	431 Broadway St.	Frank Ullman	650	1943
Escondido	RITZ	300 E. Grand Ave.	Dan Johnstone	796	1943
Fresno	REX	909 F St.	Gustavo A. Acosta	350	1943
Fresno	AZTECA	838 St.	Gustavo A. Acosta	800	1948
Gonzalez	SYLVIA		John Martese	187	1943
Guadalupe	ROYAL	437 Guadalupe St.	Affiliated Theatres	500	1943
Hanford	ROYAL		R. Lippertt	350	1943
La Habra	LA HABRA	Central Ave.	Decker. Joseph	350	1943
Los Angeles	PRINCIPAL	N. Main St.			1926
Los Angeles	ELECTRIC	262 N. Main St.		345	1920
Los Angeles	ESTELLA				1926
Los Angeles	HIDALGO	373 N. Main St.		700	1926
Los Angeles	MÉXICO (GRAND)	110 S. Main St.	West Coast Thea.	700	1927
Los Angeles	BONITO	410 N. Ford St. (Belvedere)	A. J. Olander	700	1943
Los Angeles	HUB	1007 S. Central	Colorado Corp./ A. Snadow	475	1943
Los Angeles	CALIFORNIA	810 S. Main St.	Frank Fouce	1,500	1932
Los Angeles	MASON	127 S. Broadway	Frank Fouce	850	1937
Los Angeles	MONTEREY	2312 Whiter	James C. Quinn	800	1943
Los Angeles	BARBARA	147 E. Santa Barbara Ave.			1942
Los Angeles	ROOSEVELT	212 N. Main	Frank Fouce	345	1937
Los Angeles	UNIQUE	3645 E. First St.	Robbins & James C. Quinn	1,100	1943
Los Angeles	VARIETY	5253 W. Adams Blvd.	J.C. Quinn		1957
Los Angeles	VICTOR	S. Main St.		750	1949
Los Angeles	LIBERTY	S. Main St.	Frank Fouce		1943
Los Angeles	MAYAN	1044 S. Hill St.	Frank Fouce	1,700	1949
Los Angeles	MILLION DOLLAR	307 S. Broadway	Frank Fouce		1952
Los Angeles	NUART	11272 Sta. Monica Blvd.		660	1952
Madera	REX	223 E. Yosemite Ave.	Henry Preciado	460	1950
Marysville	STATE	515 E St.	Redwood Midland Theatres	1,667	1943
Marysville	TOWER	103 O St.	Redwood Midland Theatres	772	1943
Mendota	MENDOTA	7 Que St.	Anthony Bou	150	1943
Merced	RIO	16th & L St.	Paul Bush	400	1943
Merced	STRAND	659 17th St.	Golden State Theatres	600	1943
Modesto	STRAND	1021 10th St.	Redwood Midland Theatres	1,806	1943
Mountain View	CINEMA	892 Dana St.	B. Viccarelli	438	1943
Niles	NILES	First St.	Petersen Theatres	400	1943
Oakland	REX	1011 Broadway	Arthur Barnett	550	1943
Oakland	STAR	717 Market St.		600	1947
Oakland	SUTTER				1947
Oakley	OAKLEY	Borden Highway	Petersen Theatres	250	1943
Oxnard	BOULEVARD	624 Oxnard St.	Dietrich & Feldstein	500	1943
Pittsburg	ENEAN	325 10St.	Enean Bros.	1,000	1943
Placentia	PLACENTIA	202 W. Santa Fe Ave.	Hollis Scheirmeir	275	1943
Pomona	CALIFORNIA	235 W. 3rd St.	Sidney Pink, Mgr.	1,212	1946
Pomona	SUNKIST	445 N. Garey		880	1943
Pomona	UNITED ARTISTS				1952

City	Theater	Address	Owner	Seats	*Showing Mexican Films Since*
Porterville	SUTTER		Charles Emanuel	500	1943
Redlands	STATE		Vanderburg	400	1943
Richmond	GRAND	1142 23rd St.	Affiliated Theatres	600	1943
Riverside	GOLDEN STATE	3745 7th St.		950	1943
Riverside	ARENA	2958 8th Ave.		550	1943
Sacramento	LYRIC	212 K St.	J. Esteves & P. Enriquez	375	1938
Sacramento	LOMPOC ?				1938
Sacramento	MÉXICO				1930
Salinas	CRYSTAL	137 Main St.	John Peters	650	1943
San Bernardino	AZTECA	798 Mt. Vermon Ave.	Feldstein & Dietrich	500	1943
San Diego	METRO	2175 Logan Ave.	Freehof Thea. Corp.	400	1943
San Diego	MISSION	1245 5th Ave.	Fox West Coast	800	1943
San Diego	U.S. THEATRE				1929
San Fernando	SAN FERNANDO	303 S. Brand Blvd.	Dietrich & Fedelstein	800	1943
San Francisco	VERDI	644 Broadway		900	1935
San Francisco	SUTTER	2030 Sutter St.	480		1942
San Pedro	BARTON	211 N. Pacific Ave.	Herbert Shute	430	1943
San Pedro	GLOBE	204 W. Sixth Ave.		415	1943
Sanger	ROYAL	738 L St.	Affiliated Theatres	350	1943
Santa Ana	PRINCESS	218 4th St.	c.e. Walker	300	1945
Santa Barbara	BARBARA		M. Cinift	370	1942
Santa Barbara	MISSION	618 State St.	Warner Bros. By Lu Harper	1,000	1943
Santa Barbara	STATE	1217 State St.	Mr. Dow	685	1943
Santa Clara	SANTA CLARA	956 Franklin St.	Harvey Amusement Co.	1,000	1943
Santa Paula	TOWER	976 Main St.	Fox West Coast	338	1943
Selma	SELMA	1963 High St.	Sam Levin	500	1943
Sierra Madre	WISTERIAL			400	1943
Stockton	IMPERIAL	19 S. El Dorado St.	H. Hayashino	400	1943
Tehachapi	BEEKAY	110 Green St.	F.W. Base	450	1943
Tulare	STATE	225 E. Kearn St.	Golden State Theatres	425	1943
Upland	UPLAND		B.G. Meyers	300	1944
Vacaville	VACAVILLE	308 Main St.	Redwood Midland Theatres	590	1943
Visalia	BIJOU	112 W. Main St.	O. Nakamichi	360	1943
Watts	LINDA		Eastland Thea. Corp.	500	1943
Wilmington	AUDITORIUM		M. Rocco		1943

Colorado

City	Theater	Address	Owner	Seats	*Showing Mexican Films Since*
Aguilar	UTE		S. Kelloff	250	1943
Alamosa	GROVE	615 Main St.			1946
Antonito	LA PLAZA		Chick Kelloff	150	1943
Brighton	REX		Atlas Theatre Corp.	400	1943
Buena Vista	ORPHEUM		Rock & Lovisone	240	1943
Brush	EMERSON		Ray L. Katzenbach	361	1943
Center	FAWN		R. H. Krivohlavek	300	1943
Cheyenne	STRAND				1945
Colo. Springs	FINE ARTS CENTER		Stanley Lathrop	300	1943
Cortez	CORTEZ		John Survant	250	1943
Crested Butte	PRINCESS	218 Elk Ave.	Fisher Bros.	200	1943
Del Norte	PRINCESS		Everett Cole	372	1943
Delta	EGYPTIAN	452 Main St.	Fox Rainbow Theatres, Inc.	656	1943
Denver	CAMERON	721 Santa Fe Dr.	Walter McKinney	728	
Denver	KIVA		Sam Fernstein	448	1943
Denver	MÉXICO	2118 Larimer St.	Albert Coppel	415	1943

City	Theater	Address	Owner	Seats	Showing Mexican Films Since
Denver	PALACE	1647 Curtis St.	Church & Co.	170	1943
Denver	PLAZA	1721 Curtis St.	Denham Theatres	889	1943
Denver	SANTA FE	974 Santa Fe Dr.	Altos Amusement	894	1943
Dolores	PHYTHIAN		Mrs. Earl Vance	240	1943
Durango	KIVA	813 Main St.	Fox Trinidad Theatres	635	1943
Eads	PLAINS	Main St.	Geo W. Lawton	200	1943
Eaton	EATON		H.F. Lauck	200	1943
Fort Collins	STATE		Fox	375	1943
Fort Lupton	STAR		E.K. Menagh	340	1943
Ft. Morgan	COVER	314 Main St.	J.C. Parker		1943
Fruita	RIALTO		C.J. Colosimo		1943
Fowler	STAR	Main St.	Mrs. C. Bevard	400	1943
Grand Junct.	KIVA		Westland Thea.	403	1943
Grand Junct.	MISSION		J.H. Cooper Enterprises	298	1943
Greeley	PARK	Campus Court	J.H. Cooper Ent.	420	1943
Greeley	KIVA	9th St.	Westland Thea.	508	1943
Gunnison	UNIQUE	228 Main St.	Snyder & Basse	375	1943
Ignacio	UTE	L.C.Snyder Theatres	200		1943
Julesburg	HIPPODROME		Mrs. P.J. Zorn	500	1943
Lafayette	JEWEL		L.F. Flower	300	1943
La Jara	LA JARA		S.E. Newcomb	240	1943
La Junta	KIT CARSON		Fox Lincoln Thea.	273	1943
La Junta	SCOUT			305	1945
Lamar	IRIS		Atlas Theatre Corp	468	1943
Las Animas	KIVA		c.e. Laughlin	500	1943
La Veta	RIALTO		Roberta Boyd	155	1943
Longmont	LONGMONT	336 Main St.	Fox	538	1943
Loveland	RIALTO	228 E. 4th	Gibralter Entertainment	740	1943
Manassa	VALLEY		Dr. G.A. Van Fradenburg	160	1943
Mancos	MANCOS		L.C. Snyder Thea.	300	1943
Manzanola	COMET		Eleanor H. Graham	200	1943
Monte Vista	GRANADA		Atlas Theatre Corp.	610	1943
Montrose	FOX		Rainbow Thea.	789	1943
Ordway	PRINCESS		D.J. Mooney	272	1943
Pagosa Spr.	LIBERTY	418 N. Pagosa	Chas F. Rumbaugh	200	1943
Palisade	ALBERTA			250	1943
Pueblo	CHIEF	611 N.Main St.	Westland Theatres	741	1943
Pueblo	CLYNE	421 W. Northern	J. Clyne Theatre Corp.	400	1943
Pueblo	COLONIAL		Mrs. p.m. Gayton	450	1943
Pueblo	AVALON	1301 E. Routt	S.H. Cain	530	1943
Pueblo	UPTOWN	125 E. Abriendo	J.H. Cooper Ent.	812	1943
Pueblo	VICTORY	S. Union Ave.	S. Union Ave.	620	1947
Rocky Ford	GRAND	405 S. Main	Gibraltar Ent.	598	1943
Rocky Ford	REX	4199 Main St.		650	1945
Saguache	CANADA		C.L. Canda Jr.	183	1943
Salida	SALIDA		Atlas Theatres	689	1943
San Luis	LA PLAZA		Chick Kelloff	300	1943
San Luis	SAN LUIS		Slazar & Cooper	350	1943
Segundo	SEGUNDO			100	1947
Sterling	RIALTO		Fox Lincoln Corp.	539	1943
Trinidad	ISIS	114 W. Main St.	Rocco D. Paolo	260	1943
Trinidad	RIALTO	209 W. Main St.		379	1943
Trinidad	STRAND	446 N. Commercial	M.S. Sawaya	525	1943
Valdez	YMCA		Mrs. S. Kelloff		1943
Walsenburg	VALENCIA		Fox Lincoln Thea.	669	1943

Florida

City	Theater	Address	Owner	Showing Mexican Films Since
Immokalee	CARPA		Porfirio G. Olson	1952

City	Theater	Address	Owner	Seats	Showing Mexican Films Since
Key West	MONROE	612 Duval St.		450	1947
Key West	SAN CARLOS				1952
Miami	CAPITOL	310 N. Miami Ave.		1,230	1950
Miami	FLAGLER	313 W. Flagler	Oscar D. Ramírez	725	1952
Miami	TIVOLI	744 W. Flagler St.	Charles Walder	975	1958
Miami	TOWN	265 E. Flagler St.		472	1948
West Tampa	ROYAL		Joe Chamoun	800	1943
Ybor City	CASINO		Joe Chamoun	700	1941

Illinois

City	Theater	Address	Owner	Seats	Showing Mexican Films Since
Chicago	ATLANTIC	26th & Pulaski			
Chicago	CONGRESS (AZTECA, MÉXICO)	Milwakee Ave.			
Chicago	GAYETY	9205 S. Commercial Ave.		823	1952
Chicago	GLOBE	1145 Blue Island Ave.		850	1943
Chicago	JOY	9223 Commerce Ave.		299	1943
Chicago	LAS AMERICAS	Ashland & Madison			
Chicago	MARSHALL	22nd & California St.			
Chicago	SENATE	Madison St.			
Chicago	TAMPICO	Roosevelt & Paulina St.	Abraham Gómez		1952
Chicago	VILLA	1821 S. Loomis Ave.	Henry Erenberg	500	1946
Rock Falls	STRAND			300	1950

Indiana

City	Theater	Address	Owner	Seats	Showing Mexican Films Since
Gary	GARY	475 Broadway		980	1951
Indiana Harbor	BROADWAY	2205 Broadway		440	1943
Medaryville	HARPER				1950

Iowa

City	Theater	Address	Owner	Seats	Showing Mexican Films Since
W. Des Moines	LYRIC	5th & Maple St.		350	1947

Kansas

City	Theater	Address	Owner	Seats	Showing Mexican Films Since
Emporia	K.S.T.C.				1943
Kansas City	TAMPICO				1947
Newton	REX			235	1947
Topeka	BEST				1939
Topeka	KAW	825 N. Kansas		287	1945
Whichita	ROXY	121 W. Douglas		350	1946

Louisiana

City	Theater	Address	Owner	Seats	Showing Mexican Films Since
Carville	CLUB MÉXICO				1939
Carville	MARINE				1947
New Orleans	GARDEN	3312 Magazine St.	H. Greenlin	800	1959

Michigan

City	Theater	Address	Owner	Seats	Showing Mexican Films Since
Detroit	AZTECA	1302 Michigan			1947
Detroit	DALE	Michigan Ave.		504	1946
Detroit	MODEL	3301 Michigan		504	1951
Flint	TILDEN			200	1947
Saginaw	GEM	1221 N. Sixth St.		350	1945

Minnesota

City	Theater	Address	Owner	Seats	Showing Mexican Films Since
St. Paul	NEW RAY	183 Fairfield Ave.		300 seats	1944

Missouri

City	Theater	Address	Owner	Seats	Showing Mexican Films Since
Kansas City	ROANOKE	Summit St.		500	1945
Portageville	MAXON			243	1949
Risco	ALGERIAN			390	1951

Nebraska

City	Theater	Address	Owner	Seats	Showing Mexican Films Since
Imperial	STAR		R.M. Hough	280	1943
Lyman	LYMAN		Goodall Industries	275	1943
Madrid	AMERICAN		Goodall Industries, E.J. Tuey	150	1943
McCook	FOX		Fox/ Nebraska Theatres	1,014	1943
Minitare	ALADDIN		Gordon H. Cary	200	1943
Mitchell	NILE		McMonald Bros. & Bob Spahn	550	1943
Morrill	DELMAR		Midwest Amuse & Realty Co.	250	1943
North Platte	STATE	705 N. Jeffers	Geo. Allen	700	1943
Rushville	PLAINS		D.I. Chapman	350	1943
Scottsbluff	OTO		Gibraltar Ent. & Chas Gilmour	300	1943
Sutherland	STAR		Goodall Industries & Tuey	225	1943
Wauneta	CHATEAU		Dr. F.E. Rider	300	1943

New Mexico

City	Theater	Address	Owner	Seats	Showing Mexican Films Since
Alamogordo	ALAMENTO			360	1943
Alamogordo	WHITE SANDS	798 New York Ave.	R. E. Griffith	384	1943
Albuquerque	MESA	300 Central Ave.		450	1935
Albuquerque	LA SANDIA	1220 S. Third St.			1937
Albuquerque	CHIEF		Albuquerque Theatres Inc.	356	1943
Albuquerque	CORONADO	100 1st St. SW	Claude de Graves	408	1943
Albuquerque	ISLETA				1950
Albuquerque	MISSION	Central Ave.	Interstate Circuit	400	1943
Artesia	OCOTILLO		C.W. Bartlett & Son	550	1943
Artesia	HERMOSA DRIVE IN	201 Hermosa Dr.			1960
Artesia	VALLEY			400	1946
Aztec	AZTEC		E.K. Balone Jr.	250	1943
Belen	CENTRAL		Mrs. Ruth Hicks	150	1943
Belen	CORTEZ			470	1947
Belen	OÑATE	700 Dalies Ave.		300	1943
Belen	ZIA		Graves & Baca	400	1943
Bernalillo	TIGUEZ		Graves & Baca	200	1943
Bernalillo	CORONADO		Urrea & Castillo	200	1943
Carlsbad	CAVERN		R.E. Davis/ Griffith Theatres	440	1943
Carrizozo	LYRIC	. 12th St.	R.A. Walker	200	1943
Champa	KELLY HALL		Mike Kelly	200	1943
Cimarron	NEW		Narciso Frederici	150	1943
Clayton	LUNA		Hubbard & Murphy (Gibralter)	400	1943
Cloudcroft	PAVILLON		T.J. Pittman	300	1943 (summer only)
Clovis	LYCEUM	411 Main St.	R. E. Griffith Theatres	848	1943
Clovis	MESA	206 Main St.		899	1945
Dawson	OPERA HOUSE	Phelps Dodge Corp.		450	1943
Deming	LUNA		R.E. Davis/Griffith Theatres	592	1943
Estancia	STAR		Grace Sturges	180	1943
Española	EL CINE		John C. Wood	125	1943
Española	EL RIO			650	1947
Eunice	LEA		R. E. Griffith	426	1943
Farmington	ALLEN'S		Mrs. Augusta Allen	350	1943
Ft. Sumner	GRANADA		J.W. Allen	150	1943
Gallup	EL MORRO	W. Coal Ave.	H.A. Funk & Wm. Nagle	887	1943
Gallup	NAVAJO		R.E. Davis	900	1943
Gallup	REX		R.E. Davis	500	1943
Glenwood	RITZY		B.B. Oliver	100	1943
Grants	LUX		P.H. Souris	500	1943
Hagerman	UNIVERSAL			130	1947
Hatch	BOHANNON			388	1948
Hatch	MISSION		J.B. McMahan	250	1943
Hot Springs	EL CORTEZ		B.P. McCormick	540	1943
Hurley	TEJO		Silco Theatres, Gibraltar, Gilmour	385	1943
Jal	REX		R.E. Griffith	370	1943
Las Cruces	DEL RIO		Fox New Mexico Theatres	342	1943
Las Cruces	STATE		Fox Inter Mt. Thea.	563	1943
Las Vegas	CORONADO	625 6th Ave.	Fox New Mexico Thea.	733	1943
Las Vegas	KIVA	109 Bridge St.	Fox	400	1943
Las Vegas	McROE				1945
Lordsburg	PALACE		S.E. Allen	300	1943
Los Alamos	HILL			300	1947
Los Pinitos	VICTORY				1947
Magdalena	ARAGON		Mrs. Eleanor Graham	300	1943
Madrid	MADRID HALL		E. M. Kaylor	200	1943
Maxwell	MAXWELL			100	1943
Melrose	RIALTO		G.G. Stahl	225	1943
Mesa Roca	NEW		Jim Thompson	400	1943
Mora	MONTERREY			250	1943

City	Theater	Address	Owner	Seats	Showing Mexican Films Since
Mountainair	PINTO			451	1947
Mountainair	REAL		H.H. Butler	200	1944
Mogollon	RITZY		B.B. Oliver	100	1943
Peñasco	PEÑASCO				1950
Portales	PORTOLA		R.E. Griffith	402	1943
Ranches Taos	EL CORTEZ			324	1954
Raton	EL RATON	115 N. Second St.		500	1943
Raton	SCHULER	141 N. Second St.		739	1948
Reserve	RITZY		B.B. Oliver	100	1943
Roswell	CHAVEZ	105 N. Main St.		477	1945
Roswell	EL CAPITAN	14 N. Main St.	Civic Theatre Inc.	450	1943
Roswell	YUCCA	124 W. 3rd St.	R.E. Griffith, by Lester Dollison	1,140	1944
Roy	MESA		Western Thea., by Lester Dollison	270	1944
Ruidoso	CRYSTAL		T.J. Pittman	200	1944
Santa Fe	BURRO ALLEY	201 San Francisco		550	1949
Santa Fe	LENSIC	210 San Francisco	Salmon Greer Inc., Gibraltar	1,000	1944
Santa Fe	RICO				1949
Santa Rita	EL COBRE		Silco Theatres, Chas Gilmour	317	1943
Santa Rosa	PECOS		Ira Smith	300	1944
Silver City	EL SOL		Silco Theatres, Chas Gilmour	303	1943
Silver City	SILCO			490	1946
Socorro	LOMA		Gibraltar Ent., & Chas Gilmour	365	1943
Springer	ZIA	306 Colbert Ave.	Gibraltar Ent. Inc., by Chas Gilmour	240	1944
Taos	TAOS			350	1945
Tierra Amarilla	VALLEY			250	1947
Tucumcari	ODEON		Hurley & Hurley	500	1944
Tucumcari	PRINCESS		Hurley & Hurley	600	1943
Tererro	DIXIE		A.R. Nelson	200	1944
Tularosa	MUSEUM		A.P. Sitton Jr.	200	1944
Vaughn	STUDIO			300	1945
Vaughn	WEST		L. Dollison, B. Brown Mgr.	220	1944

New York

City	Theater	Address	Owner	Seats	Showing Mexican Films Since
NYC	AMOR	(Brooklyn)	Jeanne Ansell		
NYC	ANTILLAS		Harry Harris		
NYC	ART	1077 Southern Blvd.	Jeanne Ansell	580	1944
NYC	ASTER		Max Cohen		
NYC	ATLANTIC	205 Flatbush Ave.	Harry Harris	997	1950
NYC	AZTECA	1492 Madison Ave.	Jeanne Ansell	530	1948
NYC	BELMONT	123 W. 48th St.	Gilbert Josephson	550	1943
NYC	BORICUA (STAR)	1714 Lexington Ave.	Harry Harris	2,296	1952
NYC	BORINQUEN (JACKSON)	745 Westchester Ave.	Jeanne Ansell	600	1949
NYC	BORO HALL	752 Melrose Ave.	Jeanne Ansell	559	1950
NYC	CARIBE (ARDEN)	878 Columbus Ave.	Harry Harris	594	1950
NYC	COLON	504 Columbus Ave.	Harry Harris	600	1950
NYC	COSTELLO	23 Ft. Washington Ave.		590	1948

City	Theater	Address	Owner	Seats	Showing Mexican Films Since
NYC	DEL MAR (GOTHAM)	1576 Broadway	Harry Harris	2,500	1950
NYC	EDISON	2700 Broadway	Max Cohen	600	1950
NYC	HEIGHTS	159 Washington St.	Jeanne Ansell	880	1944
NYC	HISPANO (CAMPOAMOR, CERVANTES)	Fifth and 116th St.		1,500	1934
NYC	ISLA (TIFFANY)	1007 Tiffany St.		582	1944
NYC	LATINO (SAN JOSE)	Fifth and 110th St.			1933
NYC	MANHATTAN	213 Manhattan Ave.	Jeanne Ansell	500	1944
NYC	MARCY	302 Broadway Ave.	Max Cohen	710	
NYC	METROPOLITAN	235 E. 14th St.	Max Cohen		1950
NYC	MUNICIPAL	1714 Madison Ave.		512	1948
NYC	PRESIDENT	827 Westchester Ave.		800	1950
NYC	PROSPECT	851 Prospect Ave.	Max Cohen	2,380	1950
NYC	PUERTO RICO (FORUM)	138th St. & Brook Ave.	Jeanne Ansell	2,200	1948
NYC	SAN JUAN (AUDUBON)	3934 B'Way	Harry Harris	2,600	1950
NYC	STRAND	647 Fulton St.	Harry Harris	2,894	1950
NYC	STUDIO	1931 Broadway Ave.	Max Cohen	560	
NYC	TRIBORO	165 E. 125th St.		571	1950
NYC	WORLD	153 W. 149th St.	Gilbert Josephson		1943

North Carolina

City	Theater	Address	Owner	Seats	Showing Mexican Films Since
Charlotte	LOPEZ				1947

Ohio

City	Theater	Address	Owner	Seats	Showing Mexican Films Since
Leipsic	OHIO (?)	139 Defiance St.		286	1953
Ottawa	HOLLYWOOD	Court St.	Theo. Chifos	515	1953
Toledo	(?)				1953

Oklahoma

City	Theater	Address	Owner	Seats	Showing Mexican Films Since
Oklahoma City	VICTORIA	1901 Classen		806	1950

South Dakota

City	Theater	Address	Owner	Seats	Showing Mexican Films Since
Newell	ARCADE		Raeburn (Portable)	200	1944

Tennessee

City	Theater	Address	Owner	Seats	Showing Mexican Films Since
Memphis	LIGA PANAMERICANA				1949

Texas

City	Theater	Address	Owner	Seats	*Showing Mexican Films Since*
Abernathy	RITA			240	1949
Abilene	GRAND	441 Walnut	G. H. Likins	375	1943
Abilene	STATE				1952
Alamo	ALAMO		A.R. Peña		1938
Alice	IRIS (MANVELL)		Mateo Vela	200	1945
Alice	JACKSON'S TENT		Stout Jackson	500	1939
Alice	RANCH DRIVE IN	Solis Bros.	500 cars		1954
Alice	RIO		T. L. Harville	500	1952
Alice	VELA				1946
Alpine	GRANADA		Frontier Theaters	1,000	1939
Alpine	JOHNNY				1950
Alpine	TIVOLI			430	1946
Alpine	TWIN PEAKS DRIVE IN				1952
Amarillo	RIALTO	313 S. Taylor		692	1948
Amarillo	SKYWAY DRIVE IN		Sam Jacobson	500 cars	1960
Amherst	84 DRIVE IN		E.F. Ray		1960
Anthony	ANTHONY			400	1948
Anthony	JOY				1960
Anthony	NEW-TEX		L.O. McCormick		1943
Anson	LYRIC	N. Commerce	Will Pence	350	1950
Anton	LA HARTE		W.J. Chesher	225	1949
Asherton	NACIONAL		José García		1939
Asherton	SILVA'S	Zaragoza Ave.	Antonio Silva	350	1946
Austin	CAPITOL	120 W. Sixth St.		1,092	1942
Austin	HARLEM	1800 E. 12th St.		260	1946
Austin	IRIS	306 E. Sixth St.	Eddie Joseph	290	1945
Austin	LONG HORN DRIVE IN				1960
Austin	YANK	222 E. Sixth St.	Eddie Joseph	435	1957
Ballinger	PALACE			519	1953
Ballinger	RITZ			450	1945
Balmorhea	LYRIC		C.H. Crenshaw	250	1959
Balmorhea	TEXAS			275	1944
Bay City	FRANKLIN	1704 Sixth St.		441	1952
Bay City	STATE	Main St.		453	1939
Baytown	HERRERA				1946
Beeville	ALTAVISTA		Genaro R. Treviño		1950
Beeville	AZTECA	George West Highway			1944
Beeville	GEM			490	1946
Beeville	RIO		Hall Industries, Inc.	500	1947
Benavides	EMPRESS			360	1944
Benavides	RITA			450	1943
Big Springs	LYRIC	110 E. Third St.		500	1943
Big Springs	QUEEN	206 Main St.		500	1939
Big Springs	RIO	309 NW Fourth		650	1947
Big Wells	AZTECA			350	1944
Big Wells	EL DESPLUMADERO		Wm. C. Buffington		1944
Bishop	RIO			295	1945
Bishop	TEXAS			500	1945
Bracketville	PALACE			226	1941
Brady	PIX			190	1946
Brownfield	RIO		Mrs. Tobe Howze	450	1945
Brownsville	DITTMAN			300	1934
Brownsville	IRIS	1037 Washington St.	D.J. Young	454	1946
Brownsville	EL TIRO	1100 Washington St.	D.J. Young	400	1937
Brownsville	FIESTA DRIVE IN	2950 Southmost Rd.	D. Young		1954
Brownsville	GRANDE	E. Washington St.	Leon Circuit of Dallas	550	1952
Brownsville	MEXICO	1100 Washington St.	D.J. Young	900	1940
Brownsville	VICTORIA	Harrison & 14th	Brady & Ruenes	1,000	1946
Brownsville	QUEEN	1125 S. E. Elizabeth	L.D. Brown	630	1935
Brownwood	TEXAS	205 W. Broadway		300	1946
Bryan	AZTECA				1946

City	Theater	Address	Owner	Seats	Showing Mexican Films Since
Carrizo Springs	MEXICO	Texas St.		350	1943
Carrizo Springs	TEXAS			600	1943
Carrizo Springs	WINTERGARDEN DRIVE IN				1959
Castroville	RAINBOW	Lorenzo St.	Carl P. Anderka	390	1953
Charlotte	LOPEZ				1947
Charlotte	TROPICAL				1944
Clint	CLINT				1945
Coleman	GEM			300	1946
Colorado City	GEM			200	1943
Colorado City	RITZ		Rowley United Thea.	595	1952
Concepción	ALAMO				1950
Concepción	GARCÍA				1947
Corpus Christi	AGNES	1522 Agnes St.		748	1941
Corpus Christi	APOLO	Mrs E.G. Caballero			1953
Corpus Christi	AVALON	127 N. Brownlee	A. González	521	1943
Corpus Christi	BUCCANEER DRIVE IN	Arnulfo González	250 cars		1960
Corpus Christi	GLOBE				1948
Corpus Christi	MELBA	1016 Leopard St.		1,000	1943
Corpus Christi	PANAMERICAN	2937 Ruth St.	A. González	448	1944
Corpus Christi	PORT			748	1947
Corpus Christi	RIO GRANDE				1946
Cotulla	JUNCO				1943
Cotulla	RAMIREZ	Main St.		400	1939
Cotulla	VICTORIA				1945
Crosbyton	EL CHARRO		Wallace Theaters		1953
Crystal City	ALAMEDA		H.A. Daniels	300	1949
Crystal City	GUILD		H.A. Daniels	575	1943
Crystal City	IDEAL				1941
Crystal City	LUNA	W. Sabine St.	Ignacio Luna	550	1946
Crystal City	NACIONAL			300	1943
Cuero	TROT	129 E. Main St.		440	1941
D'Harris	TEXAS				1944
Dallas	COLONIA			400	1939
Dallas	EAGLE		Ned M. Edwards	800	1953
Dallas	EL PATIO				1943
Dallas	PANAMERICANO	3104 Maple	J.J. Rodríguez	350	1943
Dallas	VARSITY	6815 Snider Plaza	Mr. Scott		1936
DeHanis	TEXAS		George E. Waites		1944
Del Rio	PRINCESS			486	1943
Del Rio	RIO	Main St.		400	1947
Del Rio	RITA			860	1943
Del Rio	TEXAS			430	1943
Denton	T.S.C.W.				1944
Devine	MAJESTIC			250	1944
Dilley	ANAHUAC		Gustavo Lavenant García		1943
Dilley	DILLEY				1959
Dilley	HAYDE		G. Lavenant García	300	1948
Dilley	MURILLO		A.R. Peña	250	1956
Dilley	ROCQUE	Main St.		200	1946
Dimmitt	CARLILE		H.H. Carlile		1953
Donna	CHAPULTEPEC		Candelario Muñoz	315	1938
Donna	EL PATIO			400	1946
Donna	PALMA		Albert Womble		1949
Donna	PALACIO		Miguel Benítez		1950
Donna	REY		Manuel M. Womble		1955
Donna	RIO		Albert Womble	490	1939
Eagle Pass	AZTEC	398 Main St.	400		1944
Eagle Pass	CENIZO DRIVE IN		Sam Schwartz		1956
Eagle Pass	IRIS		E.L. Walter	700	1960
Eagle Pass	RIVERA				1946
Eagle Pass	YOLANDA	Main St.	Sam Schwartz	350	1939

City	Theater	Address	Owner	Seats	Showing Mexican Films Since
Earth	EARTH			318	1949
Earth	LYRIC		E.T. Borum	200	1947
Edcouch	TEXAS		Miguel Benítez	300	1939
Eden	LINDA				1948
Edinburg	ALAMEDA		Miguel Benítez, Jr.	866	1952
Edinburg	AZTECA	214 E. Cano	c.e. Montague	560	1939
Edinburg	EL PATIO DRIVE IN		Fred Crowson		1956
Edinburg	JUAREZ	222 E. Harriman	Mrs. B.M. Sohn	400	1940
Edinburg	ROXY		Miguel Benítez	600	1946
El Campo	LIBERTY		Long Theaters, Inc.	318	1945
El Campo	NORMANA	Main St.	Rubin Frels	750	1939
El Paso	ALCÁZAR		Calderón & Salas Porras	800	1919
El Paso	AZCÁRATE DRIVE IN				1957
El Paso	BRONCO DRIVE IN				1957
El Paso	COLON	507 El Paso St.	Rafael Calderón	750	1921
El Paso	DEL RIO	3031 Alameda Ave.	B.F. Van Horne		1956
El Paso	ESTRELLA		Silvio Lacoma		1924
El Paso	EUREKA				1919
El Paso	IRIS				1919
El Paso	MISSION	3031 Alameda	James Dodd	585	1950
El Paso	REX				1919
El Paso	TRAIL DRIVE IN	6031 Conley Rd.	Leon Bernstein.	350 cars	1953
Elgin	ELGIN		Dale Wilson	200	1953
Elgin	ELTEX				1946
Elsa	ALAMEDA (BALLI, ROXY)		M. Benítez	350	1943
Elsa	PARIS (ELSA)			285	1946
Elsa	SKY VUE DRIVE IN		Miguel Benitez		1957
Elsa	TROPIC		H. Edwin Harris	740	1950
Encinal	PEREZ			200	1944
Encinal	RIO				1953
Encino	FOX				1950
Escobares	RAU-CON DRIVE IN	Ravel Peña	150 cars		1952
Fabens	RIO		Roy Pringle	400	1944
Fabens	TROPICAL		Inez García		1953
Falfurrias	ALAMEDA		M.H. Taulbee/ Stout Jackson	500	1948
Falfurrias	CACTUS	Main St.	R.N. Smith	425	1947
Falfurrias	JACKSON'S TENT		Stout Jackson	400	1942
Floresville	GEM			230	1946
Floresville	PARKER TENT				1953
Floydada	RITZ			200	1953
Fort Davis	APACHE			250	1948
Fort Hancock	VALLEY		Orin J. Sears	200	1953
Fort Stockton	GRAND			312	1945
Fort Stockton	TRAIL DRIVE IN		Frontier Theaters	350 cars	1948
Fort Worth	IDEAL	1408 Main St.		450	1944
Fort Worth	MAJESTIC	1101 Commerce St.		1,350	
Fort Worth	MARINE	1438 N. Main St.		500	1945
Fort Worth	ROSE			400	1944
Freeport	FREEPORT			500	1944
Galveston	AZTECA		Roy Fiedel	200	1944
Galveston	ENCANTO		C. López	200	1954
Galveston	QUEEN	2107 Market St.		790	1944
Galveston	REY				1960
Galveston	TREMONT	409 Tremont		524	1944
Ganado	GANADO		Long Theaters, Inc.	322	1953
Georgetown	RITZ		Theater Enterprises, Inc.	306	1953
Goliad	GOLIAD	Main St.		500	1943
Gonzales	CRYSTAL		Theater Enterprises, Inc.	550	1953
Gonzalez	PIX			292	1944
Grand Falls	FALLS			400	1944
Granger	GRAND	Main St.		375	1944
Gregory	VALENCIA				1949
Hale Center	RITZ		J.B. Prather	300	1949

City	Theater	Address	Owner	Seats	Showing Mexican Films Since
Hargill	HARGILL				1948
Harlingen	AZTECA	472 S. F St.		600	1946
Harlingen	GRANDE	507 N. Harrison	Interstate Circuit	700	1942
Harlingen	ROYAL				1940
Harlingen	STRAND	111 S. Jackson		400	1941
Haskell	RITA			325	1946
Hearne	SPARKS TENT				1958
Hebbronville	CASINO		J.G. Long	350	1943
Hebbronville	EL RANCHO		J.G. Long		1954
Hebbronville	LONGHORN DRIVE IN		Gustavo A. Vásquez		1958
Hebbronville	TEXAS			430	1952
Hebbronville	TITO'S DRIVE IN		Tito Muñoz		1954
Hereford	TEXAS		Theater Enterprises, Inc.	588	1950
Hondo	PARK		R.L. Jennings	250	1944
Hondo	RAYE			520	1939
Houston	AZTECA	1809 Congress	Fco. Torres	400	1937
Houston	IRIS	612 Travis St.		900	1943
Houston	JOY				1944
Houston	PALACE			940	1943
Houston	RITZ	911 Preston Ave.	F. Fletcher	900	1946
Houston	RIVER OAKS	2009 W. Gray		972	1946
Idalou	CARPA				1950
Idalou	LOU		Truett Fulcher	600	1953
Ingleside	MUSTANG				1949
Junction	BROYLES				1945
Karnes City	KARNES			298	1943
Karnes City	VIC		Dave Smason	300	1949
Kenedy	MONSIVAIS TENT			350	1943
Kingsville	IRIS				1946
Kingsville	HI-WAY DRIVE IN	Chester Kyle	250 cars		1950
Kingsville	JACKSON'S TENT	804 E. Alice	S. Jackson	600	1939
Kingsville	RANCHO DRIVE IN				1954
Knott	KNOTT TENT				1951
Knox City	TEXAS			380	1949
La Feria	EL PATIO		Condron	500	1942
La Feria	ROYAL		Womble Bros.	250	1944
La Gloria	GARCIA				1952
La Grulla	GUERRA				1945
La Pryor	DELGADO	(portable house)		200	1946
La Pryor	LUNA				1943
La Villa	BALLI		A.B. Balli		1944
Lamesa	ALAMEDA		John A. Flache	380	1947
Lamesa	FIESTA DRIVE IN		J. A. Flache	300 cars	1956
Lampasas	RIO			350	1944
Laredo	AZTECA	313 Lincoln	Rowley United Theaters	400	1939
Laredo	BUENOS AIRES		G. Gallegos	650	1946
Laredo	MÉXICO	1313 Sta. María	Rowley United	400	1939
Laredo	PLAZA		Rowley United Thea.	1,600	1960
Laredo	EL RANCHO DRIVE IN		Rowley United	350 cars	1950
Laredo	RIALTO	1216 Hidalgo		500	1948
Laredo	ROYAL	1211 Hidalgo		1,000	1943
Laredo	TIVOLI (old STRAND)	510 Flores		930	1943
Laredo	TOWER DRIVE IN		Arnulfo Gonzalez	300 cars	1950
Levelland	EL CHARRO		Wallace Theaters, Inc.		1953
Levelland	OLD ROSE		Wallace Theaters, Inc.	200	1952
Littlefield	RIO		W.J. Chesher	400	1949
Littlefield	RITZ			420	1952
Lockhart	AZTECA				1954
Lockhart	PIX			261	1944
Lockney	MESA		J.B. Seale		1953
Loraine	LOREX		Percy Bond	375	1946
Lorenzo	WALLACE		Wallace Theaters, Inc.	185	1953

City	Theater	Address	Owner	Seats	*Showing Mexican Films Since*
Los Fresnos	NACIONAL (GUADALUPE)		Samuel Tijerina		1947
Loving	APACHE				1950
Lubbock	EL CAPITAN		Hiram Parks	750	1952
Lubbock	JACKSON'S TENT				1940
Lubbock	LLANOS	1419 Ave.G	Hiram Parks	500	1943
Lubbock	LONE STAR DRIVE IN		Hiram Parks		1958
Lubbock	PLAINS	717 Broadway	Hiram Parks	300	1954
Luling	TEX			325	1946
Lyford	LACOMA		V.H. Craig	270	1946
Malakoff	DODD				1939
Marfa	MARFA DRIVE IN		Frontier Thea.	211 cars	1960
Marfa	PALACE		Frontier Theaters	475	1953
Marfa	TEXAS			350	1943
Marlin	FALLS	357 Live Oak	Homer E. Walters	303	1953
Mathis	AZTECA		W.H. Hendricks	400	1943
McAllen	MÉXICO (AZTECA)	200 S. Guerra St.		600	1939
McAllen	EL REY	311 S. 17th St.	Interstate Circuit	684	1947
McAllen	FIESTA DRIVE IN		H.C. Gunter		1956
McAllen	MEXICO		E.R. Ruenes	400	1949
Melvin	MELBA		300		1949
Menard	MISSION			500	1944
Mercedes	RIO		Interstate Circuit	630	1935
Midland	JUAREZ				1946
Midland	TROPICAL		José Suarez	200	1951
Mirando City	MIRANDO				1945
Mirando City	TRINITY			200	1944
Mission	BUCKHORN DRIVE IN	Highway 83	Ruenes&Izaguirre		1959
Mission	CARPA CONCORDIA		Raúl Salinas		1938
Mission	LOMITA				1937
Mission	REX	507 Conway St.	E. Izaguirre	600	1942
Mission	RIO	516 Doherty	Enrique Flores	600	1945
Monte Alto	ROLO				1948
Mooring	PARKER TENT				1953
Morton	WALLACE		Wallace Theaters, Inc.	350	1952
Muleshoe	EL CHARRO				1953
Munday	ROY		P.V. Williams		1947
Natalia	AZTECA				1947
New Braunfels	CAPITOL	Main Plaza	Rubin Frels	700	1942
New Braunfels	COLE			450	1944
New Braunfels	PEÑA	157 W. San Antonio		300	1946
New Braunfels	REX			450	1939
New Gulf	TEXAS			400	1940
New Home	NEW HOME		Estes Burgamy		1953
New Home	PARKER'S TENT				1952
Nixon	NIXON	Main St.	450		1953
Odem	ODEM			336	1947
Odessa	AZTEC		c.e. Walters		1953
Odessa	EL MEXICANO	818 Humble Ave.	Suarez	150	1951
Odessa	S & S				1949
Oilton	LAUREL				1946
Olton	ALAMEDA				1952
Orange Grove	COZY			176	1944
Orange Grove	STAR	Main St.		216	1946
Ozona	PALACE				1944
Palacios	GRANADA			800	1944
Palacios	HOLLYWOOD			400	1953
Pearsall	IDEAL		Frank Treviño	400	1943
Pearsall	RIO			300	1944
Pecos	CACTUS		Frontier Theaters	400	1953
Pecos	FUENTES				1951
Pecos	PECOS			375	1943
Pecos	RIO				1952

City	Theater	Address	Owner	Seats	Showing Mexican Films Since
Petersburg	WALLACE		Wallace Theaters, Inc.	180	1953
Pharr	CACTUS DRIVE IN		Interstate Circuit		1948
Pharr	EL CAPITAN	Cage Blvd.	Miguel Benítez, Jr.	250	1954
Pharr	ESPAÑA		Brewer & Britten	400	1942
Plainview	TEXAS	630 Broadway		539	1953
Pleasanton	JUAREZ				1946
Pleasanton	PLESTEX		Glasscock Theaters	300	1954
Port Arthur	MAJESTIC	1520 Hosuton		438	1945
Port Arthur	PEOPLE'S	425 Proctor		926	1953
Port Arthur	VALENCIA				1939
Port Isabel	GRANADA		Ramiro T. Ramírez	250	1945
Port Isabel	ROXY		Ramiro T. Ramírez		1946
Port Lavaca	LONG			223	1944
Port Lavaca	PORT LAVACA		Long Theaters, Inc.	365	1953
Poteet	AVON			350	1953
Poteet	JUAREZ				1944
Premont	EL TROPICO		Manuel Peña	550	1950
Premont	REX	Main St.		300	1947
Presidio	PRESIDIO		Clyde Vaught	240	1948
Presidio	RIO			250	1940
Ralls	EL CHARRO		Wallace Theaters, Inc.		1952
Raymondville	CORRAL DRIVE IN				1956
Raymondville	MEXICO	6th & Main St.	María C. Gómez	380	1940
Raymondville	RAMON	Main St.	Texas Border Thea.	480	1958
Raymondville	REY		Ruenes/García		1956
Raymondville	RIO	Main St.		300	1948
Refugio	RIG			430	1944
Rio Grande City	AZTECA		Miguel F. García	270	1942
Rio Grande City	DREAMLAND			400	1939
Rio Grande City	GARMON		M.F. García	500	1944
Rio Grande City	H & H DRIVE IN				1954
Rio Grande City	HUT		M.F. García	500	1949
Rio Grande City	MEXICO		M.F. García	500	1956
Rio Hondo	RIO (IDEAL, REX)		F.R. Cañas	250	1945
Roaring Springs	SPRING		216		1952
Robstown	AIRPORT DRIVE IN				1959
Robstown	JACKSON'S TENT		Stout Jackson	600	1935
Robstown	SAN PEDRO				1955
Rochester	REX		R.A. Greenwade	225	1950
Rockport	SURF		Long Theaters, Inc.		1953
Rock Springs	ANGORA			400	1950
Rock Springs	O. & S.				1939
Roma	ROMA		Ernesto Ramírez	325	1942
Ropesville	ROPES		Estes Burgamy		1953
Rosenberg	STATE			300	1943
Rotan	MAJESTIC			400	1944
Rotan	ROTAN				1952
Round Rock	ROCK			300	1943
Rule	RULE		E.B. Whorton	353	1953
Runge	RUNGE			400	1948
Sabinal	ROSS			285	1944
San Angelo	REX		W.V. Adwell	425	1943
San Angelo	RITA		Rowley United Theaters	300	1946
San Angelo	PALACE		W.V. Adwell		1944
San Antonio	ALAMEDA	318 W. Houston St.	G.A. Lucchese	2,500	1949
San Antonio	EL CAPITAN DRIVE IN				1953
San Antonio	EL CHARRO DRIVE IN				1955
San Antonio	CIRCLE 81 DRIVE IN				1960
San Antonio	EMPIRE	Empire Bldg. (226 N. St. Mary's)		1,200	1957
San Antonio	FIESTA DRIVE IN				1960
San Antonio	FOLLIES		Paul Garza		1948
San Antonio	GUADALUPE	1301 Guadalupe St.	G.A. Lucchese	600	1942

City	Theater	Address	Owner	Seats	Showing Mexican Films Since
San Antonio	MAYA	5045 W. Commerce			1946
San Antonio	NACIONAL	819 N. Commerce St.	G.A. Lucchese	1,000	1920
San Antonio	PROGRESO	1306 Guadalupe St.	Juan, Paul Garza	550	1937
San Antonio	RIO				1948
San Antonio	STATE	209 Main Ave.		1,900	1959
San Antonio	TOWNE TWIN DRIVE IN				1960
San Antonio	ZARAGOZA	815 N. Commerce St.	Sam Lucchese	800	1920
San Benito	JUAREZ	Hidalgo & Landrum St.	Ramón Ruenes	200	1939
San Benito	PALACE		Interstate Circuit	600	1942
San Benito	RUENES	569 W. Robertson	Ramón Ruenes	600	1944
San Diego	REGIS			350	1938
San Diego	RIO			300	1936
San Diego	VICTORIA				1946
San Juan	CARPA JALISCO		A.R. Peña		1938
San Juan	MURILLO		A.R. Peña	430	1941
San Juan	REX			312	1955
San Marcos	HAYS		F.W. Zimmermann	513	1952
San Marcos	PALACE		D.J. McCarthy	500	1957
San Marcos	PLAZA			350	1943
San Marcos	TEXAS		D.J. McCarthy	769	1957
San Perlita	MELBA (REFORMA)		G. Elizondo		1950
San Ygnacio	REX				1947
Sanderson	PRINCESS			364	1939
Santa María	MEXICO		Miguel Benítez	200	1944
Santa Marta	RIO				1950
Santa Rosa	REX (RIO)		Miguel Benítez	300	1944
Seagraves	WALLACE			375	1952
Sebastian	ALAMEDA		E.C. Gómez		1949
Sebastian	FRONTIER (FARMERS)				1947
Seguin	TEXAS	Austin St.		480	1943
Seminole	DRIVE IN		W.E Cox, Jr.		1959
Seminole	PALACE			300	1952
Seymour	RITZ		P.V. Williams	470	1947
Shafter	SHAFTER				1941
Sierra Blanca	BLANCA		A. Morales	200	1944
Sierra Blanca	STATE		G.L. Morales	200	1953
Sinton	CARPA				1940
Sinton	JUAREZ		Francisco Zapata	400	1943
Sinton	ZAPATA				1948
Slaton	PALACE			500	1949
Snyder	RITZ			540	1947
Snyder	TEXAS		Joe L. Love	400	1953
Sonora	HALL		G.H. Hall	250	1944
Sonora	LA VISTA		G.H. Hall	320	1960
Spur	SPUR			429	1945
Stamford	PALACE		Dee Smith	200	1952
Stanton	TEXAS		R.B. Whitaker	300	1944
Sugarland	PALMS		Mart Cole		1953
Sweetwater	AZTECA				1947
Sweetwater	NOLAN	210 Locust		420	1946
Taft	LELAND		Harry J. Ellis	450	1952
Taft	TENT SHOW				1939
Taft	ZARAGOZA		J.G. Long	300	1942
Tahoka	LYNN		W.B. Blankenship	320	1947
Tahoka	WALLACE		Blankenship	400	1952
Taylor	DON		Rowley United Theaters	408	1949
Taylor	RITA	308 N. Main		500	1946
Temple	RIO			288	1947
Texas City	JEWEL	518 6th St.		498	1945
Three Rivers	AZTECA				1945
Three Rivers	CARPA				1950
Tulia	GAY		Mrs. Howard Hotchkiss	350	1953
Uvalde	RITZ	227 N. Getty		400	1943

City	Theater	Address	Owner	Seats	Showing Mexican Films Since
Uvalde	STARDUST DRIVE IN		Frontier Thea.	400 cars	1959
Uvalde	TEJAS	W. Main St.		521	1946
Van Horn	COMMUNITY			200	1944
Van Horn	SAGE	Lee Welch	350		1952
Verhalen	HARLOW		Harlow & Brown		1953
Victoria	TRINITARIAN HALL				1946
Victoria	UPTOWN			740	1943
Victoria	VENUS		Rubin Frels		1952
Victoria	VICTORIA	206 E. Constitution	600		1943
Waco	CORONET		Eddie W. Fadal		1953
Waco	FOX	203 S. Third St.		550	1939
Waco	STRAND	518 Austin St.	E.W. Hammer	522	1944
Waxahachie	EMPIRE	337			1947
Weimert	TENT		Tommy Parker		1951
Weslaco	BENITEZ DRIVE IN		Miguel Benítez, Jr.		1956
Weslaco	IRIS		Miguel Benítez	400	1946
Weslaco	NACIONAL	108 N. Texas St.	Miguel Benítez	800	1935
Weslaco	RITZ	325 Texas St.	W.H. Durham	600	1959
Wharton	QUEEN			428	1952
Wharton	RIO	Main St.		450	1943
Wichita Falls	AZTECA			200	1947
Wichita Falls	ROXY	1523 Monroe	300		1946
Wilson	ALTO				1953
Woodsboro	ARCADIA	Main St.		450	1944
Yorktown	L'ARCADE			400	1943
Yorktown	YORK	Main St.		500	1953
Ysleta	TEXAS		300		1946
Zapata	REX		Humberto González	300	1944

Utah

City	Theater	Address	Owner	Seats	Showing Mexican Films Since
Bingham Can.	PRINCESS	496 Main St.		400	1944
Salt Lake	CLUB MÉXICO				1947

Wisconsin

City	Theater	Address	Owner	Seats	Showing Mexican Films Since
Milwaukee	WORLD	830 S. Sixth St.		850	1946
Racine	DOUGLAS	1639 Douglas Ave.		750	1952

Wyoming

City	Theater	Address	Owner	Seats	Showing Mexican Films Since
Lovell	ARMADA		H. Bischoff	400	1944
Worland	KIRBY		Tom Kerby	350	1944

Notes

1. The Appeal of Mexican Cinema for Hispanics in the United States

1. Clasa-Mohme Papers, Gordon B. Dunlap to Juan Bueno, 27 March 1959. Subsequent endnotes use the abbreviation C.M. Papers.

2. Sergio Valadés Bernal et al. *La lengua española en los Estados Unidos* (Cuba: Editorial Academia, 1997), p. 14.

3. Manuel G. Gonzales. *Mexicanos: A History of Mexicans in the United States* (Bloomington: Indiana University Press, 2000), pp 121, 142.

4. Valadés, p. 11.

5. *La Prensa*, San Antonio, Texas, 26 June 1938.

6. *Cinema Reporter*, 23 October 1943.

7. Constantine Panunzio, *How Mexicans Earn and Live* (Berkeley: University of California), pp. 49, 104. Douglas Monroy, *Rebirth: Mexican Los Angeles from the Great Migration to the Great Depression* (Berkeley: University of California, 1999), p. 173.

8. C. M. Papers, Gordon B. Dunlap to Bob Dunn, 12 March 1957.

9. Emilio García Riera, *Historia documental del cine mexicano* (México: Ediciones Era, 1970), Vol. 2. p. 50; *The Saturday Evening Post*, 22 July 1944; *Cinema Reporter*, 17 March 1951.

10. See, for example: Kimberly Ayn Beckwith "Thomas Jefferson *Stout* Jackson: Texas Strongman, in *Iron Game History*, Vol. 3, No. 2. Also see: *Caller Times*, Corpus Christi, Texas, 15 June 1947.

11. *The Texas Spectator*, 16 August 1946.

12. C.M. Papers, Gordon B.Dunlap to Juan Bueno, 15 June 1959.

13. Manuel G. Gonzales, *Mexicanos: A History of Mexicans in the United States* (Bloomington: Indiana University Press, 2000), pp.171, 173.

14. C.M. Papers, Mrs. R. F. Cañas to Gordon B. Dunlap, 14 July 1956.

15. C.M. Papers, Dunlap to Louis B. Hess, September 18, 1957. Theatre Reports by Eddie Noonan, 9 October 1951.

16. C.M. Papers, Dunlap to Louis B. Hess, 12 October 1953.

17. *El Cinegráfico: Anuario 1944–1945*. Mexico City, pp. 415–416.

18. C.M. Papers. Theater Receipt Records.

19. C.M. Papers, Dunlap to Ed Edwards, 13 October 1944.

20. C.M. Papers, Dunlap to Miss Fay Anthony O'Connor, 2 April 1943.

21. Alex M. Saragoza, *Mexican Cinema in Cold War America, 1940–1958: An Inquiry into the Interface Between Mexico and Mexicans in the United States.* Chicano Political Economy Working Paper Series #108 (Berkeley: University of California) 1983, p. 27.

22. *El Cinegráfico: Anuario 1944–1945*, p. 115.

23. David Maciel interviewed by author, 18 April 1997.

24. Charles Ramírez-Berg, *Cinema of Solitude: A Critical Study of Mexican Film, 1967–1983* (Austin: University of Texas, 1992), p. 115.

25. C.M. Papers, Dunlap to Minnie M. Miller, 20 October 1944.

26. *Cinema Reporter*, 1 February 1947.

27. *The New York Times*, 20 September 1953, sec. X, p. 6.

28. C.M. Papers, Dunlap to Juan Bueno, 21 March 1960.

29. C.M. Papers, ibid.

30. C.M. Papers, Dunlap to Juan Bueno, 4 November 1959.

31. C.M. Papers, ibid.

32. C.M. Papers, Frank M. Fletcher to Gordon B. Dunlap, 18 November 1955.

33. Alfonso Rodríguez, "Crossing Borders from the Beginning," in William S. Penn, Ed., *As We Are Now, Mixblood Essays on Race and Identity* (Berkeley: University of California Press, 1997), pp 57–59.

34. *The New York Times*, 8 March 1959, sec X, p. 7.

35. C.M. Papers, Dunlap to Juan Bueno, 27 March 1959.

36. Gaizka S. de Usabel, *The High Noon of American Films in Latin America* (Ann Arbor, Michigan: UMI Research Press, 1982), p. 141.

37. *Los Angeles Times*, 18 November 1947.

38. C.M. Papers, Dunalp to Max Ehrenreich, 26 January 1953.

39. Tomás Pérez Turrent. *Alfredo Ripstein, productor* (México: Universidad de Guadalajara, 2003), p. 16.

40. Rogelio Agrasánchez, Jr., *Miguel Zacarías: creador*

de estrellas (México: Archivo Fílmico Agrasánchez, Universidad de Guadalajara, 2000), pp 91–96.

41. C.M. Papers, Dunlap to Max Ehrenreich, 5 June 1958.

42. *Daily News*, Los Angeles, California, 24 August 1948.

43. C.M. Papers, Box Office Statements for *El derecho de nacer.*

44. C.M. papers, Dunlap to the Denton College, 11 December 1944.

45. C.M. Papers, Dunlap to Harry E. Fulgham, 7 December 1944.

46. C.M. Papers, Dunlap to Bob Abbuehl, 11 December 1957.

47. C.M. Papers, Theater Records, Church Accounts.

48. C.M. Papers, Dunlap to Sister Carmen of the Sacred Heart Convent, 15 February 1957. For the Church's official censorship listing, see *Apreciaciones: catálogo de los espectáculos censurados por la Legión Mexicana de la Decencia, de 1931 a 1958*. México, D.F., 1959.

49. C.M. Papers, Dunlap to Juan Bueno, 15 January 1959.

50. C.M. Papers, Dunlap to Louis B. Hess, 1 March 1956.

51. C.M. Papers. Theater Reports by Eddie Noonan, 5 and 9 October 1951.

52. C.M. Papers, ibid.

53. C.M. Papers, ibid.

54. *www.farmworkers.orj/bracentx.html* (as consulted on 22 April 2004).

55. *Southwestern Historical Quarterly,* vol. LXXV, No. 1, July 1981, p. 59.

56. *La Prensa*, San Antonio, Texas, 15 September 1935.

57. C.M. Papers, Robert Jones to Gordon B. Dunlap, 5 March 1944.

58. C.M. Papers, ibid. See also *The Daily Texan*, Austin, Texas, 10 September 1944.

59. *La Prensa*, 27 August 1939. *Mundo Cinematográfico,* June 1934.

60. C.M. Papers, Advertising, Box Office Tonic.

61. C.M. Papers, Dunlap to Ehrenreich, 4 March 1950. 70 C.M. Papers, Dunlap to Gustav Mohme (Reply on hand-written note), 27 November 1955.

62. C.M. Papers, Dunlap to Louis B. Hess, 9 November 1953.

63. C.M. Papers, Dunlap to Louis B. Hess, 19 January 1954.

64. C.M. Papers, Dunlap to Prof. Holden B. Bickford, 13 March 1959.

65. *Daily News*, 18 December 1946.

66. C.M. Papers, Dunlap to Juan Bueno, 29 September 1959.

67. C.M. Papers, Dunlap to Juan Bueno, 22 March 1960.

68. C.M. Papers, Dunlap to Juan Bueno, 15 January 1959.

69. Carlos Hinojosa interviewed by author, 10 October 2004.

71. *Southwestern Historical Quarterly*, vol. LXXXV, No. 1, July 1981, p. 63.

72. *The Texas Spectator*, 16 August 1946.

73. C.M. Papers, Dunlap to J.B. Arthur, 13 November 1944.

74. C.M. Papers, Dunlap to Juan Bueno, 2 October 1958.

75. C.M. Papers, Dunlap to Juan Bueno, 26 December 1958.

76. C.M. Papers, Dunlap to John W. Bauer, 27 March 1953. *La Novela Cinegráfica*, September 1952.

77. C.M. Papers, Dunlap to Louis B. Hess, 12 July 1954.

78. C.M. Papers, James A. Card to Gordon B. Dunlap, 23 August 1945.

79. C.M. Papers, Dunlap to Louis B. Hess, 2 June 1954.

80. C.M. Papers, Gustav Mohme to Gordon B. Dunlap, 19 February 1947.

81. C.M. Papers, Dunlap to Juan Bueno, 1 April 1960.

82. C.M. Papers, Dunlap to Juan Bueno, 15 April 1960.

83. C.M. Papers, Dunlap to Juan Bueno, 11 March 1960.

84. C.M. Papers, Dunlap to M. J. Dowling, 28 October 1944.

85. C.M. Papers, Dunlap to J. B. Arthur, 13 November 1944.

86. C.M. Papers, Dunlap to Louis B. Hess, 12 December 1957.

87. C.M. Papers, Advertising, Box Office Tonic.

88. Virginia E. Sánchez Korrol, *From Colonia to Community: The History of Puerto Ricans in New York City* (Berkeley: University of California, 1994), p. 76. *Alianza Hispano-Americana*, Tucson, Arizona, 1950.

89. *La Novela Cinegráfica*, September 1950.

90. Miguel Contreras Torres, *El libro negro del cine mexicano* (México: Author's edition, 1960), p. 264.

91. *Cinema Reporter*, 17 March 1951, pp. 39–45. This article contains several interesting photographs of the offices of Clasa-Mohme in Los Angeles, California.

92. C.M. Papers, Memorandum of the History of Distribution of Mexican Pictures in the United States as Known to Richard H. Dunlap, pp 1–2.

93. C.M. Papers, Gordon B. Dunlap to E. W. Hammer, 6 November 1944.

94. C.M. Papers, Memorandum of the History ... p. 8. Richard H. Dunlap interviewed by author. 1 October 1991.

95. See Amy B. Beer's dissertation *From the Bronx to Brooklyn: Spanish-Language Movie Theaters and Their Audiences in New York City, 1930–1999* (Illinois: Northwestern University, 2001), Chapter 2.

96. Fernando J. Obledo interviewed by author, 16 November 2003.

97. Alfonso Rosas Priego Rosales, *La intervención del Estado en la industria cinematográfica*. Thesis (México: UNAM, 1970), pp 127–131.

2. Los Angeles, California

1. Manuel G. Gonzales. *Mexicanos: A History of Mexicans in the United States* (Bloomington: Indiana University Press, 2000), pp 146–147.

2. José Juan Tablada. "Los mexicanos en Norteamérica," *Excélsior*, México City, 18 February 1921.

2. *La Opinión*, Los Angeles, California, 2 and 29 November 1926; 28 January 1927.

3. *La Opinión*, 19 October; 1926.

4. *La Opinión*, ibid. 18 and 23 March 1928.

5. *La Opinión*, 31 March; 1,7, and 13 April 1928.

6. Juan B. Heinink and Robert G. Dickson. *Cita en Hollywood* (Bilbao: Ediciones Mensajero, 1990), p. 26.

7. Juan B. Heinink, ibid.

8. *La Opinión*, 14 May 1932.

9. *La Opinión*, 22 May 1932.

10. *Mundo Cinematográfico* (México City), March 1934.

11. *La Opinión*, 14 September 1934.

12. *La Opinión*, 15 August 1937.

13. Chris Strachwitz, *Lydia Mendoza: A Family Autobiography* (Houston: Arte Público Press, 1993), p. 137.

14. Chris Strachwitz, ibid. p. 346.

15. Francisco M. Peredo, *Cine e Historia: Discurso Histórico y Producción Cinematográfica, 1940–1952*, (Ph.D. Dissertation: UNAM, 2000), p. 490.

16. Francisco M. Peredo, ibid. p. 339.

17. *La Opinión*, 13 September 1942.

18. *La Opinión*, 11 September 1943.

19. *El Cine Gráfico: Anuario 1943–1944* (México City), p. 415.

20. *La Opinión*, 22, 29 September 1946.

21. *Cinema Reporter* (México City), 1 February 1947.

22. *La Opinión*, 26 December 1948.

23. *La Novela Cinegráfica* (Los Angeles, California), February 1949.

24. Diana Negrete, *Jorge Negrete: biografía autorizada* (México: Ed. Diana, 1987), pp. 356–369.

25. *La Novela Cinegráfica*, June 1952.

26. Eduardo Quezada, *KMEX-TV Comienzos*. *www.eduardo.quezada.net/album/kmex/notas.htm* (as consulted on 24 February 2004).

27. *Cinema Reporter*, 8 March 1952.

28. *Cinema Reporter*, ibid.

29. *Cinema Reporter*, 21 March 1956; 20 June 1956.

30. Clasa-Mohme Papers. Gordon B. Dunlap to Miguel Benítez, Jr., 24 May 1960. *La Novela Cinegráfica*, June 1959.

31. *La Opinión*, 5 July 1964.

32. *The Mexican Film Industry on the World* (México: Banco Nacional Cinematográfico, 1975), p. 19.

3. Pomona Valley, California

1. T. H. Watkins, *California: An Illustrated History* (New York: American Legacy Press, 1983), p. 414.

2. Rob Hughes, *Where is Home? www.liferaft.com* (as consulted on 11 July 2004).

3. *El Espectador*, Pomona, California, 19 November 1937.

4. *El Espectador*, 11 November 1938.

5. *El Espectador*, 1 July 1938.

6. *El Espectador*, 23 December 1938.

7. *El Espectador*, 17 February 1939.

8. *El Espectador*, ibid.

9. *El Espectador*, ibid.

10. *El Espectador*, 3 March 1939.

11. *El Espectador*, 11 June 1943.

12. *El Espectador*, 13 December 1946.

13. Paul S. Taylor, "Mexican Labor in the Calumet Region," in *Forging a Community: The Latino Experience in Northwest Indiana, 1919–1975* (Chicago: Cattails Press, 1987), p. 67. Estela S. De la Fuente interviewed by author, 21 October 2004.

14. *El Espectador*, 1 March 1946.

15. "Corona building falling to mall, and with it memories of another day." Unidentified newspaper (13 January 1970), kept at the Corona Public Library. Corona, California.

16. *El Espectador*, 11 May 1956.

17. *El Espectador*, 24 October 1958.

4. New York City

1. *The New York Times Film Reviews: 1933–1940*. Subsequent notes from this source are cited: *NYTFR*. Ruth Glasser, *My Music is my Flag: Puerto Rican Musicians and Their New York Communities, 1917–1940* (Berkeley: University of California Press, 1995), p. 96.

2. *Estreno de la película Cuesta Abajo ... www.gardelweb.com* (as consulted on 6 January 2004).

3. *Cinema Reporter* (México City), 22 May 1948. Subsequent notes from this source are cited: *CR*.

4. *Mundo Cinematográfico* (México City), June 1934.

5. *NYTFR*, 10 October 1934.

6. *NYTFR*, 24 September 1940.

7. *NYTFR*, 6 April 1935.

8. *NYTFR*, 9 April 1938.

9. *NYTFR*, 24 April 1943.

10. *The New York Times*, 4 April 1943. Subsequent notes from this source are cited *NYT*.

11. *NYTFR*, 7 August 1943; 7 November 1944.

12. *CR*, 12 March 1947.

13. *Bronx Times Reporter* (New York City), 16 November 2000.

14. *El Cine Gráfico: Anuario 1944–1945* (México City), p. 406.

15. Amy Barnes Beer, *From the Bronx to Brooklyn: Spanish-Language Movie Theaters and Their Audiences in New York City, 1930–1999* (Doctoral dissertation: Northwestern University, Illinois, 2001), p. 75.

16. *CR*, 10 February 1945.

17. *CR*, 4 December 1948.

18. *CR*, 3 December 1949.

19. *CR*, 17 December 1949.

20. *CR*, 25 March 1950.

21. *CR*, 15 April 1950.

22. Carl J. Mora. "Reminiscences of Mexican Movies in New York City." Unpublished manuscript (2005). pp. 2–3. Agrasanchez Film Archive.

23. *CR*, 13 January 1951.

24. *CR*, 9 February 1952.

25. Amy B. Beer, *From the Bronx to Brooklyn*, pp. 76–77.

26. Amy B. Beer, *From the Bronx to Brooklyn*, pp. 76–77.

27. *CR*, 5 July 1952. *NYT*, 21 December 1955.

28. Fernando J. Obledo interviewed by author, 21 June 2004.

29. Amy B. Beer, *From the Bronx to Brooklyn*, p. 89.

30. *CR*, 22 May 1948; 20 October 1951. See also *NYT*, 8 March 1959.
31. *Columbia Pictures Corp.* Film catalog, ca. 1970.

5. El Paso, Texas

1. *La República* (El Paso, Texas), 1 November 1919.
2. *La República*, 3 November 1919.
3. *La Patria* (El Paso, Texas), 7, 21, and 30 April 1921; 9, 14, and 28 May 1921.
4. *La Patria*, 11 October 1924.
5. *Mundo Cinematográfico* (Mexico City), June 1930, p. 14.
6. *El Continental* (El Paso, Texas), 6 May 1931; 21, 29 November 1931.
7. *El Continental*, 24 November 1931.
8. *El Continental*, August; September; November; December 1935; September; October 1936.
9. Clasa-Mohme Papers. Theater Receipt Records, Teatro Colón. Subsequent notes from this source are cited: C.M. Papers.
10. C.M. Papers, Gordon B. Dunlap to Juan Bueno, 2 December 1958.
11. C.M. Papers, ibid. 26 December 1958; 30 May 1960.
12. C.M. Papers. Theater Receipt Records. Azcárate Drive-In.
13. Denise Chávez, *Loving Pedro Infante* (New York: Farrar, Straus and Giroux, 2001), pp 3–4, 7, 14.
14. I. C. Jarvie, *Movies and Society* (New York: Basic Books, Inc., 1970), p. 106.
15. C.M. Papers, Dunlap to Juan Bueno, 8 December 1959; 9 January 1960.
16. C.M. Papers. Theater Receipt Records. Teatro Colón.
17. C.M. Papers, ibid.

6. San Antonio, Texas

1. Daniel D. Arreola, *Tejano South Texas: A Mexican American Cultural Province* (Austin: University of Texas Press, 2002), pp. 50, 136.
2. Richard A. García, *Rise of Mexican American Middle Class: San Antonio, 1929–1941* (College Station: Texas A&M University Press, 1990), p. 78.
3. *San Antonio Express* (San Antonio, Texas), 20 June 1926.
4. *San Antonio Express,* ibid. See also *La Prensa* (San Antonio, Texas), 23 September 1921.
5. Nicolas Kanellos, *A History of Hispanic Theatre in the United States: Origins to 1940* (Austin: University of Texas Press, 1990), pp 78–79.
6. *La Prensa*, February, November 1921.
7. *San Antonio Express*, 20 June 1926.
8. *La Prensa*, 28 July, 8 November 1920; 8 January 1922.
9. *La Prensa*, 24 April, 19 September 1921.
10. *La Prensa*, 20, 27 October 1921.
11. *La Prensa*, 25 December 1924.
12. *La Prensa*, 9 June 1929.

13. Interview with G.J. Lucchese, 19 August 1982, The Institute of Texan Cultures, Oral History Program. Since 1945, Gaetano's brothers, Frank and Sam II, operated movie houses for African-Americans in Austin and Dallas, Texas. See Dan Streible, "The Harlem Theater: Black Film Exhibition in Austin, Texas: 1920–1973, in Gregory A. Waller, ed., *Moviegoing in America* (Malden, Massachusetts: Blackwell Publishers, 2002), pp. 268–278.
14. *Mundo Cinematográfico* (Mexico City), June 1934.
15. *La Prensa*, 22 May 1932.
16. *La Prensa*, 26 November 1933; 22 November 1936.
17. *La Prensa,* 23 June 1937.
18. *La Prensa,* 9 April 1939.
19. *La Prensa,* 24 March 1938.
20. *La Prensa,* 3 December 1939.
21. *La Prensa,* 23 December 1939.
22. *La Prensa*, 2, 3 July 1942. *Tonantzin, Chicano Arts in San Antonio,* January 1984.
23. *La Prensa,* 21 November 1938.
24. Clasa-Mohme Papers, Teatro Progreso Folder, Paul Garza to Gordon B. Dunlap, 20 March 1947.
25. C.M. Papers, Theater Receipt Records, Teatro Maya.
26. C.M. Papers, Theater Receipt Records, Teatro Follies.
27. *La Prensa,* 23 February 1949.
28. *La Prensa,* 3 March 1949.
29. *La Prensa,* 13 March 1949.
30. The naming of San Antonio's Alameda was inspired in turn by a México City theater of the same name, which opened in 1936 and was located across from the Alameda Park, in downtown.
31. C.M. Papers, Reports 1947.
32. C.M. Papers, Gordon B. Dunlap to Juan Bueno, 16 April, 5 May 1959.
33. C.M. Papers, Dunlap to Juan Bueno, 11 June 1959.
34. C.M. Papers, ibid.
35. C.M. Papers, 20 October, 16 November 1959.
36. C.M. Papers, 26 December 1959.
37. C.M. Papers, 22 January 1960.
38. C.M. Papers, ibid.
39. C.M. Papers, 19 May 1960.
40. C.M. Papers. Advertising. Box Office Tonic. *El derecho de nacer.*
41. C.M. Papers, Box Office Statements, *El derecho de nacer.*
42. C.M. Papers, Dunlap to Louis Hess, 23 November 1957.
43. C.M. Papers, ibid.
44. C.M. Papers, Juan Bueno to Gordon B. Dunlap, 4 December 1958.
45. C.M. Papers, Zaragoza Amusement Co. Folder.
46. C.M. Papers, Dunlap to Juan Bueno, 17, 31 October 1959.
47. C.M. Papers, Dunlap to Juan Bueno 24 October 1958.
48. C.M. Papers, *The Wall Street Journal*, 11 December 1957.
49. C.M. Papers, Dunlap to Juan Bueno, 10 November 1958.
50. C.M. Papers, Dunlap to Juan Bueno, 6 August 1959.

51. C.M. Papers, ibid.

52. C.M. Papers, Dunlap to Juan Bueno, 21 April 1960.

53. C.M. Papers, Dunlap to Juan Bueno, 11 June 1959.

54. C.M. Papers, Dunlap to Juan Bueno, 29 January 1960.

55. C.M. Papers, Dunlap to Juan Bueno, 23 March 1960.

56. C.M. Papers, Dunlap to Juan Bueno, 5 March 1960.

57. C.M. Papers, Dunlap to Juan Bueno, 9 January 1960.

58. Arnulfo Arias (Azteca Films manager) interviewed by author. 15 November 2003. "Programa de Re-Inauguración. Teatro Alameda. Miércoles 17 de Enero de 1962," Alameda Theater Folder, San Antonio Public Library, San Antonio, Texas.

59. "Alameda Theater may be demolished," *The San Antonio Light* (San Antonio, Texas), 5 June 1982, p. 9A.

60. "¿Qué pasa con el Cine Alameda?," *El Heraldo* (San Antonio, Texas), 19 March 1987.

61. *San Antonio Express News* (San Antonio, Texas), 7 July 1996, p. 13-A.

7. The Rio Grande Valley

1. *El Puerto de Brownsville* (Brownsville, Texas), 31 July, 23 October 1954.

2. Clasa-Mohme Papers, Gordon B. Dunlap to Juan Bueno, 10 April 1959; Dunlap to Miguel Benitez, Jr., 20 July 1960. Subsequent notes from this source are cited: C.M. Papers.

3. C.M. Papers, Theater Receipt Records. Theaters of the Rio Grande Valley.

4. C.M. Papers, ibid.

5. *La Prensa* (San Antonio, Texas), 19 May 1929. *El Defensor* (Edinburg, Texas), 21 March 1930.

6. *La Prensa*, 28 March 1930.

7. *La Prensa*, January, February, March, 1938. Carlos Hinojosa interviewed by author, 6 December 2003.

8. *McAllen Daily Monitor* (McAllen, Texas), September, October, November 1937.

9. *La Prensa*, 10 March 1938.

10. *La Prensa*, 27 March 1939.

11. C.M. Papers, Gordon B. Dunlap to Miguel Benitez, Jr., 24 March 1960.

12. "The Benitez Theaters," Oral history program, The Museum of Weslaco, Texas.

13. C.M. Papers, Theater Receipt Records, Teatro Nacional (Weslaco).

14. *La Prensa*, 15 February 1939. *Éxito, revista mensual ilustrada*, Weslaco, Texas, 1 April 1940. *The Weslaco News*, 14 March 1946. C.M. Papers, Theater Receipt Records, Teatro Rex (Santa Rosa).

15. C.M. Papers, Dunlap to Juan Bueno, 27 February 1959.

16. C.M. Papers, Dunlap to Juan Bueno, 5 February 1959.

17. C.M. Papers, Folder: Miguel Benitez, Jr. Confidential, 8 August 1952.

18. C.M. Papers, Theater Receipt Records, Teatro Alameda (Edinburg).

19. Carlos Hinojosa interviewed by author, 6 December 2003.

20. *San Benito News* (San Benito, Texas), 30 November 1986.

21. *Valley Evening Monitor* (McAllen, Texas), 18 October 1949.

22. *San Benito News*, 30 November 1986.

23. C.M. Papers, Rex Theater Folder, 1957.

24. C.M. Papers, Dunlap to Juan Bueno, 25 September 1959.

25. *The Brownsville Herald* (Brownsville, Texas), 21 October 1934; 29 December 1935; 26 January 1936.

27. C.M. Papers, Theater Receipt Records, Teatro México (Brownsville), Teatro Azteca (McAllen).

28. C.M. Papers, ibid., Teatro México (Brownsville).

29. *The Brownsville Herald*, 23 April 1945.

30. C.M. Papers, Theater Receipt Records, Teatro México (Brownsville).

31. C.M. Papers, ibid.

32. C.M. Papers, Box Office Statements, Teatro México (Brownsville): *El derecho de nacer*.

33. C.M. Papers, Dunlap to Juan Bueno, 19 May 1959.

34. *The Brownsville Herald*, 24 November 1946.

35. *Brownsville Herald,* ibid.

36. C.M. Papers, Theater Receipt Records, Teatro Grande (Brownsville).

37. C.M. Papers, ibid., Teatro Grande (Harlingen).

38. *Cinema Reporter* (México City), 10 November 1951.

39. *Cinema Reporter*, 15 November 1952.

40. C.M. Papers, Theater Receipt Records, Teatro El Rey (McAllen).

41. C.M. Papers. Dunlap to Bill Rast, 3 May 1956.

42. C.M. Papers, Dunlap to R.E.M. Gilbert, 21 May 1958.

43. Estela De la Fuente interviewed by author, 21 September 2004.

44. *El Puerto de Brownsville*, 12 June 1954.

45. *La Prensa*, 21 March 1949.

46. C.M. Papers, Dunlap to Vean Gregg, 4 December 1959.

47. Alton Moore. *Drive-In Memories.* http://www.angelfire.com/tx3/herguy/ (as consulted on 13 January 2004).

Epilogue

1. For a contemporary assessment of the progress of Mexican films in the decade of the 1930s and their popular appeal among Spanish speaking audiences, see Elgin Groseclose, "Film Making Below the Rio Grande" in *Mexican Life* (Mexico City), December 1935; see also this magazine's illuminating articles written by Vane C. Dalton: February and April 1938.

2. Amy Barnes Beer, *From the Bronx to Brooklyn: Spanish-Language Movie Theaters and Their Audiences in New York City, 1930–1999* (Doctoral dissertation: Northwestern University, Illinois, 2001), p. 95.

3. Judith Mayne, *Cinema and Spectatorship* (New York: Routledge, 1993), pp. 20–21.

4. See, for example, Jorge Calderón González, *Nosotros, la música y el cine* (México: Universidad Veracruzana, 1997).

Bibliography

Archival Sources

Clasa-Mohme, Inc., Papers and Theater Records. Agrasánchez Film Archive. Harlingen, Texas.
Frank Torres Papers. Harry Ransom Humanities Research Center. The University of Texas, Austin.
Hoblitzelle Interstate Theatre Circuit Collection. Harry Ransom Humanities Research Center. The University of Texas, Austin.
Edinburg Theater File. The Museum of South Texas History. Edinburg, Texas.
Lucchese Family File. San Antonio Public Library. San Antonio, Texas.
San Antonio Theaters File. The Institute of Texan Cultures. The University of Texas. San Antonio, Texas.
San Antonio Theaters File. The San Antonio Conservation Society. San Antonio, Texas.
Stout Jackson File. The Museum of Robstown. Robstown, Texas.
Teatro Chapultepec File. Corona Public Library. The W.D. Addison Heritage Room. Corona, California.
Theaters File. The Museum of Weslaco. Weslaco, Texas.
Theaters File. Arnulfo L. Oliveira Memorial Library. Hunter Room. The University of Texas at Brownsville-TSC. Brownsville, Texas.

Interviews

Arias, Arnulfo. Interview by author. San Antonio, Texas, 15 November 2003.
De la Fuente, Estela S. Interviews by author. Harlingen, Texas, 21 September and 21 October 2004.
Dunlap, Richard H. Interview by author. Los Angeles, California, 1 October 1991.
González, David. Interview by author. San Antonio, Texas. 15 November 2004.
Hinojosa, Carlos. Interview by author. Pharr, Texas, 6 December 2003.
Huerta, Alberto. Interview by author. Falfurrias, Texas, 28 May 2004.
Maciel, David. Interview by author. Guadalajara, Jalisco (México), 18 April 1997.
Obledo, Fernando J. Interviews by author. San Antonio, Texas, 16 November 2003 and 21 June 2004.

Periodicals

Newspapers

La Bandera Americana. Albuquerque, New Mexico, 1935–1937.
The Brownsville Herald. Brownsville, Texas, 1934–1979.

Bronx Times Reporter. Bronx, New York. 2000.
Challenge. Denver, Colorado, 1946.
El Continental. El Paso, Texas, 1931–1938.
El Cronista del Valle. Brownsville, Texas, 1924–1925.
The Daily Texan. Austin, Texas, 1944.
El Defensor. Edinburg, Texas, 1930–1931.
El Espectador del Valle. Pomona, California, 1937–1958.
La Estrella. Las Cruces, New Mexico, 1930–1931.
The Galveston News. Galveston, Texas, 1944.
El Hispano. Albuquerque, New Mexico, 1966–1970.
Hispano América. San Francisco, California, 1920–1925.
El Heraldo Dominical. Tampa, Florida, 1941.
Hidalgo County News. Edinburg, Texas, 1950–1953.
The Houston Post. Houston, Texas, 1946.
The Laredo Times. Laredo, Texas, 1945–1954.
McAllen Daily Monitor. McAllen, Texas, 1937.
The New York Times Film Reviews. 1931–1948.
Notas de Kingsville. Kingsville, Texas, 1948–1950.
La Opinión. Los Angeles, California, 1926–1971.
La Patria. El Paso, Texas, 1921–1925.
The Pharr News. Pharr, Texas. 1945.
La Prensa. Los Angeles, California, 1920–1922.
La Prensa. San Antonio, Texas, 1913–1960.
La Prensa. Tampa, Florida, 1951–1953.
La Prensa Libre. Berkeley, California, 1971.
El Puerto de Brownsville. Brownsville, Texas, 1954–1957.
La Raza. Chicago, Illinois, 1974–1975.
La República. El Paso, Texas, 1919–1923.
San Antonio Express News. San Antonio, Texas, 1926.
The San Antonio Light. San Antonio, Texas, 1982, 1985.
San Benito News. San Benito, Texas, 1986.
Semanario Imparcial. San Francisco, California, 1935–1938.
El Sol. San Marcos, Texas, 1956.
The Texas Spectator. Austin, Texas, 1946.
Valley Evening Monitor. McAllen, Texas, 1949.
Valley Morning News. McAllen, Texas, 1934–1938.
Valley Morning Star. Harlingen, Texas, 1941–1945.
La Verdad. Corpus Christi, Texas, 1957.
La Voz. San Diego, Texas, 1936.

Magazines

Alianza. Tucson, Arizona, 1950.
Cinema Reporter. México City, 1942–1960.
Éxito, Revista mensual ilustrada. Weslaco, Texas, 1940.
Filmográfico. México City, 1932–1937.
Mexican Life. México City, 1935, 1938.
La Novela Cinegráfica. Los Angeles, California, 1947–1967.
Tonantzin, Chicano Arts in San Antonio. San Antonio, Texas, 1984.

Official and Trade Publications

American General Film Distribution, Inc., Film Catalog 1983–1984.
Azteca Films, Inc., Film Catalogs: 1953, 1956, 1959.
Brownsville, Texas. City Directories: 1929–1930, 1931, 1938.

Catálogo de los espectáculos censurados por la Legión Mexicana de la Decencia de 1931 a 1958. México, D. F. 1959.
El Cinegráfico, Anuario 1943–1944. México, 1944.
Cinevoz: Boletín de la Comisión Nacional de Cinematografía. México, 1948.
Clasa-Mohme, Inc., Film Catalog ca. 1959.
Columbia Pictures Corp. Film Catalog ca. 1970.
Directorio cinematográfico internacional de México: 1938–1939.
The Film Daily Year Book of Motion Pictures. New York, 1936–1956.
Guía oficial del cine en México: 1943–1944. México: Alberto Monroy, 1943.
Mundo Cinematográfico. México, 1930–1937.
San Antonio City Directory, 1948. San Antonio, Texas. 1948.
Texas Theatre Guide: 1956–1957. Dallas, Texas, 1957.
The Year Book of the Lower Rio Grande Valley. 1945–1958.

Secondary Sources

Agrasánchez, Rogelio, Jr. *Miguel Zacarías, creador de estrellas.* México: Archivo Fílmico Agrasánchez y Universidad de Guadalajara, 2000.
Arreola, Daniel D. *Tejano South Texas: A Mexican American Cultural Province.* Austin: University of Texas Press, 2002.
Ayala Blanco, Jorge. *Cartelera cinematográfica: 1930–1939.* México: Filmoteca UNAM, 1977.
Beer, Amy Barnes. *From the Bronx to Brooklyn: Spanish-Language Movie Theaters and Their Audiences in New York City, 1930–1999.* Doctoral dissertation: Northwestern University, Illinois, 2001.
Calderón González, Jorge. *Nosotros, la música y el cine.* México: Universidad Veracruzana, 1997.
Cárdenas, Cipriano A. "Hispanic Journalism in Brownsville, Texas," in *Studies in Matamoros and Cameron County History.* Brownsville: University of Texas at Brownsville, 1997.
Cien años del cine mexicano [CD Rom]. IMCINE-Univ. de Colima-CONACULTA, 1999.
Cine El Rey. History. http://www.cineelrey.com/pages/1/page1.html (as consulted on 20 December 2004).
Ciuk, Perla. *Diccionario de directores del cine mexicano.* México: CONACULTA-Cineteca Nacional, 2001.
Contreras Torres, Miguel. *El libro Negro del cine mexicano.* México: Ed. Hispano Continental, 1960.
Chávez, Denise. *Loving Pedro Infante.* New York: Farrar, Straus and Giroux, 2001.
Dávalos Orozco, Federico. *Albores del cine mexicano.* México: Clío, 1996.
Delson, Don. *The Dictionary of Marketing and Related Terms in the Motion Picture Industry.* California: Bradson Press, 1979.
Driscoll, Barbara A. *The Tracks North: The Railroad Bracero Program of World War II.* Austin: Center for Mexican American Studies, University of Texas, 1999.
Durán, Ignacio, et al. *México-Estados Unidos: Encuentros y desencuentros en el cine.* México: UNAM, CONACULTA, 1996.
Filmografía mexicana. [Online database]. Filmoteca de la UNAM. *http://www.unam.mx/filmoteca* (as consulted on 20 December 2004).
Foley, Neil. *The White Scourge: Mexicans, Blacks, and Poor Whites in Texas Cotton Culture.* Berkeley: University of California Press, 1997.
Gamboa, Erasmo. *Mexican Labor and World War II: Braceros in the Pacific Northwest 1942–1947.* Austin: University of Texas Press, 1990.
García Riera, Emilio. *La guía del cine mexicano: de la pantalla grande a la televisión (1919–1984).* México: Ed. Patria, 1988.
_____. *Historia documental del cine mexicano.* 2nd edition. Guadalajara: Universidad de Guadalajara, 1992.
Glasner, Ruth. *My Music is my Flag: Puerto Rican Musicians and Their New York Communities, 1917–1940.* Berkeley: University of California Press, 1995.
Gonzales, Manuel G. *Mexicanos: A History of Mexicans in the United States.* Bloomington, Indiana: Indiana University Press, 2000.
_____. *Arturo Tirado and the Teatro Azteca: Mexican Popular Culture in the Central San Joaquín Valley.* Unpublished Manuscript.

Granados, Pável. *XEW, 70 años en el aire.* México: Editorial Clío, 2000.

Heinink, Juan B. and Robert G. Dickson. *Cita en Hollywood: Antología de las películas Norteamericanas habladas en castellano.* Bilbao: Ed. Mensajero, 1990.

Hershfield, Joanne and David R. Maciel. *Mexico's Cinema: A Century of Film and Filmmakers.* Wilmington, Delaware: Scholarly Resources, 1999.

Hughes, Rob. *Where is Home? www.liferaft.com.*, (as consulted on 11 July 2004).

Jarvie, I. C. *Movies and Society.* New York: Basic Books, Inc., 1970.

Kanellos, Nicolás. *A History of Hispanic Theatre in the United States: Origins to 1940.* Austin: University of Texas Press, 1990.

Kibbe, Pauline R. *Latin Americans in Texas*, cited in "El trato a los braceros en Texas" *www.farmworkers.org/bracentx.html*, (as consulted on 22 April 2004).

Mayne, Judith. *Cinema and Spectatorship.* New York: Routledge, 1993.

Miquel, Ángel. *Mimí Derba.* México: Agrasánchez Film Archive-Filmoteca de la UNAM, 2000.

Monroy, Douglas. *Rebirth: Mexican Los Angeles from the Great Migration to the Great Depression.* Berkeley: University of California Press, 1999.

Moore, Alton. *Drive-In Memories. http://www.angelfire.com/tx3/herguy/* (as consulted on 13 January 2004).

Mora, Carl J. *Mexican Cinema: Reflections of a Society, 1896–2004*, 3rd edition. Jefferson, North Carolina: McFarland Publishers, 2005.

_____. *Reminiscences of Mexican Movies in New York City.* Unpublished Manuscript.

Negrete, Diana. *Jorge Negrete: biografía autorizada.* México: Ed. Diana, 1987,

Oroz, Silvia. *Melodrama: El cine de lágrimas de América Latina.* México: UNAM, 1995.

Panunzio, Constantine. *How Mexicans Earn and Live.* Berkeley: University of California Press, 1933.

Paranaguá, Paulo Antonio. *Mexican Cinema.* London: British Film Institute, 1995.

Penn, William S. Ed. *As We Are Now: Mixblood Essays on Race and Identity.* Berkeley: University of California Press, 1997.

Peredo, Francisco M. *Cine e historia: Discurso histórico y producción cinematográfica (1940–1952).* Tesis doctoral. México: UNAM, 2000.

Pérez Montfort, Ricardo. *Estampas de nacionalismo popular mexicano.* México: CIESAS, 2003.

Pérez Turrent, Tomás. *Arturo Ripstein, productor.* Guadalajara, Jalisco: Universidad de Guadalajara, 2003.

Prida Santacilia, Pablo. *Y se levanta el telón: Mi vida dentro del teatro.* México: Ed. Botas, 1960.

Quezada, Eduardo. *KMEX-TV Comienzos www.eduardoquezada.net/album/kmex/notas* (as consulted on 24 February 2004).

Rae Hark, Ina. *Exhibition, The Film Reader.* New York: Routledge, 2002.

Ramírez, Elizabeth C. *Foot Lights Across the Border: A History of Spanish-Language Professional Theatre on Texas Stage.* New York: Peter Lang, 1990.

Ramírez, Gabriel. *Miguel Contreras Torres.* México: Universidad de Guadalajara, 1994.

Ramírez-Berg, Charles. *Cinema of Solitude: A Critical Study of Mexican Film, 1967–1983.* Austin: University of Texas Press, 1992.

Reyes de la Maza, Luis. *El cine sonoro en México.* México: UNAM, 1973.

Rodríguez Mas, Juan. *La vida del inventor y pionero del cine sonoro mexicano, Joselito Rodríguez.* México: Author's edition, 1990.

Rosas Priego, Alfonso. *La intervención del estado en la industria cinematográfica.* Tesis profesional. México: UNAM, 1970.

Rubel, Arthur J. *Across the Tracks: Mexican-Americans in a Texas City.* Austin: University of Texas Press, 1966.

Sánchez Korrol, Virginia E. *From Colonia to Community: The History of Puerto Ricans in New York City.* Berkeley: University of California Press, 1983.

Sewell, Philip Winston. *Texas's Theater Monopoly: A History of Interstate Theaters, 1905–1951.* M.A. Thesis: University of Texas at Austin, 1996.

Strachwitz, Chris. *Lydia Mendoza: A Family Autobiography.* Houston: Arte Público Press, 1993.

Taylor, Paul. *Mexican Labor in the United States: Chicago and the Calumet Region.* Berkeley: University of California Press, 1932.

Usabel, Gaizka S. de. *The High Noon of American Films in Latin America.* Ann Arbor, Michigan: UMI Research Press, 1982.

Valdés Bernal, Sergio and Nuria Gregori Torada. *La lengua española en los Estados Unidos.* La Habana: Editorial Academia, 1997.

Vargas, Zaragosa. *Proletarians of the North: A History of the Mexican Industrial Workers in Detroit and the Midwest, 1917–1933.* Berkeley: University of California Press, 1999.

Vega, Eduardo de la. *Gabriel Soria.* México: Universidad de Guadalajara, 1992.

_____. Coordinador. *Microhistorias del cine en México.* México: Universidad de Guadalajara, 2000.

Viñas, Moisés. *Índice cronológico del cine mexicano (1896–1992).* México: UNAM, 1992.

Waller, Gregory A. *Moviegoing in America: A Sourcebook in the History of Film Exhibition.* Malden, Massachusetts: Blackwell Publishers, 2002.

Watkins, T. H. *California: An Illustrated History.* New York: American Legacy Press, 1983.

Wilt, David E. *The Mexican Filmography, 1916 through 2001.* Jefferson, North Carolina: McFarland Publishers, 2004.

Zaragoza, Alex M. *Mexican Cinema in Cold War America, 1940–1958: An Inquiry into the Mexican Interface Between Mexico and Mexicans in the United States.* Berkeley: Chicano Studies Library Publications, 1983.

Index